# THE KAMA SUTRA
## AND
# ANANGA RANGA

# THE KAMA SUTRA
## AND
# ANANGA RANGA

TRANSLATED BY SIR RICHARD FRANCIS BURTON

INTRODUCTION TO THE NEW EDITION
BY ANNE HARDGROVE

**BARNES & NOBLE**
NEW YORK

THE BARNES & NOBLE
LIBRARY OF ESSENTIAL READING

Introduction and Suggested Reading
Copyright © 2006 by Barnes & Noble Publishing, Inc.

*The Kama Sutra* written in the third century AD; this translation first
published in 1883. *Ananga Ranga* written in the fifteenth century AD;
this translation first published in 1885

This edition published by Barnes & Noble Publishing, Inc.

Cover design by Stacey May

2006 Barnes & Noble Publishing

ISBN-13: 978-0-7607-7899-9
ISBN-10: 0-7607-7899-X

Printed and bound in the United States of America

1 3 5 7 9 10 8 6 4 2

# CONTENTS

## PART FOUR
## ABOUT A WIFE

## PART FIVE
## ABOUT THE WIVES
## OF OTHER MEN

PART SIX

ABOUT COURTESANS

PART SEVEN

ON THE MEANS OF ATTRACTING

OTHERS TO YOURSELF

ANANGA RANGA

# INTRODUCTION TO
# THE NEW EDITION

ALMOST TWO THOUSAND YEARS OLD, *THE KAMA SUTRA* IS A compilation of timeless wisdom about the arts of pleasurable living. Written during the third century AD in Sanskrit, the literary language of ancient India, the text known as *The Kama Sutra* contains detailed inventories and lists of advice on topics ranging from homemaking to lovemaking, covering the arts of attraction, courtship, seduction, marriage, and sexual union. Also written in Sanskrit, but some twelve hundred years later, the *Ananga Ranga* is an updated version, drawing extensively upon the cornucopia of sexual positions that *The Kama Sutra* first proposed. Their sexual candor, along with vivid descriptions of sexual positions, make *The Kama Sutra* and the *Ananga Ranga* indispensable guides to couples seeking to enhance their sexual relationship.

In 1883, Richard F. Burton produced an edition of *The Kama Sutra* translated from the ancient Sanskrit to English. The English version was scandalous for its time, and in the first edition, only 250 copies were secretly printed. The *Ananga Ranga* came out two years later, enveloped in the same veils of secrecy. The 1880s were, after all, the Victorian era, a time of strictly regulated public morals. European publishers could be imprisoned for printing what was considered to be obscene literature. This was also the era of colonialism and empire, and Burton's translations of Eastern classics could be read as a threat to British ideas of racial and cultural superiority. As a result, *The Kama Sutra* and *Ananga Ranga* appeared subsequently only in limited private editions, ostensibly for medical professionals and scholarly researchers, along with numerous pirated editions printed in Brussels and Paris. The legal editions were—and in some cases still in fact are—kept under lock and key in public libraries. Only in the 1960s, as part of the rising countercultural interest in Asian religions, were Burton's *Kama Sutra* and *Ananga Ranga* made available to a larger reading public in America and Britain, and they quickly became required reading during the sexual revolution, reinvigorating the idea that ancient Hindu culture holds special wisdom for modern peoples. Today, the Western fascination with Eastern spirituality, including traditions of religious wisdom, yoga, diet, and meditation, remains as strong as ever, often serving as an antidote to a frenetic American lifestyle too often filled with stress, disenchantment, and information overload. The wisdom of *The Kama Sutra* and the *Ananga Ranga* provide a way for modern readers to bring such insight and sacred spirituality into the most intimate domains of sex and sexual relationships.

These two translations by Richard F. Burton, the British adventurer and linguist, have been pivotal to the widespread global popularization of these texts. Throughout his varied and fascinating career as an explorer and linguist, soldier and swordsman, travel writer and polymath Orientalist, translator and poet, geographer and anthropologist, archaeologist and geologist, and—toward the end of his life—diplomat and consul, Burton spent a great deal of his time searching out and documenting erotic customs and translating erotic literature from societies all over the globe. His various journeys and travels led him to work in and explore places as far-flung as India, Arabia, Africa, and even included a stint in America, where he studied practices of polygamy among the Mormons of Salt Lake City, Utah. Along with his friend John Speke, Richard Burton set out on a famous exploration to find the source of the Nile River. As a result of his linguistic skills—he was fluent in at least twenty-five languages—Burton could pass himself off as a native speaker. His adventures included traveling to Mecca and Medina disguised as a pilgrim, where he witnessed ceremonies at holy sites that were strictly off-limits to non-Muslims.

Throughout his life, Burton kept copious notes on human sexual behavior. These observations would later influence his translations of the *Ananga Ranga, The Kama Sutra,* and other erotic texts. Burton always considered himself an outsider to English polite society, and his resentment of strict Victorian codes gave both purpose and impetus to his studies. He often wrote the most explicit material in his footnotes in Latin, and elsewhere was very careful in his wording, especially when it came to female sexuality. Conducting this work at a time when translating and publishing ancient erotic literature could have led to his prosecution under the British Obscene Publications Act, Burton sought to challenge the environment of legal censorship of the Victorian age. His goal was to have the study of sexuality undertaken as a serious intellectual pursuit, and not dismissed merely as a social perversion. As co-founder of the Anthropological Society of London, he helped establish an institutional forum for the scientific study of sexuality.

Born in the English seaside resort town of Torquay in 1821, Richard Burton was the eldest of three children born to Captain Joseph Netterville Burton and his wife, Martha. His half-Irish father came from a well-to-do Protestant family, and whose own father served as a Protestant minister in Galway, Ireland. After serving in the British army in Italy, Joseph met Martha Baker at a military ball and they married in 1820.

Joseph went on sick leave due to asthma, and the family moved to Europe when Richard was five years old. The family lived in English expatriate communities in France and Italy, and had a comfortable existence thanks to Martha's large inheritance. Richard was a precocious child, learning both Latin and Greek at age four. His education was eclectic: sometimes he studied in small schools for English expatriates or with private tutors employed for him and his brother. At the age of nineteen, Richard entered Oxford University where he often found himself unfamiliar with the codes of etiquette of English high society. After about a year and a half, he dropped out of the university to join the Bombay Infantry. As a member of the British military, Burton spent about six years in the Indian subcontinent, where he had relationships with Indian women and mastered a number of modern Indian languages. He was a prolific writer, publishing books on a wide variety of topics stemming from his explorations and travels. Toward the end of his life as his health declined, Burton pursued translations of literary erotica with great enthusiasm.

Burton first encountered the *Ananga Ranga* in the early 1870s, in collaboration with his friend F. F. Arbuthnot, a civil service employee and fellow linguist. In 1873, Burton and Arbuthnot arranged with a London printer to publish the *Ananga Ranga* in English. The text was given the title "*Kama-Shastra*," or, *The Hindoo Art of Love (Ars Amoris Indica)*. This text was well known through the Indian subcontinent and Arabia, having been translated already into many local languages. Burton and Arbuthnot used only their initials—written backwards—to identify themselves as the translators, and noted in their introduction that the book was intended "for the private use of the translators only, in connection with a work on the Hindoo religion, and on the manners and customs of the Hindoos." Despite these precautions, only four copies of the *Kama Shastra* were printed. The printer abruptly cancelled the printing after realizing the text was of an erotic nature and questionable legal status. The actions of this printer made Burton realize that he could only achieve his dreams of bringing this literature to the attention of his contemporaries by a different path. It would be more than a decade before publication.

It was through these labors on the *Ananga Ranga*, however, that Burton came to know about the classic *Kama Sutra*. The author of the *Ananga Ranga*, Kalyanamalla, made numerous mentions to an earlier text upon which he had drawn extensively. *The Kama Sutra* was composed in a more difficult classical Sanskrit, making the text less well known across India despite its once foundational status.[1] Burton and Arbuthnot approached Indian Sanskrit experts, known as pundits, to find a copy of this manuscript for their literary explorations. These personal connections with Indian scholars, who had the requisite language skills to read and interpret Sanskrit, made Burton successful in his work.

While Burton is almost always given sole credit for his translations from ancient Sanskrit to English, in fact he relied heavily on the help of his collaborators, both Indian and British. Burton's role in both translation projects was to polish up the text produced by Arbuthnot, who himself commissioned the Sanskrit-English translations. In the case of *The Kama Sutra*, the work of translation was done by Indian pundits Bhagvanlal Indrajit and Shivaram Parashuram Bhide. In preparing their text, Indrajit and Bhide consulted a number of versions of *The Kama Sutra* kept in different libraries, along with the major commentaries. As recent translators of *The Kama Sutra* have noted, these commentaries tended to incorporate a male bias that pervades the Burton text, and is not as apparent in the original Sanskrit edition. Burton himself took some liberties with the translation, including the use of Sanskrit terms *yoni* and *lingam* for female and male genitals, which appear respectively nowhere or only infrequently in the original Sanskrit text.[2]

In the early 1880s, with these two translations completed, Burton was ready to again tackle the tricky task of having these works published. As part of their determined project to print a number of translations of erotic texts and make them available to readers, Burton and Arbuthnot, along with erotic literary enthusiast Lord Monckton Milnes, formed the Kama Shastra Society of London and Benaras, whose purpose was to publish ancient and medieval erotic literature, ostensibly for "private subscribers only." This so-called society existed in name only, and their place of publishing, Cosmopoli, was a thinly veiled euphemism for London. In addition to *The Kama Sutra* and the *Ananga Ranga*, the Kama Shastra Society published translations of the *Arabian Nights* (a collection of tales about Sindbad, Ali Baba, and Aladdin), *The Perfumed Garden* (a text on sex by sixteenth-century author Shaykh Umar ibn Muhammed al-Nefzawi), *Beharistan* ("Abode of Spring," an erotic poem by Persian poet Jâmi), and *Gulistan* ("Rose Garden," homoerotic stories by thirteenth-century Persian writer Sadi).

The ancient corpus of practical knowledge about pursuing the life of pleasure, *The Kama Sutra*, was compiled originally in the third century AD by the Indian sage Vatsyayana. During much of his life Vatsyayana was based near the modern city of Patna, Bihar, in an ancient city known as Pataliputra. A celibate monk, Vatsyayana had retired to the banks of the Ganges River in Varanasi to meditate and prepare spiritually for his old age and eventual death. He claims that writing *The Kama Sutra* was strictly an exercise of mental concentration. Vatsyayana clearly was familiar with many regions of the Indian subcontinent. He sometimes refers to the unique sexual practices of different regions of India, such as the area now known as Maharashtra, in describing different groups of people and their sexual preferences.[3] Almost nothing is known about Vatsyayana outside of *The Kama Sutra*—our only clues are what he has provided in the text itself.

Vatsyayana did not claim that *The Kama Sutra* was an original work. His text summarizes the writings of earlier writers on love and sex. The book, essentially a marriage manual, is divided into seven sections. The topics explored include Society and Social Concepts, On Sexual Union, About the Acquisition of a Wife, About a Wife, About the Wives of Other Men, About Courtesans, and On the Means of Attracting Others to Yourself. In *The Kama Sutra*, pleasure refers to the fruits of wealth and culture, including those pleasures of an erotic variety. Since there are no other surviving firsthand accounts of social and political life of this period, the text offers the unique opportunity to learn about the social and cultural practices of upper-class India during ancient times.

Many readers in modern times have assumed that *The Kama Sutra* is a book merely about sexual positions and erotic acrobatics. But sexual positions are only a small part of what *The Kama Sutra* encompasses. The book is framed within the trinity of life aims comprised of religious duty, wealth and status, and the pursuit of pleasure. The book is entitled *The Kama Sutra* because the Sanskrit word "Kama" encompasses the ideas of love, affection, desire, sensuousness, and sexual pleasures. The second word of the title, "Sutra," refers to the genre of the book, which is written in the form of short aphorisms, or rules. Combined, then, the words *Kama Sutra* could be read as "A Treatise on Pleasure."

One of the most fascinating aspects of *The Kama Sutra* is that it was written for both men and women. Studying the famous "sixty-four arts," which is a list of the essential knowledge a lover must possess, provides the basic education that needs to be mastered by practitioners of *Kama Sutra*. Significantly, *The Kama Sutra* provided a major contribution to sexual knowledge because of its emphasis on female pleasure. According to *The Kama Sutra*, for a marriage to be successful, happy, and stable, it is the man's responsibility and duty that his wife should derive pleasure from sex. The book contains detailed advice on what a man must do to win over a woman, what a woman must do to win over a man, the states of a woman's mind, the role of a go-between, and the reasons why women might reject the advances of men. In terms of choosing a mate, *The Kama Sutra* advises on whether to consider fellow students or childhood friends. It provides charts that categorize male and female physical types and their compatibility with their lover's body. Varieties of embracing, kissing, scratching, biting, oral sex, and sexual intercourse are elaborated. The text also incorporates instruction on extramarital relationships, including with "the wives of other men," and devotes many pages to the methods of seduction—and methods of extortion—practiced by the courtesan. Finally, in case all of that knowledge should fail in winning the love that one seeks, the final chapter of *The Kama Sutra* contains recipes for tonics, powders, and foods that have the power to help attract others to oneself.

*The Kama Sutra* is not only a book with appeal to modern reading publics in America and Britain. It is a very important text in Indian literature. Since the third century CE, *The Kama Sutra* has been a key Sanskrit text in the literary history of India, considered the foundational text for works on erotica onwards, including the erotic texts called *Kokashastra* (Ratirahasya) and the *Ananga Ranga* (eleventh and fifteenth centuries, respectively), and inspiring renowned commentaries by major critics such as Yashodhara Indrapada in the thirteenth century. It also influenced Persian and Arabic erotic texts through the eighteenth century.

In the twentieth century, commentaries have been written in the modern Indian languages of Hindi, Bengali, Tamil, and Telegu. Burton's edition inspired Indian scholars to publish their own translations of *The Kama Sutra*, in English and local vernacular languages, sometimes editing out parts concerning the courtesans and references to homosexuality. In the sixties, the legal re-publication of *The Kama Sutra* prompted Alex Comfort to translate German editions of the *Kokashastra* (erotic verse poetry by Kokkoka) into English, which along with the line drawings became the basis for his seminal book, *The Joy of Sex*.

Along with Burton's *Kama Sutra*, Burton's *Ananga Ranga* is included in this edition, giving readers two major treatises on love, sex, and desire from India. The *Ananga Ranga* was the last major work in a whole genre of erotic literature inspired by *The Kama Sutra*. The name *Ananga Ranga* has been variously rendered in English as *The Hindu Art of Love*, *Stage of the Bodiless One*, *The Pleasures of Women*, and *Theater of the Love God*. The purpose of the *Ananga Ranga* is to promote marital fidelity by teaching married couples to bring variety to their physical pleasures to prevent monotony in monogamy. The author of the treatise, Kalyanamalla (1460–1530), was a Hindu poet who purportedly assembled the text for a Lodi monarch, a member of the powerful dynasty of Muslim rulers known as the Delhi Sultanate. Like that of Vatsyayana, little is known about the life of Kalyanamalla. He was presumably of the Brahmin caste and hailed from Kalinga. He dedicated the book to an official of the Lodi dynasty, which lasted from 1450 to 1526 AD. Kalyanamalla's patron was a nobleman called Ladakhana, son of King Ahmad. The royal patronage of the *Ananga Ranga*, along with its more accessible Sanskrit style, ensured that the work enjoyed a wide circulation. Translators produced versions of the text in Arabic, Persian, and Urdu, so it became known in many languages across a variety of places.

Like *The Kama Sutra,* the *Ananga Ranga* melds together sexuality and spirituality. The *Ananga Ranga* opens with a salutation to the god of love, followed by a dedication to the author's patron, Ladakhana. The *Ananga Ranga* is divided into ten chapters, and contains prescriptions for both social and sexual conduct for married couples. It begins with a detailed description of female bodies, and includes "centers of passion," erogenous zones, classifications of body types and the timeliness of their potential sexual pleasures. Classification and compatibility of males and females by their genital size is explored in various combinations and to their degree of passion. Many scholars speculate that Kalyanamalla lived in a more sexist society than earlier writers, noting that Kalyanamalla deviates from other writers by encouraging female stimulation without the use of fingers, a method that other texts heartily endorse.

It is a clichéd understatement to say that Burton's *Kama Sutra* and *Ananga Ranga* have had a lasting impact. Burton's *Kama Sutra* especially has served as the basis of subsequent re-translations of the book into dozens of languages. In terms of their impact on Western culture, Burton's translations contributed significantly to the popular image of a romantically mysterious Orient. His writing creates an image of the sexually libertine, uninhibited Orient in a rather subversive manner, as a counterpoint to the public tensions over sexuality expressed by his co-Victorians. The potential danger of Burton's texts did not lie in merely its relating customs of an erotic nature. *The Kama Sutra* and *Ananga Ranga* stood as threats to the presumed superiority of Western civilization, particularly relating to women. Presented by Burton as trans-historical and transcendent texts, *The Kama Sutra* and *Ananga Ranga* implied that Eastern women possessed a knowledge and freedom of sex far greater than their Victorian counterparts, who were still decades away from the discovery of the female orgasm. By translating them into English, Burton hoped to propagate this sexual knowledge for the enlightenment of his countrymen. In the 1960s, publishers in the United States and Britain sought to challenge obscenity laws on the basis of the right to freedom of speech. They daringly published *The Kama Sutra* and the *Ananga Ranga*, pointing to the texts' scholarly and cultural merit. This rediscovery of Eastern candor about sex helped pave the way for ideas of sexual liberation. Today, there are no longer any legal obstacles to the publication of erotic literature, and globalization has largely replaced the political climate of colonialism. In today's more open society, many Westerners seek enlightenment and escape from the pressures of an increasingly complex world by turning to the wisdom of texts from ancient Eastern spiritual traditions. By providing a "treatise on pleasure" that Easterners and Westerners have turned to for centuries, *The Kama Sutra* and *Ananga Ranga* remain relevant over hundreds of years.

***Anne Hardgrove*** is a historian and anthropologist of India, and author of *Community and Public Culture: The Marwaris in Calcutta c. 1897-1997*. She is currently writing a book on the history of translations of *The Kama Sutra*, which is tentatively titled *The Global Erotic: Translating The Kama Sutra*.

# THE KAMA SUTRA

# SOCIETY AND
# SOCIAL CONCEPTS

# ⊰ PART ONE ⊱

# INTRODUCTORY PREFACE

*Salutation to Dharma, Artha, and Kama*

IN THE BEGINNING THE LORD OF BEINGS (BRAHMA) CREATED MEN and women, and in the form of commandments in one hundred thousand chapters laid down rules for regulating their existence with regard to Dharma,[1] Artha,[2] and Kama.[3] Some

> These three words are retained throughout in their original, as technical terms. They may also be defined as virtue, wealth, and pleasure, the three things repeatedly spoken of in the Laws of Manu.

of these commandments, namely, those which treated of Dharma, were separately written by Swayambhu Manu; those that related to Artha were compiled by Brihaspati; and those that referred to Kama were expounded by Nandi, the follower of Mahadeva, in one thousand chapters.

Now, these *Kama Sutra* (Aphorisms on Love), written by Nandi in one thousand chapters, were reproduced by Shvetaketu, the son of Uddvalaka, in an abbreviated form in five hundred chapters, and this work was again similarly reproduced in an abridged form, in one hundred and fifty chapters, by Babhravya, an inhabitant of the Panchala (South of Delhi) country. These one hundred and fifty chapters were then put together under seven heads or parts named severally:

1. Sadharana (general topics)
2. Samprayogika (embraces, and so on)
3. Kanya Samprayuktaka (union of males and females)
4. Bharyadhikarika (on one's own wife)
5. Paradarika (on the wives of other people)
6. Vaisika (on courtesans)
7. Aupamishadika (on the arts of seduction, tonic medicines, and so on)

The sixth part of this last work was separately expounded by Dattaka at the request of the public women of Pataliputra (Patna), and in the same way Charayana explained the first part of it. The remaining parts, namely, the second, third, fourth, fifth, and seventh, were separately expounded by:

Suvarnanabha (second part).
Ghotakamukha (third part).
Gonardiya (fourth part).
Gonikaputra (fifth part).
Kuchumara (seventh part).

Thus the work, being written in parts by different authors, was almost unobtainable, and as the parts which were expounded by Dattaka and the others treated only of the particular branches of the subject to which each part related, and moreover as the original work of Babhravya was difficult to be mastered on account of its length, Vatsyayana composed this work in a small volume as an abstract of the whole of the works of the above-named authors.

# → CHAPTER ONE ←

# BEING THE INDEX TO OR CONTENTS OF THE WORK

VIII  About females acting the part of males
IX  On holding the lingam in the mouth
X  How to begin and how to end the congress. Different kinds of congress, and love quarrels

## PART THREE: *ABOUT THE ACQUISITION OF A WIFE*

I  Observations on betrothal and marriage
II  On creating confidence in the girl
III  On courtship, and the manifestation of the feelings by outward signs and deeds
IV  On things to be done only by the man, and the acquisition of the girl thereby. Also, what is to be done by a girl to gain over a man, and subject him to her
V  On certain forms *of marriage*

## PART FOUR: *ABOUT A WIFE*

I  On the manner of living of a virtuous woman, and of her behavior during the absence of her husband
II  On the conduct of the eldest wife toward the other wives of her husband, and of a younger wife toward the elder ones. On the conduct of a virgin widow remarried; on a wife disliked by her husband; on the women in the king's harem; and on a husband who has more than one wife

## PART FIVE: *ABOUT THE WIVES OF OTHER MEN*

I  On the characteristics of men and women, and the reasons why women reject the addresses of men. About men who have success with women, and about women who are easily gained over

## → CHAPTER TWO ←

# ON THE ACQUISITION OF
# DHARMA, ARTHA, AND KAMA

MAN, THE PERIOD OF WHOSE LIFE IS ONE HUNDRED YEARS, should practice Dharma, Artha, and Kama at different times and in such a manner that they may harmonize, and not clash in any way. He should acquire learning in his childhood; in his youth and middle age he should attend to Artha and Kama; and in his old age he should perform Dharma, and thus seek to gain Moksha, that is, release from further transmigration. Or, because of the uncertainty of life, he may practice them at times when they are enjoined to be practiced. But one thing is to be noted: he should lead the life of a religious student until he finishes his education.

*Dharma* is obedience to the command of the Shastra, or Holy Writ, of the Hindus to do certain things, such as the performance of sacrifices, which are not generally done because they do not belong to this world, and produce no visible effect; and not do other things, such as eating meat, which is often done because it belongs to this world, and has visible effects.

Dharma should be learned from the Shruti (Holy Writ), and from those conversant with it.

*Artha* is the acquisition of arts, land, gold, cattle, wealth, equipages, and friends. It is also the protection of what is acquired, and the increase of what is protected.

10

Artha should be learned from the King's officers, and from merchants who may be versed in the ways of commerce.

*Kama* is the enjoyment of appropriate objects by the five senses of hearing, feeling, seeing, tasting, and smelling, assisted by the mind together with the soul. The ingredient in this is a peculiar contact between the organ of sense and its object, and the consciousness of pleasure that arises from that contact is called Kama.

Kama is to be learned from the *Kama Sutra* (aphorisms on love) and the practice of citizens.

When all three, Dharma, Artha, and Kama, come together, the former is better than the one which follows it; that is, Dharma is better than Artha, and Artha is better than Kama. But Artha should always be first practiced by the king, for the livelihood of men is to be obtained from it only. Again, Kama being the occupation of public women, they should prefer it to the other two, and these are exceptions to the general rule.

*Objection*

Some learned men say that as Dharma is connected with things not belonging to this world, it is appropriately treated of in a book; and so also is Artha, because it is practiced only by the application of proper means, and a knowledge of those means can be obtained only by study and from books. But Kama being a thing which is practiced even by the brute creation, and which is to be found everywhere, does not want any work on the subject.

*Answer*

This is not so. Sexual intercourse, being a thing dependent on man and woman, requires the application of proper means by them, and those means are to be learned from the *Kama Shastra*. The nonapplication of proper means, which we see in the brute creation, is caused by their being unrestrained, and by the females among them being fit for sexual intercourse at certain seasons only and no more, and by their intercourse not being preceded by thought of any kind.

## Objection

The Lokayatikas[1] say: Religious ordinances should not be observed, for they bear a future fruit, and at the same time it is also doubtful whether they will bear any fruit at all. What foolish person will give away that which is in his own hands into the hands of another? Moreover, it is better to have a pigeon today than a peacock tomorrow; and a copper coin we have the certainty of obtaining is better than a gold coin the possession of which is doubtful.

## Answer

It is not so. First, Holy Writ, which ordains the practice of Dharma, does not admit of a doubt.

Second, sacrifices such as those made for the destruction of enemies, or for the fall of rain, are seen to bear fruit.

Third, the sun, moon, stars, planets, and other heavenly bodies appear to work intentionally for the good of the world.

Fourth, the existence of this world is effected by the observance of the rules respecting the four classes[2] of men and their four stages of life.

Fifth, we see that seed is thrown into the ground with the hope of future crops.

Vatsyayana is therefore of the opinion that the ordinances of religion must be obeyed.

## Objection

Those who believe that destiny is the prime mover of all things say: We should not exert ourselves to acquire wealth, for sometimes it is not acquired although we strive to get it, while at other times it comes to us of itself without any exertion on our part. Everything is therefore in the power of destiny, who is the lord of gain and loss, of success and defeat, of pleasure and pain. Thus we see that Bali[3] was raised to the throne of Indra by destiny, and was also put down by the same power, and only destiny can reinstate him.

*Answer*

It is not right to say so. As the acquisition of every object presupposes at all events some exertion on the part of man, the application of proper means may be said to be the cause of gaining all our ends, and this application of proper means being thus necessary (even where a thing is destined to happen), it follows that a person who does nothing will enjoy no happiness.

*Objection*

Those who are inclined to think that Artha is the chief object to be obtained argue thus: Pleasures should not be sought for, because they are obstacles to the practice of Dharma and Artha, which are both superior to them, and are also disliked by meritorious persons. Pleasures also bring a man into distress, and into contact with low persons; they cause him to commit unrighteous deeds, and produce impurity in him; they make him regardless of the future, and encourage carelessness and levity. And, lastly, they cause him to be disbelieved by all, received by none, and despised by everybody, including himself. It is notorious, moreover, that many men who have given themselves up to pleasure alone have been ruined along with their families and relations. Thus King Dandakya,[4] of the Bhoja dynasty, carried off a Brahman's daughter with evil intent, and was eventually ruined and lost his kingdom. Indra, too, having violated the chastity of Ahalya,[5] was made to suffer for it. In like manner the mighty Kichaka,[6] who tried to seduce Draupadi; and Ravana,[7] who attempted to gain over Sita, were punished for their crimes. These and many others fell by reason of their pleasures.

*Answer*

This objection cannot be sustained, for pleasures, being as necessary for the existence and well-being of the body as food, are consequently equally required. They are, moreover, the results of Dharma and Artha. Pleasures are, therefore, to be followed with moderation and caution. No one refrains from cooking food because there are beggars to ask for it, or from sowing seed because there are deer to destroy the corn when it has grown up.

Thus a man practicing Dharma, Artha, and Kama enjoys happiness both in this world and in the world to come. The good perform those actions in which there is no fear as to what is to result from them in the next world, and in which there is no danger to their welfare. Any action which conduces to the practice of Dharma, Artha, and Kama together, or of any two, or even of one of them, should be performed, but an action which conduces to the practice of one of them at the expense of the remaining two should not be performed.

→ CHAPTER THREE ←

# ON THE ARTS AND
# SCIENCES TO BE STUDIED

MAN SHOULD STUDY THE *KAMA SUTRA* AND THE ARTS AND SCIENCES subordinate thereto, in addition to the study of the arts and sciences contained in Dharma and Artha. Even young maids should study this *Kama Sutra*, along with its arts and sciences, before marriage, and after it they should continue to do so with the consent of their husbands.

Here some learned men object, and say that females, not being allowed to study any science, should not study the *Kama Sutra*.

But Vatsyayana is of opinion that this objection does not hold good, for women already know the practice of *Kama Sutra*, and that practice is derived from the *Kama Shastra*, or the science of Kama itself. Moreover, it is not only in this but in many other cases that, though the practice of a science is known to all, only a few persons are acquainted with the rules and laws on which the science is based. Thus the Yajnikas, or sacrificers, though ignorant of grammar, make use of appropriate words when addressing the different deities, and do not know how these words are framed. Again, persons do the duties required of them on auspicious days, which are fixed by astrology, though they are not acquainted with the science of astrology. In a like manner riders of horses and elephants train these animals without knowing the science of training animals, but from practice only.

And similarly the people of the most distant provinces obey the laws of the kingdom from practice, and because there is a king over them, and without further reason.[1] And from experience we find that some women, such as the daughters of princes and their ministers, and public women, are actually versed in the *Kama Shastra*.

A female, therefore, should learn the *Kama Shastra*, or at least a part of it, by studying its practice from some confidential friend. She should study alone, in private, the sixty-four practices that form a part of the *Kama Shastra*. Her teacher should be one of the following persons; namely, the daughter of a nurse brought up with her and already married,[2] or a female friend who can be trusted in everything, or the sister of her mother (that is, her aunt), or an old female servant, or a female beggar who may have formerly lived in the family, or her own sister, who can always be trusted.

The following are the arts to be studied, together with the *Kama Sutra*:

1. Singing.
2. Playing on musical instruments.
3. Dancing.
4. Union of dancing, singing, and playing instrumental music.
5. Writing and drawing.
6. Tattooing.
7. Arraying and adorning an idol with rice and flowers.
8. Spreading and arranging beds or couches of flowers, or flowers upon the ground.
9. Coloring the teeth, garments, hair, nails and bodies, that is, staining, dyeing, coloring, and painting them.
10. Fixing stained glass into a floor.
11. The art of making beds, and spreading out carpets and cushions for reclining.

12. Playing on musical glasses filled with water.

13. Storing and accumulating water in aqueducts, cisterns, and reservoirs.

14. Picture making, trimming and decorating.

15. Stringing of rosaries, necklaces, garlands, and wreaths.

16. Binding of turbans and chaplets, and making crests and topknots of flowers.

17. Scenic representations. Stage playing.

18. Art of making ear ornaments.

19. Art of preparing perfumes and odors.

20. Proper disposition of jewels and decorations, and adornment in dress.

21. Magic or sorcery.

22. Quickness and dexterity in manual skill.

23. Culinary art, that is, cooking and cookery.

24. Making lemonades, sherbets, acidulated drinks, and spirituous extracts with proper flavor and color.

25. Tailor's work and sewing.

26. Making parrots, flowers, tufts, tassels, bunches, bosses, knobs, and so on, out of yarn or thread.

27. Solution of riddles, enigmas, covert speeches, verbal puzzles, and enigmatical questions.

28. A game, which consists in repeating verses, and as one person finishes, another person has to commence at once, repeating another verse, beginning with the same letter with which the last speaker's verse ended. Whoever fails to repeat, is considered to have lost and to be subject to pay a forfeit or stake of some kind.

29. The art of mimicry or imitation.

30. Reading, including chanting and intoning.

31. Study of sentences difficult to pronounce. It is played as a game, chiefly by women and children, and consists of a difficult sentence being given; and when it is repeated quickly, the words are often transposed or badly pronounced.

32. Practice with sword, single-stick, quarterstaff, and bow and arrow.

33. Drawing inferences, reasoning or inferring.

34. Carpentry, or the work of a carpenter.

35. Architecture, or the art of building.

36. Knowledge about gold and silver coins, and jewels and gems.

37. Chemistry and mineralogy.

38. Coloring jewels, gems, and beads.

39. Knowledge of mines and quarries.

40. Gardening; knowledge of treating the diseases of trees and plants, of nourishing them, and determining their ages.

41. Arts of cockfighting, quail fighting, and ram fighting.

42. Art of teaching parrots and starlings to speak.

43. Art of applying perfumed ointments to the body, and of dressing the hair with unguents and perfumes, and braiding it.

44. The art of understanding writing in cipher and the writing of words in a peculiar way.

45. The art of speaking by changing the forms of words. It is of various kinds. Some speak by changing the beginning and end of words, others by adding unnecessary letters between every syllable of a word, and so on.

46. Knowledge of languages and of the vernacular dialects.

47. Art of making flower carriages.

48. Art of framing mystical diagrams, of addressing spells and charms, and binding armlets.

49. Mental exercises, such as completing stanzas or verses on receiving a part of them; or supplying one, two, or three lines when the remaining lines are given indiscriminately from different verses, so as to make the whole an entire verse with regard to its meaning; or arranging the words of a verse written irregularly by separating the vowels from the consonants, or

leaving them out altogether; or putting into verse or prose sentences represented by signs or symbols. There are many other such exercises.

50. Composing poems.

51. Knowledge of dictionaries and vocabularies.

52. Knowledge of ways of changing and disguising the appearance of persons.

53. Knowledge of the art of changing the appearance of things, such as making cotton to appear as silk, coarse and common things to appear as fine and good.

54. Various ways of gambling.

55. Art of obtaining possession of the property of others by means of muntras or incantations.

56. Skill in youthful sports.

57. Knowledge of the rules of society, and of how to pay respects and compliments to others.

58. Knowledge of the art of war, of arms, armies, and so on.

59. Knowledge of gymnastics.

60. Art of knowing the character of a man from his features.

61. Knowledge of scanning or constructing verses.

62. Arithmetical recreations.

63. Making artificial flowers.

64. Making figures and images in clay.

A public woman, endowed with a good disposition, beauty, and other winning qualities, and also versed in the above arts, obtains the name of a Ganika, or public woman of high quality, and receives a seat of honor in an assemblage of men. She is, moreover, always respected by the king, and praised by learned men, and her favor being sought for by all, she becomes an object of universal regard. The daughter of a king, too, as well as the daughter of a minister, being learned in the above arts, can make their husbands favorable to them, even though these may have thousands of other wives besides themselves. And in the same manner, if a wife becomes separated from her husband, and falls into distress, she can support herself easily, even in a foreign country, by means of her knowledge of these arts. Even the bare knowledge of them gives attractiveness to a woman, though the practice of them may be possible only according to the circumstances of each case. A man who is versed in these arts, who is loquacious and acquainted with the arts of gallantry, gains very soon the hearts of women, even though he is acquainted with them for only a short time.

## CHAPTER FOUR

# THE LIFE OF THE CITIZEN[1]

HAVING THUS ACQUIRED LEARNING, A MAN, WITH THE WEALTH that he may have gained by gift, conquest, purchase, deposit,[2] or inheritance from his ancestors, should become a householder (Grihastha), and pass the life of a citizen. He should take a house in a city or large village, or in the vicinity of good men, or in a place which is the resort of many persons. This abode should be situated near some water, and divided into different compartments for different purposes. It should be surrounded by a garden, and also contain two rooms, an outer and an inner one. The inner room should be occupied by the females, while the outer room, balmy with rich perfumes, should contain a bed, soft, agreeable to the sight, covered with a clean white cloth, low in the middle part, having garlands and bunches of flowers[3] upon it, and a canopy above it, and two pillows, one at the top, another at the bottom. There should be also a sort of couch, and at the head of this a sort of stool, on which should be placed the fragrant ointments for the night, such as flowers, pots containing collyrium and other fragrant substances, things used for perfuming the mouth, and the bark of the common citron tree. Near the couch, on the ground, there should be a pot for spitting, a box containing ornaments, and also a lute hanging from a peg made of the tooth of an elephant, a board for drawing, a pot containing perfume, some books, and some garlands of the yellow amaranth flowers. Not far from the couch, and on the ground, there should be a round seat, a toy cart, and a board for playing with dice; outside the outer room there should be cages of birds,[4] and a separate place for spinning, carving and suchlike diversions. In the garden there should be a whirling swing and a common swing, as well as a bower of creepers covered with flowers, in which a raised parterre should be made for sitting.

Now, the householder, having got up in the morning and performed his necessary duties,[5] should wash his teeth, apply a limited quantity of ointments and perfumes to his body, put some ornaments on his person and collyrium on his eyelids and below his eyes, color his lips with alacktaka,[6] and look at himself in the glass. Having then eaten betel leaves, with other things that give fragrance to the mouth, he should perform his usual business. He should bathe daily, anoint his body with oil every other day, apply a lathering[7] substance to his body every three days, get his head (including face) shaved every four days and the other parts of his body every five or ten days.[8] All these things should be done without fail, and the sweat of the armpits should also be removed. Meals should be taken in the forenoon, in the afternoon, and again at night, according to Charayana. After breakfast, parrots and other birds should be taught to speak, and the fighting of cocks, quails, and rams should follow. A limited time should be devoted to diversions with Pithamardas, Vitas, and Vidushakas,[9] and then the midday sleep should be taken.[10] After this, the householder, having put on his clothes and ornaments, should, during the afternoon, converse with his friends. In the evening there should be singing, and after that the householder, along with his friend, should await in his room, previously decorated and perfumed, the arrival of the woman that may be attached to him, or he may send a female messenger for her or go to her himself. After her arrival at his house, he and his friends should welcome her and entertain her with a loving and agreeable conversation. Thus end the duties of the day.

The following are the things to be done occasionally as diversions or amusements:

1. Holding festival[11] in honor of different deities
2. Social gatherings of both sexes
3. Drinking parties
4. Picnics
5. Other social diversions

*Festivals*

On some particularly auspicious day, an assembly of citizens should be convened in the temple of Saraswati.[12] There the skill of singers, and of others who may have come recently to the town, should be tested, and on the following day they should always be given some rewards. After that, they may either be retained or dismissed, according as their performances are liked or not by the assembly. The members of the assembly should act in concert both in times of distress as well as in times of prosperity, and it is also the duty of these citizens to show hospitality to strangers who may have come to the assembly. What is said above should be understood to apply to all the other festivals which may be held in honor of the different deities according to the present rules.

*Social Gatherings*

When men of the same age, disposition, and talents, fond of the same diversions and with the same degree of education, sit together in company with public women,[13] or in an assembly of citizens, or at the abode of one among themselves, and engage in agreeable discourse with each other, such is called a sitting in company or a social gathering. The subjects of discourse are to be the completion of verses half composed by others, and the testing of the knowledge of one another in the various arts. The women who may be the most beautiful, who may like the same things that the men like, and who may have power to attract the minds of others, are here done homage to.

## Drinking Parties

Men and women should drink in one another's houses. And here the men should cause the public women to drink, and should then drink themselves, liquors such as the Madhu, Aireya, Sura, and Asawa, which are of bitter and sour taste; also drinks concocted from the barks of various trees, wild fruits, and leaves.

## Going to Gardens or Picnics

In the forenoon, men, having dressed themselves, should go to gardens on horseback, accompanied by public women and followed by servants. And having done there all the duties of the day, and passed the time in various agreeable diversions, such as the fighting of quails, cocks, and rams, and other spectacles, they should return home in the afternoon in the same manner, bringing with them bunches of flowers, and so on.

The same also applies to bathing in summer in water from which poisonous or dangerous animals have previously been taken out, and which has been built in on all sides.

## Other Social Diversions

Spending nights playing with dice. Going out on moonlight nights. Keeping the festive day in honor of spring. Plucking the sprouts and fruits of the mango trees. Eating the fibers of lotuses. Eating the tender ears of corn. Picniking in the forests when the trees get their new foliage. The Udakakshvedika, or sporting in the water. Decorating each other with the flowers of some trees.

Pelting each other with the flowers of the Kadamba tree, and many other sports which may either be known to the whole country or may be peculiar to particular parts of it. These and similar amusements should always be carried on by citizens.

The above amusements should be followed by a person who diverts himself alone in company with a courtesan, as well as by a courtesan who can do the same in company with her maidservants or with citizens.

A Pithamarda[14] is a man without wealth, alone in the world, whose only property consists of his Mallika,[15] some lathering substance, and a red cloth, who comes from a good country, and who is skilled in all the arts; and by teaching these arts is received in the company of citizens, and in the abode of public women.

A Vita[16] is a man who has enjoyed the pleasures of fortune, who is a compatriot of the citizens with whom he associates, who is possessed of the qualities of a householder, who has his wife with him, and who is honored in the assembly of citizens and in the abodes of public women, and lives on their means and on them.

A Vidushaka[17] (also called a Vaihasaka, that is, one who provokes laughter) is a person acquainted with only some of the arts, who is a jester, and who is trusted by all.

These persons are employed in matters of quarrels and reconciliations between citizens and public women. This remark applies also to female beggars, to women with their heads shaven, to adulterous women, and to old public women skilled in all the various arts.

Thus a citizen living in his town or village, respected by all, should call on the persons of his own caste who may be worth knowing. He should converse in company and gratify his friends by his society; and obliging others by his assistance in various matters, he should cause them to assist one another in the same way.

There are some verses on this subject, as follows:

"A citizen discoursing, not entirely in the Sanskrit language[18] nor wholly in the dialects of the country, on various topics in society, obtains great respect. The wise should not resort to a society disliked by the public, governed by no rules, and intent on the destruction of others. But a learned man living in a society which acts according to the wishes of the people and which has pleasure for its only object is highly respected in this world."

## CHAPTER FIVE

# ON THE KINDS OF WOMEN
# RESORTED TO BY THE CITIZEN;
# AND ON FRIENDS AND MESSENGERS

WHEN KAMA IS PRACTICED BY MEN OF THE FOUR CLASSES, according to the rules of the Holy Writ (that is, by lawful marriage), with virgins of their own caste, it then becomes a means of acquiring lawful progeny and good fame, and it is not opposed to the customs of the world. On the contrary, the practice of Kama with women of the higher castes, and with those previously enjoyed by others, even though they be of the same caste, is prohibited. But the practice of Kama with women of the lower castes, with women excommunicated from their own caste, with public women, and with women twice married,[1] is neither enjoined nor prohibited. The object of practicing Kama with such women is pleasure only.

Nayikas,[2] therefore, are of three kinds, namely, maids, women twice married, and public women. Gonikaputra has expressed an opinion that there is a fourth kind of Nayika: a woman who is resorted to on some special occasion even though she be previously married to another. These special occasions are when a man thinks thus:

> This woman is self-willed, and has been previously enjoyed by many others besides myself. I may therefore safely resort to her as to a public woman though she belongs to

a higher caste than mine, and in so doing I shall not be violating the ordinances of Dharma.

Or thus:

This is a twice-married woman and has been enjoyed by others before me; there is, therefore, no objection to my resorting to her.

Or thus:

This woman has gained the heart of her great and powerful husband, and exercises a mastery over him, who is a friend of my enemy; if, therefore, she becomes united with me she will cause her husband to abandon my enemy.

Or thus:

This woman will turn the mind of her husband, who is very powerful, in my favor, he being at present disaffected toward me, and intent on doing me some harm.

Or thus:

By making this woman my friend I shall gain the object of some friend of mine, or shall be able to effect the ruin of some enemy, or shall accomplish some other difficult purpose.

Or thus:

By being united with this woman, I shall kill her husband, and so obtain his vast riches which I covet.

Or thus:

The union of this woman with me is not attended with any danger, and will bring me wealth, of which, on account of my poverty and inability to support myself, I am very much in need. I shall, therefore, obtain her vast riches in this way without any difficulty.

Or thus:
This woman loves me ardently, and knows all my weak points; if therefore I am unwilling to be united with her, she will make my faults public, and thus tarnish my character and reputation. Or she will bring some gross accusation against me, of which it may be hard to clear myself, and I shall be ruined. Or perhaps she will detach from me her husband, who is powerful and yet under her control, and will unite him to my enemy, or will herself join the latter.

Or thus:
The husband of this woman has violated the chastity of my wives; I shall therefore return that injury by seducing his wives.

Or thus:
By the help of this woman I shall kill an enemy of the king, who has taken shelter with her and whom I am ordered by the king to destroy.

Or thus:
The woman I love is under the control of this woman. I shall, through the influence of the latter, be able to get at the former.

Or thus:
This woman will bring to me a maid who possesses wealth and beauty but who is hard to get at, and under the control of another.

Or lastly thus:

My enemy is a friend of this woman's husband; I shall
therefore cause her to join him, and will thus create an
enmity between her husband and him.

For these and similar reasons the wives of other men may be
resorted to; but it must be distinctly understood that it is allowed
only for special reasons, and not for mere carnal desire.

Charayana thinks that under these circumstances there is
also a fifth kind of Nayika; namely, a woman who is kept by
a minister, or who repairs to him occasionally; or a widow
who accomplishes the purpose of a man with the person to
whom she resorts.

Suvarnanabha adds that a woman who passes the life of an
ascetic and in the condition of a widow may be considered as a
sixth kind of Nayika.

Ghotakamukha cites the daughter of a public woman, and a
female servant, who are still virgins, for a seventh kind of Nayika.

Gonardiya puts forth his doctrine that any woman born of
good family, after she has come of age, is an eighth kind of Nayika.

But these last four kinds of Nayikas do not differ much from the
first four kinds of them, as there is no separate object in resorting
to them. Therefore, Vatsyayana is of opinion that there are only
four kinds of Nayikas: the maid, the twice-married woman, the
public woman, and the woman resorted to for a special purpose.

The following women are not to be enjoyed:

A leper
A lunatic
A woman turned out of caste
A woman who reveals secrets
A woman who publicly expresses a desire for sexual intercourse

A woman who is extremely white
A woman who is extremely black
A bad-smelling woman
A woman who is a near relative
A woman who is a female friend
A woman who leads the life of an ascetic
And, lastly, the wife of a relative, of a friend, of a learned Brahman, and of the king

The followers of Babhravya say that any woman who has been enjoyed by five men is a fit and proper person to be enjoyed. But Gonikaputra is of opinion that even when this is the case, the wives of a relative, of a learned Brahman, and of a king should be excepted.

The following are the kind of friends:

One who has played with you in the dust, that is, in childhood
One who is bound by an obligation
One who is of the same disposition and fond of the same things
One who is a fellow student
One who is acquainted with your secrets and faults, and whose faults and secrets are also known to you
One who is a child of your nurse
One who is brought up with you
One who is a hereditary friend

These friends should possess the following qualities:

They should tell the truth.
They should not be changed by time.
They should be favorable to your designs.
They should be firm.

They should be free from covetousness.
They should not be capable of being gained over by others.
They should not reveal your secrets.

Charayana says that citizens form friendships with washermen, barbers, cowherds, florists, druggists, betel-leaf sellers, tavern keepers, beggars, Pithamardas, Vitas, and Vidushakas, as also with the wives of all these people.

A messenger should possess the following qualities:

Skillfulness
Boldness
Knowledge of the intention of men by their outward signs
Absence of confusion, that is, no shyness
Knowledge of the exact meaning of what others do or say
Good manners
Knowledge of appropriate times and places for doing different things
Ingenuity in business
Quick comprehension
Quick application of remedies, that is, quick and ready resources

And this part ends with a verse:
"The man who is ingenious and wise, who is accompanied by a friend, and who knows the intentions of others, as well as the proper time and place for doing everything, can gain over, very easily, even a woman who is very hard to be obtained."

# On Sexual Union

## ❧ Part Two ❧

## CHAPTER ONE

# KINDS OF UNION ACCORDING TO DIMENSIONS, FORCE OF DESIRE OR PASSION, AND TIME

MAN IS DIVIDED INTO THREE CLASSES: THE HARE MAN, THE BULL man, and the horse man, according to the size of his lingam.

Woman also, according to the depth of her yoni is either a female deer, a mare, or a female elephant.

There are thus three equal unions between persons of corresponding dimensions, and there are six unequal unions when the dimensions do not correspond, or nine in all, as the following table shows:

| EQUAL | | UNEQUAL | |
|---|---|---|---|
| MEN | WOMEN | MEN | WOMEN |
| Hare | Deer | Hare | Mare |
| Bull | Mare | Hare | Elephant |
| Horse | Elephant | Bull | Deer |
| | | Bull | Elephant |
| | | Horse | Deer |
| | | Horse | Mare |

In these unequal unions, when the male exceeds the female in point of size, his union with a woman who is immediately next to him in size is called high union, and is of two kinds; while his union with the woman most remote from him in size is called the highest union, and is of one kind only. On the other hand, when the female exceeds the male in point of size, her union with a man immediately next to her in size is called low union, and is of two kinds; while her union with a man most remote from her in size is called the lowest union, and is of one kind only.

In other words, the horse and mare, the bull and deer, form the high union, while the horse and deer form the highest union. On the female side, the elephant and bull, the mare and hare, form low unions, while the elephant and the hare make the lowest unions.

There are, then, nine kinds of union according to dimensions. Among all these, equal unions are the best; those of a superlative degree, that is, the highest and the lowest, are the worst; and the rest are middling, and with them the high[1] are better than the low.

There are also nine kinds of union according to the force of passion or carnal desire, as follows:

| MEN | WOMEN | MEN | WOMEN |
|---|---|---|---|
| Small | Small | Small | Middling |
| Middling | Middling | Small | Intense |
| Intense | Intense | Middling | Small |
| | | Middling | Intense |
| | | Intense | Small |
| | | Intense | Middling |

A man is called a man of small passion whose desire at the time of sexual union is not great, whose semen is scanty, and who cannot bear the warm embraces of the female.

Those who differ from this temperament are called men of middling passion, while those of intense passion are full of desire.

In the same way, women are supposed to have the three degrees of feeling as specified above.

Lastly, according to time there are three kinds of men and women: the short-timed, the moderate-timed, and the long-timed, and of these, as in the previous statements, there are nine kinds of union.

But on this last head there is a difference of opinion about the female, which should be stated.

Auddalika says: "Females do not emit as males do. The males simply remove their desire, while the females, from their consciousness of desire, feel a certain kind of pleasure, which gives them satisfaction, but it is impossible for them to tell you what kind of pleasure they feel. The fact from which this becomes evident is that males, when engaged in coition, cease of themselves after emission, and are satisfied, but it is not so with females."

This opinion is, however, objected to on the grounds, that if a male be long-timed, the female loves him the more, but if he be short-timed she is dissatisfied with him. And this circumstance, some say, would prove that the female emits also.

But this opinion does not hold good, for if it takes a long time to allay a woman's desire, and during this time she is enjoying great pleasure, it is quite natural then that she should wish for its continuation. And on this subject there is a verse as follows:

"By union with men the lust, desire, or passion of women is satisfied, and the pleasure derived from the consciousness of it is called their satisfaction."

The followers of Babhravya, however, say that the semen of women continues to fall from the beginning of the sexual union to its end; and it is right that it should be so, for if they had no semen there would be no embryo.

To this there is an objection. In the beginning of coition the passion of the woman is middling, and she cannot bear the vigorous thrusts of her lover; but by degrees her passion increases until she ceases to think about her body, and then finally she wishes to stop from further coition.

This objection, however, does not hold good, for even in ordinary things that revolve with great force, such as a potter's wheel or a top, we find that the motion at first is slow, but by degrees it becomes very rapid. In the same way the passion of the woman having gradually increased, she has a desire to discontinue coition, when all the semen has fallen away. And there is a verse with regard to this as follows:

"The fall of the semen of the man takes place only at the end of coition, while the semen of the woman falls continually; and after the semen of both has all fallen away then they wish for the discontinuance of coition."

Lastly, Vatsyayana is of opinion that the semen of the female falls in the same way as that of the male.

Now, someone may ask here: If men and women are beings of the same kind, and are engaged in bringing about the same result, why should they have different work to do?

Vatsyayana says that this is so because the ways of working, as well as the consciousness of pleasure in men and women, are different. The difference in the ways of working, by which men are the actors and women are the persons acted upon, is owing to the nature of the male and the female; otherwise the actor would be sometimes the person acted upon, and vice versa. And from this difference in the ways of working follows the difference in the consciousness of pleasure, for a man thinks, "This woman is united with me," and a woman thinks, "I am united with this man."

It may be said that if the ways of working in men and women are different, why should there not be a difference, even in the pleasure they feel, which is the result of those ways?

But this objection is groundless, for the person acting and the person acted upon being of different kinds, there is a reason for the difference in their ways of working; but there is no reason for any difference in the pleasure they feel, because they both naturally derive pleasure from the act they perform.[2]

On this again some may say that when different persons are engaged in doing the same work, we find that they accomplish the same end or purpose; while, on the contrary, in the case of men and women we find that each of them accomplishes his or her own end separately, and this is inconsistent. But this is a mistake, for we find that sometimes two things are done at the same time; as for instance in the fighting of rams, both the rams receive the shock at the same time on their heads. Or in throwing one wood apple against another, or in a fight or struggle of wrestlers. If it be said that in these cases the things employed are of the same kind, it is answered that even in the case of men and women, the nature of the two persons is the same. And as the difference in their ways of working arises from the difference of their conformation only, it follows that men experience the same kind of pleasure as women do. There is also a verse on this subject as follows:

"Men and women being of the same nature feel the same kind of pleasure, and therefore a man should marry such a woman as will love him ever afterward."

The pleasure of men and women being thus proved to be of the same kind, it follows that in regard to time there are nine kinds of sexual intercourse, in the same way as there are nine kinds according to the force of passion.

There being thus nine kinds of union with regard to dimensions, force of passion, and time, respectively, by making combinations of them innumerable kinds of union would be produced. Therefore in each particular kind of sexual union, men should use such means as they may think suitable for the occasion.

At the first time of sexual union the passion of the male is intense, and his time is short, but in subsequent unions on the same day the reverse of this is the case. With the female, however, it is the contrary, for at the first time her passion is weak, and her time long, but on subsequent occasions on the same day her passion is intense and her time short, until her passion is satisfied.

## On the Different Kinds of Love

Men learned in the humanities are of opinion that love is of four kinds:

1. Love acquired by continual habit
2. Love resulting from the imagination
3. Love resulting from belief
4. Love resulting from the perception of external objects

(1). Love resulting from the constant and continual performance of some act is called love acquired by constant practice and habit; as for instance, the love of sexual intercourse, the love of hunting, the love of drinking, the love of gambling, and so on.

(2). Love which is felt for things to which we are not habituated, and which proceeds entirely from ideas, is called love resulting from imagination; as for instance, that love which some men and women and eunuchs feel for the Auparishtaka, or mouth congress, and that which is felt by all for such things as embracing, kissing, and so on.

(3). The love which is mutual on both sides, and proved to be true, when each looks upon the other as his or her very own; such is called love resulting from belief by the learned.

(4). The love resulting from the perception of external objects is quite evident and well known to the world, because the pleasure it affords is superior to the pleasure of the other kinds of love, which exist only for its sake.

What has been said in this chapter upon the subject of sexual union is sufficient for the learned; but for the edification of the ignorant, the same will now be treated at length and in detail.

## CHAPTER TWO

# ON THE EMBRACE

THIS PART OF THE *KAMA SHASTRA*, WHICH TREATS OF SEXUAL UNION, is also called "Sixty-four" (Chatushshashti). Some old authors say that it is called so because it contains sixty-four chapters. Others are of opinion that the author of this part being a person named Panchala, and the person who recited the part of the Rig-Veda called "Dashatapa," which contains sixty-four verses, being also called Panchala, the name "Sixty-four" has been given to the part of the work in honor of the Rig-Veda. The followers of Badhravya say on the other hand that this part contains eight subjects: the embrace, kissing, scratching with the nails or fingers, biting, lying down, making various sounds, playing the part of a man, and the Auparishataka, or mouth congress. Each of these subjects being of eight kinds, and eight multiplied by eight being sixty-four, this part is therefore named "Sixty-four." But Vatsyayana affirms that as this part contains also the following subjects, namely striking, crying, the acts of a man during congress, the various kinds of congress, and other subjects, the name "Sixty-four" is given to it only accidentally. As for instance, we say this tree is "Saptaparna," or seven-leaved; this offering of rice is "Panchavarna," or five-colored; but the tree has not seven leaves, nor has the rice five colors.

However, the part "Sixty-four" is now treated of; and the embrace, being the first subject, will now be considered.

The embrace which indicates the mutual love of a man and woman who have come together is of four kinds:

Touching
Piercing
Rubbing
Pressing

The action in each case is denoted by the meaning of the word which stands for it.

(1). When a man under some pretext or other goes in front of or alongside a woman and touches her body with his own, it is called the "touching embrace."

(2). When a woman in a lonely place bends down, as if to pick up something, and pierces, as it were, a man sitting or standing, with her breasts, and the man in return takes hold of them, it is called a "piercing embrace."

These two embraces take place only between persons who do not, as yet, speak freely with each other.

(3). When two lovers are walking slowly together, either in the dark or in a place of public resort, or in a lonely place, and rub their bodies against each other, it is called a "rubbing embrace."

(4). When on the above occasion one of them presses the other's body forcibly against a wall or pillar, it is called a "pressing embrace."

These two last embraces are peculiar to those who know the intentions of each other.

At the times of meeting, the four following kinds of embrace are used:

*Jataveshtitaka,* or the twining of a creeper.
*Vrikshadhirudhaka,* or climbing a tree.
*Tila-Tandulaka,* or the mixture of sesame seed with rice.
*Kshiraniraka,* or milk-and-water embrace.

(1). When a woman, clinging to a man as a creeper twines round a tree, bends his head down to hers with the desire of kissing him and slightly makes the sound of *Sūt, sūt,* embraces him, and looks lovingly toward him, it is called an embrace like the "twining of a creeper."

(2). When a woman, having placed one of her feet on the foot of her lover, and the other on one of his thighs, passes one of her arms round his back, and the other on his shoulders, makes slightly the sounds of singing and cooing, and wishes, as it were, to climb up him in order to have a kiss, it is called an embrace like the "climbing of a tree."

These two embraces take place when the lover is standing.

(3). When lovers lie on a bed, and embrace each other so closely that the arms and thighs of one are encircled by the arms and thighs of the other, and are, as it were rubbing up against them, this is called an embrace like "the mixture of sesame seed with rice."

(4). When a man and a woman are very much in love with each other, and, not thinking of any pain or hurt, embrace each other as if they were entering into each other's bodies either while the woman is sitting on the lap of the man or in front of him, or on a bed, then it is called an embrace like a "mixture of milk and water."

These two embraces take place at the time of sexual union.

Babhravya has thus related to us the above eight kinds of embraces.

Suvarnanabha, moreover, gives us four ways of embracing simple members of the body, which are:

The embrace of the thighs
The embrace of the *jaghana,* that is, the part of the body from the navel downward to the thighs
The embrace of the breasts
The embrace of the forehead

(1). When one of two lovers presses forcibly one or both of the thighs of the other between his or her own, it is called the "embrace of thighs."

(2). When the man presses the jaghana, or middle part, of the woman's body against his own, and mounts upon her to practice, either scratching with the nail or finger, or biting or striking or kissing, the hair of the woman being loose and flowing, it is called the "embrace of the jaghana."

(3). When a man places his breast between the breasts of a woman and presses her with it, it is called the "embrace of the breasts."

(4). When either of the lovers touches the mouth, the eyes, and the forehead of the other with his or her own, it is called the "embrace of the forehead."

Some say that even shampooing is a kind of embrace, because there is a touching of bodies in it. But Vatsyayana thinks that shampooing is performed at a different time, and for a different purpose; and as it is also of a different character, it cannot be said to be included in the embrace. There are also some verses on the subject, as follows:

"The whole subject of embracing is of such nature that men who ask questions about it, or who hear about it, or who talk about it, acquire thereby a desire for enjoyment. Even those embraces that are not mentioned in the *Kama Shastra* should be practiced at the time of sexual enjoyment, if they are in any way conducive to the increase of love or passion. The rules of the Shastra apply as long as the passion of man is middling, but when the wheel of love is once set in motion, there is then no Shastra and no order."

## CHAPTER THREE

# ON KISSING

It is said by some that there is no fixed time or order between the embrace, the kiss, and the pressing or scratching with the nails or fingers, but that all these things should be done generally before sexual union takes place, while striking and making the various sounds generally takes place at the time of the union. Vatsyayana, however, thinks that anything may take place at any time, for love does not care for time or order.

On the occasion of first congress, kissing and the other things mentioned above should be done moderately; they should not be continued for a long time, and should be done alternately. On subsequent occasions, however, the reverse of all this may take place, and moderation will not be necessary; they may continue for a long time; and for the purpose of kindling love, they may be all done at the same time.

The following are the places for kissing: the forehead, the eyes, the cheeks, the throat, the bosom, the breasts, the lips, and the interior of the mouth. Moreover, the people of the Lat country kiss also the following places: the joints of the thighs, the arms, and the navel. But Vatsyayana thinks that though kissing is practiced by these people in the above places because of the intensity of their love and the customs of their country, it is not fit to be practiced by all.

Now, with a young girl there are three sorts of kisses:

46

The nominal kiss
The throbbing kiss
The touching kiss

(1). When a girl touches only the mouth of her lover with her own, but does not herself do anything, it is called the "nominal kiss."

(2). When a girl, setting aside her bashfulness a little, wishes to touch the lip that is pressed into her mouth, and with that object moves her lower lip, but not the upper one, it is called the "throbbing kiss."

(3). When a girl touches her lover's lip with her tongue, and having shut her eyes, places her hands on those of her lover, it is called the "touching kiss."

Other authors describe four other kinds of kisses:

The straight kiss
The bent kiss
The turned kiss
The pressed kiss

(1). When the lips of two lovers are brought into direct contact with each other, it is called a "straight kiss."

(2). When the heads of two lovers are bent toward each other, and when so bent, kissing takes place, it is called a "bent kiss."

(3). When one of them turns up the face of the other by holding the head and chin, and then kissing, it is called a "turned kiss."

(4). Lastly, when the lower lip is pressed with much force, it is called "pressed kiss."

There is also a fifth kind of kiss, called the "greatly pressed kiss," which is effected by taking hold of the lower lip between two fingers, and then after touching it with the tongue, pressing it with great force with the lip.

As regards kissing, a wager may be laid as to which will get hold of the lips of the other first. If the woman loses, she should pretend to cry, should keep her lover off by shaking her hands, and turn away from him and dispute with him, saying, "Let another wager be laid." If she loses this a second time, she should appear doubly distressed, and when her lover is off his guard or asleep, she should get hold of his lower lip, and hold it in her teeth, so that it should not slip away; and then she should laugh, make a loud noise, deride him, dance about, and say whatever she likes in a joking way, moving her eyebrows, and rolling her eyes. Such are the wagers and quarrels as far as kissing is concerned, but the same may be applied with regard to the pressing or scratching with the nails and fingers, biting and striking. All these, however, are peculiar only to men and women of intense passion.

When a man kisses the upper lip of a woman, while she in return kisses his lower lip, it is called the "kiss of the upper lip."

When one of them takes both the lips of the other between his or her own, it is called "a clasping kiss." A woman, however, takes this kind of kiss only from a man who has no moustache. And on the occasion of this kiss, if one of them touches the teeth, the tongue, and the palate of the other, with his or her tongue, it is called the "fighting of the tongue." In the same way, the pressing of the teeth of the one against the mouth of the other is to be practiced.

Kissing is of four kinds: moderate, contracted, pressed, and soft, according to the different parts of the body which are kissed, for different kinds of kisses are appropriate for different parts of the body.

When a woman looks at the face of her lover while he is asleep, and kisses it to show her intention or desire, it is called a "kiss that kindles love."

When a woman kisses her lover while he is engaged in business, or while he is quarreling with her, or while he is looking at something else, so that his mind may be turned away, it is called a "kiss that turns away."

When a lover coming home late at night kisses his beloved who is asleep on her bed, in order to show her his desire, it is called a "kiss that awakens." On such an occasion the woman may pretend to be asleep at the time of her lover's arrival, so that she may know his intention and obtain respect from him.

When a person kisses the reflection of the person he loves in a mirror, in water, or on a wall, it is called a "kiss showing the intention."

When a person kisses a child sitting on his lap, or a picture or an image or figure, in the presence of the person beloved by him, it is called a "transferred kiss."

When at night at a theater, or in an assembly of caste men, a man coming up to a woman kisses a finger of her hand if she be standing, or a toe of her foot if she be sitting, or when a woman in shampooing her lover's body places her face in his thigh (as if she were sleepy) so as to inflame his passion, and kisses his thigh or great toe, it is called a "demonstrative kiss."

There is also a verse on this subject as follows:

"Whatever things may be done by one of the lovers to the other, the same should be returned by the other; that is, if the woman kisses him he should kiss her in return; if she strikes him he should also strike her in return."

## CHAPTER FOUR

# ON PRESSING OR MARKING OR SCRATCHING WITH THE NAILS

WHEN LOVE BECOMES INTENSE, PRESSING WITH THE NAILS OR scratching the body with them is practiced, and it is done on the following occasions: on the first visit; at the time of setting out on a journey; on the return from a journey; at the time when an angry lover is reconciled; and, lastly, when the woman is intoxicated.

But pressing with the nails is not a usual thing except with those who are intensely passionate. It is employed, together with biting, by those to whom the practice is agreeable.

Pressing with the nails is of the eight following kinds, according to the forms of the marks which are produced:

1. Sounding
2. Half-moon
3. A circle
4. A line
5. A tiger's nail or claw
6. A peacock's foot
7. The jump of a hare
8. The leaf of a blue lotus

The places that are to be pressed with the nails are: the armpit, the throat, the breasts, the lips, the jaghana, or middle parts of the body, and the thighs. But Suvarnanabha is of the opinion that when the impetuosity of passion is excessive, then the places need not be considered.

The qualities of good nails are that they should be bright, well set, clean, entire, convex, soft, and glossy in appearance. Nails are of three kinds according to their size:

Small
Middling
Large

Large nails, which give grace to the hands, and attract the hearts of women from their appearance, are possessed by the Bengalese.

Small nails, which can be used in various ways, and are to be applied only with the object of giving pleasure, are possessed by the people of the southern districts.

Middling nails, which contain the properties of both the above kinds, belong to the people of Maharashtra.

(1). When a person presses the chin, the breasts, the lower lip, or the jaghana of another so softly that no scratch or mark is left, but only the hair on the body becomes erect from the touch of the nails, and the nails themselves make a sound, it is called a "sounding or pressing with the nails."

This pressing is used in the case of a young girl when her lover shampoos her, scratches her head, and wants to trouble or frighten her.

(2). The curved mark with the nails, which is impressed on the neck and the breasts, is called the "half-moon."

(3). When the half-moons are impressed opposite each other, it is called a "circle." This mark with the nails is generally made on the navel, the small cavities about the buttocks, and on the joints of the thigh.

(4). A mark in the form of a small line, which can be made on any part of the body, is called a "line."

(5). This same line, when it is curved, and made on the breast, is called a "tiger's nail."

(6). When a curved mark is made on the breast by means of the five nails, it is called a "peacock's foot." This mark is made with the object of being praised, for it requires a great deal of skill to make it properly.

(7). When five marks with the nails are made close to one another near the nipple of the breast, it is called "the jump of a hare."

(8). A mark made on the breast or on the hips in the form of a leaf of the blue lotus is called the "leaf of a blue lotus."

When a person is going on a journey, and makes a mark on the thighs, or on the breast, it is called a "token of remembrance." On such an occasion three or four lines are impressed close to one another with the nails.

Here ends discourse of the marking with the nails. Marks of kinds other than the above may also be made with the nails, for the ancient authors say that as there are innumerable degrees of skill among men (the practice of this art being known to all), so there are innumerable ways of making these marks. And as pressing or marking with the nails is dependent on love, no one can say with certainty how many different kinds of marks with the nails do actually exist. The reason for this is, Vatsyayana says, that as variety is necessary in love, so love is to be produced by means of variety. It is on this account that courtesans, who are well acquainted with various ways and means, become so desirable; for if variety is sought in all the arts and amusements, such as archery and others, how much more should it be sought after in the art of love.

The marks of the nails should not be made on married women, but particular kinds of marks may be made on their private parts for the remembrance and increase of love.

There are also some verses on the subject, as follows:

"The love of a woman who sees the marks of nails on the private parts of her body, even though they are old and almost worn out, becomes again fresh and new. If there be no marks of nails to remind a person of the passages of love, then love is lessened in the same way as when no union takes place for a long time."

Even when a stranger sees at a distance a young woman with the marks of nails on her breast,[1] he is filled with love and respect for her.

A man, also, who carries the marks of nails and teeth on some parts of his body, influences the mind of a woman, even though it be ever so firm. In short, nothing tends to increase love so much as the effects of marking with the nails, and biting.

# ON BITING, AND THE MEANS TO BE EMPLOYED WITH REGARD TO WOMEN OF DIFFERENT COUNTRIES

ALL THE PLACES THAT CAN BE KISSED ARE ALSO THE PLACES THAT can be bitten, except the upper lip, the interior of the mouth, and the eyes.

The qualities of good teeth are as follows: They should be equal, possessed of a pleasing brightness, capable of being colored, of proper proportions, unbroken, and with sharp ends.

The defects of teeth, on the other hand, are that they are blunt, protruding from the gums, rough, soft, large, and loosely set.

The following are the different kinds of biting:

> The hidden bite
> The swollen bite
> The point
> The line of points
> The coral and the jewel
> The line of jewels
> The broken cloud
> The biting of the boar

(1). The biting which is shown only by the excessive redness of the skin that is bitten, is called the "hidden bite."

(2). When the skin is pressed down on both sides, it is called the "swollen bite."

(3). When a small portion of the skin is bitten with two teeth only, it is called the "point."

(4). When such small portions of the skin are bitten with all the teeth, it is called the "line of points."

(5). The biting which is done by bringing together the teeth and the lips is called the "coral and the jewel." The lips are the coral, and the teeth are the jewel.

(6). When biting is done with all the teeth, it is called the "line of jewels."

(7). The biting which consists of unequal risings in a circle, and which comes from the space between the teeth, is called the "broken cloud." This is impressed on the breasts.

(8). The biting which consists of many broad rows of marks near to one another, and with red intervals, is called the "biting of a boar." This is impressed on the breasts and the shoulders; and these two last modes of biting are peculiar to persons of intense passion.

The lower lip is the place on which the "hidden bite," the "swollen bite," and the "point" are made; the "swollen bite" and the "coral and the jewel" bite are done on the cheek. Kissing, pressing with the nails, and biting are the ornaments of the left cheek, and when the word "cheek" is used, it is to be understood as the left cheek.

Both the "line of points" and the "line of jewels" are to be impressed on the throat, the armpit, and the joints of the thighs; but the "line of points" alone is to be impressed on the forehead and the thighs.

The marking with the nails, and the biting of the following things, namely, an ornament of the forehead, an ear ornament, a bunch of flowers, a betel leaf, or a tamala leaf, which are worn by or belong to the woman who is beloved, are signs of desire of enjoyment.

Here ends discourse of the different kinds of biting.

In the affairs of love a man should do such things as are agreeable to the women of different countries.

The women of the central countries (that is, between the Ganges and the Jumna) are noble in their character, not accustomed to disgraceful practices, and dislike pressing with the nails and biting.

The women of the Balhika country are gained over by striking.

The women of Avantika are fond of foul pleasures, and have not good manners.

The women of Maharashtra are fond of practicing the sixty-four arts; they utter low and harsh words, and like to be spoken to in the same way, and have an impetuous desire of enjoyment.

The women of Pataliputra (that is, the modern Patna) are of the same nature as the women of the Maharashtra, but show their likings only in secret.

The women of the Dravidian country, though they are rubbed and pressed about at the time of sexual enjoyment, have a slow fall of semen: that is, they are very slow in the act of coition.

The women of Vanavasi are moderately passionate; they go through every kind of enjoyment, cover their bodies, and abuse those who utter low, mean, and harsh words.

The women of Avanti hate kissing, marking with the nails, and biting, but they have a fondness for various kinds of sexual union.

The women of Malwa like embracing and kissing, but not wounding, and they are gained over by striking.

The women of Abhira, and those of the country about the Indus and five rivers (that is, the Punjab), are gained over by the Auparishtaka, or mouth congress.

The women of Aparatika are full of passion, and make slowly the sound *Sit.*

The women of the Lat country have even more impetuous desire, and also make the sound *Sit.*

The women of the Stri Rajya and of Koshala (Oudh) are full of impetuous desire; their semen falls in large quantities, and they are fond of taking medicine to make it do so.

The women of the Andhra country have tender bodies; they are fond of enjoyment, and have a liking for voluptuous pleasures.

The women of Gandak have tender bodies, and speak sweetly.

Now, Suvarnanabha is of opinion that that which is agreeable to the nature of a particular person is of more consequence than that which is agreeable to a whole nation, and that therefore the peculiarities of the country should not be observed in such cases. The various pleasures, the dress, and the sports of one country are in time borrowed by another, and in such a case these things must be considered as belonging originally to that country.

Among the things mentioned above, namely, embracing, kissing, and so on, those which increase passion should be done first, and those which are only for amusement or variety should be done afterward.

There are also some verses on this subject, as follows:

"When a man bites a woman forcibly, she should angrily do the same to him with double force. Thus a 'point' should be returned with a 'line of points,' and a 'line of points' with a 'broken cloud'; and if she be excessively chaffed, she should at once begin a love quarrel with him. At such a time she should take hold of her lover by the hair, and bend his head down, and kiss his lower lip, and then, being intoxicated with love, she should shut her eyes and bite him in various places. Even by day and in a place of public resort, when her lover shows her any mark that she may have inflicted on his body, she should smile at the sight of it, and turning her face as if she were going to chide him, she should show him with an angry look the marks on her own body that have been made by him. Thus if men and women act according to each other's liking, their love for each other will not be lessened even in one hundred years."

## CHAPTER SIX

# ON THE VARIOUS WAYS OF LYING DOWN, AND THE DIFFERENT KINDS OF CONGRESS

ON THE OCCASION OF A "HIGH CONGRESS" THE MRIGI (DEER) woman should lie down in such a way as to widen her yoni, while in a "low congress" the Hastini (Elephant) woman should lie down so as to contract hers. But in an "equal congress" they should lie down in the natural position. What is said above concerning the Mrigi and the Hastini applies also to the Vadawa (Mare) woman. In a "low congress" the woman should particularly make use of medicine, to cause her desires to be satisfied quickly.

The Deer woman has the following three ways of lying down:

> The widely opened position
> The yawning position
> The position of the wife of Indra

(1). When she lowers her head and raises her middle parts, it is called the "widely opened position." At such a time the man should apply some unguent, so as to make the entrance easy.

(2). When she raises her thighs and keeps them wide apart and engages in congress, it is called the "yawning position."

(3). When she places her thighs with her legs doubled on them upon her sides, and thus engages in congress, it is called the position of Indrani, and this is learned only by practice. The position is also useful in the case of the "highest congress."

There are also the "clasping position" and the "low congress," and in the "lowest congress," together with the "pressing position," the "twining position" and the "mare's position."

When the legs of both the male and the female are stretched straight out over each other, it is called the "clasping position." It is of two kinds, the side position and the supine position, according to the way in which they lie down. In the side position the male should invariably lie on his left side, and cause the woman to lie on her right side, and this rule is to be observed in lying down with all kinds of women.

When, after congress has begun in the clasping position, the woman presses her lover with her thighs, it is called the "pressing position."

When the woman places one of her thighs across the thigh of her lover, it is called the "twining position."

When the woman forcibly holds in her yoni the lingam after it is in, it is called the "mare's position." This is learned by practice only, and is chiefly found among the women of the Andra country.

The above are the different ways of lying down, mentioned by Babhravya; Suvarnanabha, however, gives the following in addition:

When the female raises both of her thighs straight up, it is called the "rising position."

When she raises both of her legs, and places them on her lover's shoulders, it is called the "yawning position."

When the legs are contracted, and thus held by the lover before his bosom, it is called the "pressed position."

When only one of her legs is stretched out, it is called the "half-pressed position."

When the woman places one of her legs on her lover's shoulder, and stretches the other out, and then places the latter on his shoulder, and stretches out the other, and continues to do so alternately, it is called the "splitting of a bamboo."

When one of her legs is placed on the head, and the other is stretched out, it is called the "fixing of a nail." This is learned by practice only.

When both the legs of the woman are contracted, and placed on her stomach, it is called the "crab's position."

When the thighs are raised and placed one upon the other, it is called the "packed position."

When the shanks are placed one upon the other, it is called the "lotus-like position."

When a man, during congress, turns round, and enjoys the woman without leaving her, while she embraces him round the back all the time, it is called the "turning position," and is learned only by practice.

Thus, says Suvarnanabha, these different ways of lying down, sitting, and standing should be practiced in water, because it is easy to do so therein. But Vatsyayana is of opinion that congress in water is improper, because it is prohibited by the religious law.

When a man and a woman support themselves on each other's bodies, or on a wall or pillar, and thus while standing engage in congress, it is called the "supported congress."

When a man supports himself against a wall, and the woman, sitting on his hands joined together and held underneath her, throws her arms round his neck, and putting her thighs alongside his waist, moves herself by her feet, which are touching the wall against which the man is leaning, it is called the "suspended congress."

When a woman stands on her hands and feet like a quadruped, and her lover mounts her like a bull, it is called the "congress of a cow." At this time everything that is ordinarily done on the bosom should be done on the back.

In the same way can be carried on the congress of a dog, the congress of a goat, the congress of a deer, the forcible mounting of an ass, the congress of a cat, the jump of a tiger, the pressing of an elephant, the rubbing of a boar, and the mounting of a horse. And in all these cases the characteristics of the different animals should be manifested by acting like them.

When a man enjoys two women at the same time, both of whom love him equally, it is called the "united congress."

When a man enjoys many women altogether, it is called the "congress of a herd of cows."

The following kinds of congress, namely, sporting in water, or the congress of an elephant with many female elephants which is said to take place only in the water, the congress of a collection of goats, the congress of a collection of deer, take place in imitation of these animals.

In Gramaneri many young men enjoy a woman that may be married to one of them, either one after the other or at the same time. Thus one of them holds her, another enjoys her, a third uses her mouth, a fourth holds her middle part, and in this way they go on enjoying her several parts alternately.

The same things can be done when several men are sitting in company with one courtesan, or when one courtesan is alone with many men. In the same way this can be done by the women of the king's harem when they accidentally get hold of a man.

The people in the Southern countries have also a congress in the anus, that is called the "lower congress."

Thus ends the various kinds of congress. There are also two verses on the subjects, as follows:

"An ingenious person should multiply the kinds of congress after the fashion of the different kinds of beasts and of birds. For these different kinds of congress, performed according to the usage of each country, and the liking of each individual, generate love, friendship, and respect in the hearts of women."

## CHAPTER SEVEN

# ON THE VARIOUS MODES OF STRIKING, AND ON THE SOUNDS APPROPRIATE TO THEM

SEXUAL INTERCOURSE CAN BE COMPARED TO A QUARREL, ON account of the contrarieties of love and its tendency to dispute. The place of striking with passion is the body, and on the body the special places are:

The shoulders
The head
The space between the breasts
The back
The jaghana, or middle part of the body
The sides

Striking is of four kinds:

Striking with the back of the hand
Striking with the fingers a little contracted
Striking with the fist
Striking with the open palm of the hand

On account of its causing pain, striking gives rise to the kissing sound, which is of various kinds, and to the eight kinds of crying:

The sound *Hin*
The thundering sound
The cooing sound
The weeping sound
The sound *Phut*
The sound *Phât*
The sound *Sût*
The sound *Plât*

Besides these, there are also words having a meaning, such as "mother," and those that are expressive of prohibition, sufficiency, desire of liberation, pain or praise, and to which may be added sounds like those of the dove, the cuckoo, the green pigeon, the parrot, the bee, the sparrow, the flamingo, the duck, and the quail, which are all occasionally made use of.

Blows with the fist should be given on the back of the woman, while she is sitting on the lap of the man, and she should give blows in return, abusing the man as if she were angry, and making the cooing and the weeping sounds. While the woman is engaged in congress the space between the breasts should be struck with the back of the hand, slowly at first, and then proportionately to the increasing excitement, until the end.

At this time the sounds *Hin* and others may be made, alternately or optionally, according to habit. When the man, making the sound *Phât,* strikes the woman on the head with the fingers of his hand a little contracted, it is called Prasritaka, which means striking with the fingers of the hand a little contracted. In this case the appropriate sounds are the cooing sound, the sound *Phât,* and the sound *Phut* in the interior of the mouth, and at the end of congress the sighing and weeping sounds. The sound *Phât* is an imitation of the sound of a bamboo being split, while the sound *Phut* is like the sound made by something falling into water. At all times when kissing and suchlike things are begun, the woman should give a reply with a kissing sound. During the excitement, when the woman is not accustomed to striking, she continually utters words expressive of prohibition, sufficiency, or desire of liberation, as well as the words "father," "mother," intermingled with the sighing, weeping, and thundering sound. Toward the conclusion of the congress, the breasts, the jaghana, and the sides of the women should be pressed with the open palms of the hand, with some force, until the end of it, and then sounds like those of the quail or the goose should be made.

There are also two verses on the subject, as follows:

"The characteristics of manhood are said to consist of roughness and impetuosity, while weakness, tenderness, sensibility, and an inclination to turn away from unpleasant things are the distinguishing marks of womanhood. The excitement of passion, and peculiarities of habit, may sometimes cause contrary results to appear, but these do not last long, and in the end the natural state is resumed."

The wedge on the bosom, the scissors on the head, the piercing instrument on the cheeks, and the pincers on the breasts and sides may also be taken into consideration with the other four modes of striking, and thus give eight ways altogether. But these four ways of striking with instruments are peculiar to the people of the southern countries, and the marks caused by them are seen on the breasts of their women. They are local peculiarities, but Vatsyayana is of the opinion that the practice of them is painful, barbarous, and base, and quite unworthy of imitation.

In the same way anything that is a local peculiarity should not always be adopted elsewhere, and even in the place where the practice is prevalent, excess of it should always be avoided. Instances of the dangerous use of them may be given as follows. The King of the Panchalas killed the courtesan Madhavasena by means of the wedge during congress. King Satakarni Satavahana of the Kuntala, deprived his great Queen Malayavati of her life by a pair of scissors, and Naradeva, whose hand was deformed, blinded a dancing girl by directing a piercing instrument in a wrong way.

There are also two verses on the subject, as follows:

"About these things there cannot be either enumeration or any definite rule. Congress having once commenced, passion alone gives birth to all the acts of the parties."

Such passionate actions and amorous gesticulations or movements, which arise on the spur of the moment, and during sexual intercourse, cannot be defined, and are as irregular as dreams. A horse having once attained the fifth degree of motion goes on with blind speed, regardless of pits, ditches, and posts in his way; and in the same manner a loving pair become blind with passion in the heat of congress, and go on with great impetuosity, paying not the least regard to excess. For this reason one who is well acquainted with the science of love, and knowing his own strength as also the tenderness, impetuosity, and strength of the young woman, should act accordingly. The various modes of enjoyment are not for all times or for all persons, but should be used only at the proper time, and in the proper countries and places.

## CHAPTER EIGHT

# ON WOMEN ACTING THE PART OF A MAN; AND ON THE WORK OF A MAN

WHEN A WOMAN SEES THAT HER LOVER IS FATIGUED BY CONSTANT congress, without having his desire satisfied, she should, with his permission, lay him down upon his back, and give him assistance by acting his part. She may also do this to satisfy the curiosity of her lover, or her own desire of novelty.

There are two ways of doing this: the first is when during congress she turns round, and gets on top of her lover, in such a manner as to continue the congress, without obstructing the pleasure of it; and the other is when she acts the man's part from the beginning. At such a time, with flowers in her hair hanging loose, and her smiles broken by hard breathings, she should press upon her lover's bosom with her own breasts; and, lowering her head frequently, she should do in return the same actions which he used to do before, returning his blows and chaffing him. She should say, "I was laid down by you, and fatigued with hard congress; I shall now therefore lay you down in return." She should then again manifest her own bashfulness, her fatigue, and her desire of stopping the congress. In this way she should do the work of a man, which we shall presently relate.

Whatever is done by a man for giving pleasure to a woman is called the work of a man, and is as follows:

While the woman is lying on his bed, and is as it were abstracted by his conversation, he should loosen the knot of her undergarments, and when she begins to dispute with him he should overwhelm her with kisses. Then when his lingam is erect he should touch her with his hands in various places, and gently manipulate various parts of the body. If the woman is bashful, and if it is the first time that they have come together, the man should place his hands between her thighs, which she would probably keep close together; and if she is a very young girl, he should first get his hands upon her breasts, which she would probably cover with her own hands, and under her armpits and on her neck. If, however, she is a seasoned woman, he should do whatever is agreeable either to him or to her, and whatever is fitting for the occasion. After this, he should take hold of her hair, and hold her chin in his fingers for the purpose of kissing her. On this, if she is a young girl, she will become bashful and close her eyes. In any event, he should gather from the action of the woman what things would be pleasing to her during congress.

Here Suvarnanabha says that while a man is doing to the woman what he likes best during congress, he should always make a point of pressing those parts of her body on which she turns her eyes.

The signs of the enjoyment and satisfaction of the woman are as follows: her body relaxes, she closes her eyes, she puts aside all bashfulness, and shows increased willingness to unite the two organs as closely together as possible. On the other hand, the signs of her want of enjoyment and of failing to be satisfied are as follows: she shakes her hands, she does not let the man get up, feels dejected, bites the man, kicks him, and continues to go on moving after the man has finished. In such cases the man should rub the yoni of the woman with his hand and fingers (as the elephant rubs anything with his trunk) before engaging in congress, until it is softened, and after that is done he should proceed to put his lingam into her.

The acts to be done by the man are:

> Moving forward
> Friction or churning
> Piercing
> Rubbing
> Pressing
> Giving a blow
> The blow of a boar
> The blow of a bull
> The sporting of a sparrow

(1). When the organs are brought together properly and directly, it is called "moving the organ forward."

(2). When the lingam is held with the hand, and turned all round in the yoni, it is called a "churning."

(3). When the yoni is lowered, and the upper part of it is struck with the lingam, it is called "piercing."

(4). When the same thing is done on the lower part of the yoni, it is called "rubbing."

(5). When the yoni is pressed by the lingam for a long time, it is called "pressing."

(6). When the lingam is removed to some distance from the yoni, and then forcibly strikes it, it is called "giving a blow."

(7). When only one part of the yoni is rubbed with the lingam, it is called the "blow of a boar."

(8). When both sides of the yoni are rubbed in this way, it is called the "blow of a bull."

(9). When the lingam is in the yoni, and is moved up and down frequently, and without being taken out, it is called the "sporting of a sparrow." This takes place at the end of congress.

When a woman acts the part of a man, she has the following things to do in addition to the nine given above:

> The pair of tongs
> The top
> The swing

(1). When the woman holds the lingam in her yoni, draws it in, presses it, and keeps it thus in her for a long time, it is called the "pair of tongs."

(2). When, while engaged in congress, she turns round like a wheel, it is called the "top." This is learned by practice only.

(3). When, on such an occasion, the man lifts up the middle part of his body, and the woman turns round her middle part, it is called the "swing."

When the woman is tired, she should place her forehead on that of her lover, and should thus take rest without disturbing the union of the organs; and when the woman has rested herself the man should turn round and begin the congress again.

There are also some verses on the subject, as follows:

"Though a woman is reserved, and keeps her feelings concealed, yet when she gets on top a man, she then shows all her love and desire. A man should gather from the actions of the woman of what disposition she is, and in what way she likes to be enjoyed. A woman during her monthly courses, a woman who has been lately confined, and a fat woman should not be made to act the part of a man."

## CHAPTER NINE

# ON THE AUPARISHTAKA,[1]
# OR MOUTH CONGRESS

THERE ARE TWO KINDS OF EUNUCHS, THOSE THAT ARE DISGUISED as males and those that are disguised as females. Eunuchs disguised as females imitate their dress, speech, gestures, tenderness, timidity, simplicity, softness, and bashfulness. The acts that are done on the jaghana, or middle parts, of women, are done in the mouths of these eunuchs, and this is called Auparishtaka. These eunuchs derive their imaginative pleasure, and their livelihood, from this kind of congress, and they lead the life of courtesans. So much concerning eunuchs disguised as females.

Eunuchs disguised as males keep their desires secret, and when they wish to do anything they lead the life of shampooers. Under the pretense of shampooing, a eunuch of this kind embraces and draws toward himself the thighs of the man whom he is shampooing, and after this he touches the joints of the thighs and the jaghana, or central portions, of the body. Then, if he finds the lingam of the man erect, he presses it with his hands, and chaffs him for getting into that state. If after this, and after knowing the eunuch's intention, the man does not tell the eunuch to proceed, then the latter does it of his own accord and begins the congress. If, however, he is ordered by the man to do it, then he disputes with him, and consents at last, but only with difficulty.

The following eight things are then done by the eunuch one after the other:

> The nominal congress
> Biting the sides
> Pressing outside
> Pressing inside
> Kissing
> Rubbing
> Sucking a mango fruit
> Swallowing up

At the end of each of these, the eunuch expresses his wish to stop; but when one of them is finished, the man desires him to do another, and after that is done, then the one that follows it, and so on.

(1). When, holding the man's lingam with his hand, and placing it between his lips, the eunuch moves his mouth about, it is called the "nominal congress."

(2). When, covering the end of the lingam with his fingers collected together like the bud of a plant or flower, the eunuch presses the sides of it with his lips, using his teeth also, it is called "biting the sides."

(3). When, being desired to proceed, the eunuch presses the end of the lingam with his lips closed together, and kisses it as if he were drawing it out, it is called the "outside pressing."

(4). When, being asked to go on, he puts the lingam further into his mouth, and presses it with his lips and then takes it out, it is called the "inside pressing."

(5). When, holding the lingam in his hand, the eunuch kisses it as if he were kissing the lower lip, it is called "pressing."

(6). When, after kissing it, he touches it with his tongue everywhere, and passes his tongue over the end of it, it is called "rubbing."

(7). When, in the same way, he puts the half of it into his mouth, and forcibly kisses and sucks it, this is called "sucking a mango fruit."

(8). And, lastly, when with the consent of the man the eunuch puts the whole lingam into his mouth, and presses it to the very end, as if he were going to swallow it up, it is called "swallowing up."

Striking, scratching, and other things may also be done during this kind of congress.

The Auparishtaka is practiced also by unchaste and wanton women, female attendants, and serving maids, that is, those who are not married to anybody, but who live by shampooing.

The Acharyas (ancient and venerable authors) are of opinion that this Auparishtaka is the work of a dog and of a man, because it is a low practice, and opposed to the orders of the Holy Writ (Dharma Shastras), and because the man himself suffers by bringing his lingam into contact with the mouths of eunuchs and women. But Vatsyayana says that the orders of the Holy Writ do not affect those who resort to courtesans, and the law prohibits the practice of the Auparishtaka with married women only. As regards the injury to the male, that can be easily remedied.

The people of eastern India do not resort to women who practice the Auparishtaka.

The people of Ahichhatra resort to such women, but do nothing with them so far as the mouth is concerned.

The people of Saketa do with these women every kind of mouth congress, while the people of Nagara do not practice this, but do every other thing.

The people of the Shurasena country, on the southern bank of the Jumna, do everything without any hesitation, for they say that women being naturally unclean, no one can be certain about their character, their purity, their conduct, their practices, their confidences, or their speech. They are not, however, on this account to be abandoned, because religious law, on the authority of which they are reckoned pure, lays down that the udder of a cow is clean at the time of milking, though the mouth of a cow, and also the mouth of her calf, are considered unclean by the Hindus. Again, a dog is clean when he seizes a deer in hunting, though food touched by a dog is otherwise considered very unclean. A bird is clean when it causes a fruit to fall from a tree by pecking at it, though things eaten by crows and other birds are considered unclean. And the mouth of a woman is clean for kissing and suchlike things at the time of sexual intercourse. Vatsyayana, moreover, thinks that in all these things connected with love, everybody should act according to the custom of his country, and his own inclination.

There are also the following verses on the subject:

"The male servants of some men carry on the mouth congress with their masters. It is also practiced by some citizens, who know each other well, among themselves. Some women of the harem, when they are amorous, do the acts of the mouth on the yonis of one another, and some men do the same thing with women. The way of doing this (kissing the yoni) should be known from kissing the mouth. When a man and woman lie down in an inverted order, with the head of the one toward the feet of the other, and carry on this congress, it is called the "congress of a crow."

For the sake of such things, courtesans abandon men possessed of good qualities, liberal and clever, and become attached to low persons, such as slaves and elephant drivers. The Auparishtaka, or mouth congress, should never be done by a learned Brahman, by a minister that carries on the business of a state, or by a man of good reputation, because though the practice is allowed by the Shastras, there is no reason why it should be carried on, and need be practiced only in particular cases. For instance, the taste and the digestive qualities of the flesh of dogs are mentioned in works on medicine, but it does not therefore follow that it should be eaten by the wise. In the same way there are some men, some places, and some times with respect to which these practices can be made use of. A man should therefore pay regard to the place, to the time, and to the practice which is to be carried out, as also as to whether it is agreeable to his nature and to himself, and then he may or may not practice these things according to circumstances. But after all, these things being done secretly, and the mind of the man being fickle, how can it be known what any person will do at any particular time and for any particular purpose?

## CHAPTER TEN

# HOW TO BEGIN AND HOW TO END THE CONGRESS; DIFFERENT KINDS OF CONGRESS, AND LOVE QUARRELS

IN THE PLEASURE ROOM, DECORATED WITH FLOWERS, AND fragrant with perfumes, attended by his friends and servants, the citizen should receive the woman, who will come bathed and dressed, and will invite her to take refreshment and to drink freely. He should then seat her on his left side, and holding her hair, and touching also the end and knot of her garment, he should gently embrace her with his right arm. They should then carry on an amusing conversation on various subjects, and may also talk suggestively of things which would be considered as coarse, or not to be mentioned generally in society. They may then sing, either with or without gesticulations, and play on musical instruments, talk about the arts, and persuade each other to drink. At last, when the woman is overcome with love and desire, the citizen should dismiss the people that may be with him, giving them flowers, ointments, and betel leaves; and then when the two are left alone, they should proceed as has been already described in the previous chapters.

Such is the beginning of sexual union. At the end of the congress, the lovers, with modesty, and not looking at each other, should go separately to the washing room. After this, sitting in their own places, they should eat some betel leaves, and the citizen should apply with his own hand to the body of the woman some pure sandalwood ointment, or ointment of some other kind. He should then embrace her with his left arm, and with agreeable words should cause her to drink from a cup held in his own hand, or he may give her water to drink. They can then eat sweatmeats, or anything else, according to their liking, and may drink fresh juice,[1] soup, gruel, extracts of meat, sherbet, the juice of mango fruits, the extract of the juice of the citron tree mixed with sugar, or anything that may be liked in different countries, and known to be sweet, soft, and pure. The lovers may also sit on the terrace of the palace or house, and enjoy the moonlight, and carry on an agreeable conversation. At this time, too, while the woman lies in his lap, with her face toward the moon, the citizen should show her the different planets, the morning star, the polar star, and the seven Rishis, or Great Bear.

This is the end of sexual union.

Congress is of the following kinds:

> Loving congress
> Congress of subsequent love
> Congress of artificial love
> Congress of transferred love
> Congress like that of eunuchs
> Deceitful congress
> Congress of spontaneous love

(1). When a man and a woman who have been in love with each other for some time come together with great difficulty, or when one of the two returns from a journey, or is reconciled after having been separated because of a quarrel, then congress is called the "loving congress." It is carried on according to the liking of the lovers, and for as long as they choose.

(2). When two persons come together, while their love for each other is still in its infancy, their congress is called the "congress of subsequent love."

(3). When a man carries on the congress by exciting himself by means of the sixty-four ways, such as kissing, and so on, or when a man and a woman come together, though in reality they are both attached to different persons, their congress is then called "congress of artificial love." At this time all the ways and means mentioned in the *Kama Shastra* should be used.

(4). When a man, from the beginning to the end of the congress, though having connection with the woman, thinks all the time he is enjoying another one whom he loves, it is called the "congress of transferred love."

(5). Congress between a man and a female water carrier, or a female servant of a caste lower than his own, lasting only until the desire is satisfied, is called "congress like that of eunuchs." Here external touches, kisses, and manipulations are not to be employed.

(6). The congress between a courtesan and a rustic, and that between citizens and the women of villages and bordering countries, are called "deceitful congress."

(7). The congress that takes place between two persons who are attached to one another, and which is done according to their own liking, is called "spontaneous congress."

Thus ends discourse of the kinds of congress.

We shall now speak of love quarrels.

A woman who is very much in love with a man cannot bear to hear the name of her rival mentioned, or to have any conversation regarding her, or to be addressed by her name through mistake. If such takes place, a great quarrel arises, and the woman cries, becomes angry, tosses her hair about, strikes her lover, falls from her bed or seat, and, casting aside her garlands and ornaments, throws herself down on the ground.

At this time the lover should attempt to reconcile her with conciliatory words, and should take her up carefully and place her on her bed. But she, not replying to his questions, and with increased anger, should bend down his head by pulling his hair, and having kicked him once, twice, or thrice on his arms, head, bosom, or back, should then proceed to the door of the room. Dattaka says that she should then sit angrily near the door and shed tears, but should not go out, because she would be found fault with for going away. After a time, when she thinks that the conciliatory words and actions of her lover have reached their utmost, she should then embrace him, talking to him with harsh and reproachful words, but at the same time showing a loving desire for congress.

When the woman is in her own house, and has quarreled with her lover, she should go to him and show how angry she is, and leave him. Afterward the citizen having sent the Vita, the Vidushaka, or the Pithamarda to pacify her, she should accompany them back to the house, and spend the night with her lover.

Thus ends discourse of the love quarrels.

In conclusion:

A man employing the sixty-four means mentioned by Babhravya obtains his object, and enjoys the woman of the first quality. Though he may speak well on other subjects, if he does not know sixty-four divisions, no great respect is paid to him in the assembly of the learned. A man, devoid of other knowledge, but well acquainted with the sixty-four divisions, becomes a leader in any society of men and women. What man will not respect the sixty-four parts, considering they are respected by the learned, by the cunning, and by the courtesans? As the sixty-four parts are respected, are charming, and add to the talent of women, they are called by the Acharyas dear to women. A man skilled in the sixty-four parts is looked upon with love by his own wife, by the wives of others, and by courtesans.

# ABOUT THE ACQUISITION OF A WIFE

## ⊰ PART THREE ⊱

## CHAPTER ONE

# ON MARRIAGE

WHEN A GIRL OF THE SAME CASTE, AND A VIRGIN, IS MARRIED IN accordance with the precepts of Holy Writ (Dharma Shastras), the results of such a union are: the acquisition of Dharma and Artha, offspring, affinity, increase of friends, and untarnished love. For this reason a man should fix his affections upon a girl who is of good family, whose parents are alive, and who is three years or more younger than himself. She should be born of a highly respectable family, possessed of wealth, well connected, and with many relations and friends. She should also be beautiful, of a good disposition, with lucky marks on her body, and with good hair, nails, teeth, ears, eyes, and breasts, neither more nor less than they ought to be, and no one of them entirely wanting, and not troubled with a sickly body. The man should, of course, also possess these qualities himself. But at all events, says Ghotakamukha, a girl who has been already joined with others (that is, no longer a maiden) should never be loved, for it would be reproachful to do such a thing.

Now, in order to bring about a marriage with a girl such as described above, the parents and relations of the man should exert themselves, as should such friends on both sides as may be desired to assist in the matter. These friends should bring to the notice of the girl's parents, the faults, both present and future, of all the other men that may wish to marry her, and should at the same time extol even to exaggeration all the excellences, ancestral and paternal, of their friend, so as to endear him to them, and particularly to those that may be liked by the girl's mother. One of the friends should also disguise himself as an astrologer, and declare the future good fortune and wealth of his friend by showing the existence of all the lucky omens[1] and signs,[2] the good influence of planets, the auspicious entrance of the sun into a sign of the Zodiac, propitious stars and fortunate marks on his body. Others again should rouse the jealousy of the girl's mother by telling her that their friend has a chance of getting from some other quarter an even better girl than hers.

A girl should be taken as a wife, and given in marriage, when fortune, signs, omens, and the words[3] of others are favorable, for, says Ghotakamukha, a man should not marry at any time he likes. A girl who is asleep, crying, or gone out of the house when sought in marriage, or who is betrothed to another, should not be married. The following should also be avoided:

> One who is kept concealed
> One who has an ill-sounding name
> One who has her nose depressed
> One who has her nostril turned up
> One who is formed like a male
> One who is bent down
> One who has crooked thighs
> One who has a projecting forehead
> One who has a bald head
> One who does not like purity
> One who has been polluted by another
> One who is affected with the Gulma[4]
> One who is disfigured in any way
> One who has fully arrived at puberty

One who is a friend

One who is a younger sister

One who is a Varshakari[5]

In the same way a girl who is called by the name of one of the twenty-seven stars, or by the name of a tree, or of a river, is considered worthless, as also a girl whose name ends in "r" or "l." But some authors say that prosperity is gained only by marrying that girl to whom one becomes attached and that therefore no other girl but the one who is loved should be married by anyone.

When a girl becomes marriageable her parents should dress her smartly, and should place her where she can be easily seen by all. Every afternoon, having dressed her and decorated her in a becoming manner, they should send her with her female companions to sports, sacrifices, and marriage ceremonies, and thus show her to advantage in society, because she is a kind of merchandise. They should also receive with kind words and signs of friendliness those of an auspicious appearance who may come accompanied by their friends and relatives for the purpose of marrying the daughter; and, under some pretext or other having first dressed her becomingly, the parents should then present her to them. After this, they should await the pleasure of fortune, and with this object should appoint a future day on which a determination could be come to with regard to their daughter's marriage. On this occasion when the persons have come, the parents of the girl should ask them to bathe and dine, and should say, "Everything will take place at the proper time," and should not then comply with the request, but should settle the matter later.

When a girl is thus acquired, either according to the custom of the country or according to his own desire, the man should marry her in accordance with the precepts of the Holy Writ, according to one of the four kinds of marriage.

Thus ends discourse of marriage.

There are also some verses on the subject, as follows:

"Amusement in society, such as completing verses begun by others, marriages, and auspicious ceremonies, should be carried on neither with superiors nor with inferiors, but with our equals. That should be known as a high connection when a man, after marrying a girl, has to serve her and her relatives afterward like a servant, and such a connection is censured by the good. On the other hand, that reproachable connection where a man, together with his relatives, lords it over his wife is called a low connection by the wise. But when both the man and the woman afford mutual pleasure to each other, and where the relatives on both sides pay respect to one another, such is called a connection in the proper sense of the word. Therefore a man should contract neither a high connection by which he is obliged to bow down afterward to his kinsmen, nor a low connection, which is universally reprehended by all."

→ CHAPTER TWO ←

# ON CREATING CONFIDENCE
# IN THE GIRL

FOR THE FIRST THREE DAYS AFTER MARRIAGE, THE GIRL AND HER husband should sleep on the floor, abstain from sexual pleasures, and eat their food without seasoning it either with alkali or salt. For the next seven days they should bathe amidst the sounds of auspicious musical instruments, should decorate themselves, dine together, and pay attention to their relatives as well as to those who may have come to witness their marriage. This is applicable to persons of all castes. On the night of the tenth day the man should begin in a lonely place with soft words, and thus create confidence in the girl. Some authors say that for the purpose of winning her over he should not speak to her for three days; but the followers of Babhravya are of the opinion that if the man does not speak with her for three days, the girl may be discouraged by seeing him spiritless, like a pillar, and, becoming dejected, she may begin to despise him as a eunuch. Vatsyayana says that the man should begin to win her over, and to create confidence in her, but should abstain at first from sexual pleasures. Women being of a tender nature, want tender beginnings, and when they are forcibly approached by men with whom they are but slightly acquainted, they sometimes suddenly become haters of sexual connection, and sometimes even haters of the male sex. The man should therefore approach the girl according to her liking, and should make use of those devices by which he may be able to establish himself more and more in her confidence. These devices are as follows:

He should embrace her first of all in the law she likes most, because it does not last for a long time.

He should embrace her with the upper part of his body, because that is easier and simpler. If the girl is grown up, or if the man has known her for some time, he may embrace her by the light of a lamp; but if he is not well acquainted with her, or if she is a young girl, he should then embrace her in darkness.

When the girl accepts the embrace, the man should put a "tambula," or screw of betel nut and betel leaves, in her mouth, and if she will not take it, he should induce her to do so by conciliatory words, entreaties, oaths, and kneeling at her feet, for it is a universal rule that however bashful or angry a woman may be, she never disregards a man's kneeling at her feet. At the time of giving this tambula, he should kiss her mouth softly and gracefully, without making any sound. When she is gained over in this respect, he should then make her talk, and so that she may be induced to talk he should ask her questions about things of which he knows or pretends to know nothing, and which can be answered in a few words. If she does not speak to him, he should not frighten her, but should ask her the same thing again and again in a conciliatory manner. If she does not then speak, he should urge her to give a reply, because, as Ghotakamukha says, "All girls hear everything said to them by men, but do not themselves sometimes say a single word." When she is thus importuned, the girl should give replies by shakes of the head, but if she quarreled with the man she should not even do that. When she is asked by the man whether she desires him, and whether she likes him, she should remain silent for a long time, and when at last importuned to reply, should give him a favorable answer by a nod of her head. If the man is previously acquainted with the girl, he should converse with her by means of a female friend, who may be favorable to him, and in the confidence of both, and carry on the conversation on both sides. On such an occasion the girl should smile with her head bent down, and if the female friend say more on her part than she was desired to do, she should chide her and dispute with her. The female friend should say in jest even what she is not desired to say by the girl, and add, "She says so"; on which the girl should say, indistinctly and prettily, "Oh, no! I did not say so," and she should then smile, and throw an occasional glance toward the man.

If the girl is familiar with the man, she should place near him, without saying anything, the tambula, the ointment, or the garland that he may have asked for, or she may tie them up in his upper garment. While she is engaged in this, the man should touch her young breasts in the sounding way of pressing with the nails, and if she prevents him doing this he should say to her, "I will not do it again if you will embrace me," and should in this way cause her to embrace him. While he is being embraced by her he should pass his hand repeatedly over and about her body. By and by he should place her in his lap, and try more and more to gain her consent, and if she will not yield to him he should frighten her by saying: "I shall impress marks of my teeth and nails on your lips and breasts, and then make similar marks on my own body, and shall tell my friends that you did them. What will you say then?" In this and other ways, as fear and confidence are created in the minds of children, so should the man gain her over to his wishes.

On the second and third nights, after her confidence has increased still more, he should feel the whole of her body with his hands, and kiss her all over; he should also place his hands upon her thighs and shampoo them, and if he succeeds in this he should then shampoo the joints of her thighs. If she tries to prevent him doing this, he should say to her, "What harm is there in doing it?" and should persuade her to let him do it. After gaining this point he should touch her private parts, should loosen her girdle and the knot of her dress, and, turning up her lower garment, should shampoo the joints of her naked thighs. Under various pretenses he should do all these things, but he should not at that time begin actual congress. After this, he should teach her the sixty-four arts, should tell her how much he loves her, and describe to her the hopes he formerly entertained regarding her. He should also promise to be faithful to her in future, and should dispel all her fears with respect to rival women, and at last, after having overcome her bashfulness, he should begin to enjoy her in a way so as not to frighten her. So much about creating confidence in the girl; there are, moreover, some verses on the subject, as follows:

"A man acting according to the inclinations of a girl should try to gain her over so that she may love him and place her confidence in him. A man does not succeed either by implicity following the inclination of a girl or by wholly opposing her, and he should therefore adopt a middle course. He who knows how to make himself beloved by women, as well as to increase their honor and create confidence in them, becomes an object of their love. But he who neglects a girl, thinking she is too bashful, is despised by her as a beast ignorant of the working of the female mind. Moreover, a girl forcibly enjoyed by one who does not understand the hearts of girls become nervous, uneasy, and dejected, and suddenly begins to hate the man who has taken advantage of her; and then, when her love is not understood or returned, she sinks into despondency, and becomes either a hater of mankind altogether or, hating her own man, she has recourse to other men.

# → CHAPTER THREE ←

# ON COURTSHIP, AND THE MANIFESTATION OF THE FEELINGS BY OUTWARD SIGNS AND DEEDS

A POOR MAN POSSESSED OF GOOD QUALITIES, A MAN BORN OF A low family possessed of mediocre qualities, a neighbor possessed of wealth, and one under the control of his father, mother, or brothers, should not marry without endeavoring to gain over the girl from her childhood to love and esteem them. Thus a boy separated from his parents, and living in the house of his uncle, should try to gain over the daughter of his uncle, or some other girl, even though she be previously betrothed to another. And this way of gaining over a girl, says Ghotakamukha, is unexceptionable, because Dharma can be accomplished by means of it, as well as by any other way of marriage.

When a boy has thus begun to woo the girl he loves, he should spend his time with her and amuse her with various games and diversions fitted for their age and acquaintanceship, such as picking and collecting flowers, making garlands of flowers, playing the parts of members of a fictitious family, cooking food, playing with dice, playing with cards, the game of odd and even, the game of finding out the middle finger, the game of six pebbles, and such other games as may be prevalent in the country, and agreeable to the disposition of the girl. In addition to this, he should carry on various amusing games played by several persons together, such as hide-and-seek, playing with seeds, hiding things in several small heaps of wheat and looking for them, blind-man's buff, gymnastic exercises, and other games of the same sort in company with the girl, her friends, and female attendants. The man should also show great kindness to any woman whom the girl thinks fit to be trusted, and should also make new acquaintances, but above all he should attach to himself by kindness and little services the daughter of the girl's nurse, for if she be gained over, even though she comes to know of his design, she does not cause any obstruction, but is sometimes even able to effect a union between him and the girl. And though she knows the true character of the man, she always talks of his many excellent qualities to the parents and relations of the girl, even though she may not be desired to do so by him.

In this way the man should do whatever the girl takes most delight in, and he should get for her whatever she may have a desire to possess. Thus he should procure for her such playthings as may be hardly known to other girls. He may also show her a ball dyed with various colors, and other curiosities of the same sort; and should give her dolls made of cloth, wood, buffalo horn, ivory, wax, flour, or earth; also utensils for cooking food; and figures in wood, such as a man and woman standing, a pair of rams or goats or sheep; also temples made of earth, bamboo, or wood, dedicated to various goddesses, and cages for parrots, cuckoos, starlings, quails, cocks, and partridges; water vessels of different sorts and of elegant forms, machines for throwing water about, guitars, stands for putting images upon, stools, lac, red arsenic, yellow ointment, vermilion and collyrium, as well as sandalwood, saffron, betel nut and betel leaves. Such things should be given at different times whenever he gets a good opportunity of meeting her in public, according to circumstances. In short, he should try in every way to make her look upon him as one who would do for her everything that she wanted to be done.

In the next place he should get her to meet him in some place privately, and should then tell her that the reason for his giving presents to her in secret was the fear that the parents of both of them might he displeased, and then he may add that the things which he had given her had been much desired by other people. When her love begins to show signs of increasing, he should relate to her agreeable stories if she expresses a wish to hear such narratives. Or if she takes delight in legerdemain, he should amaze her by performing various tricks of jugglery; or if she feels a great curiosity to see a performance of the various arts, he should show his own skill in them. When she is delighted with singing, he should entertain her with music, and on certain days, and at the time of going together to moonlight fairs and festivals, and at the time of her return after being absent from home, he should present her with bouquets of flowers and with chaplets for the head and with ear ornaments and rings, for these are the proper occasions on which such things should be presented.

He should also teach the daughter of the girl's nurse all the sixty-four means of pleasure practiced by men, and under this pretext should also inform her of his great skill in the art of sexual enjoyment. All this time he should wear a fine dress, and make as good an appearance as possible, for young women love men who live with them, and who are handsome, good looking, and well dressed. As for the saying that though women may fall in love, they still make no effort themselves to gain over the object of their affections, that is only a matter of idle talk.

Now, a girl always shows her love by outward signs and actions such as the following: She never looks the man in the face, and becomes abashed when she is looked at by him; under some pretext or other she shows her limbs to him; she looks secretly at him, though he has gone away from her side; hangs down her head when she is asked some question by him, and answers in indistinct words and unfinished sentences, delights to be in his company for a long time, speaks to her attendants in a peculiar tone with the hope of attracting his attention toward her when she is at a distance from him, and does not wish to go from the place where he is; under some pretext or other she makes him look at different things, narrates to him tales and stories very slowly so that she may continue conversing with him for a long time; kisses and embraces before him a child sitting in her lap; draws ornamental marks on the foreheads of her female servants, performs sportive and graceful movements when her attendants speak jestingly to her in the presence of her lover; confides in her lover's friends, and respects and obeys them; shows kindness to his servants, converses with them and engages them to do her work as if she were their mistress, and listens attentively to them when they tell stories about her lover to somebody else; enters his house when induced to do so by the daughter of her nurse, and by her assistance manages to converse and play with him; avoids being seen by her lover when she is not dressed and decorated; gives him by the hand of her female friend her ear ornament, ring, or garland of flowers that he may have asked to see; always wears anything that he may have presented to her, becomes dejected when any other bridegroom is mentioned by her parents, and does not mix with those who may be of his party, or who may support his claims.

There are also some verses on the subject, as follows:

"A man who has seen and perceived the feelings of the girl toward him, and who has noticed the outward signs and movements by which those feelings are expressed, should do everything in his power to effect a union with her. He should gain over a young girl by childlike sports; a damsel come of age by his skill in the arts, and a girl that loves him, by having recourse to persons in whom she confides."

# ON THINGS TO BE DONE ONLY BY THE MAN, AND THE ACQUISITION OF THE GIRL THEREBY. ALSO, WHAT IS TO BE DONE BY A GIRL TO GAIN OVER A MAN, AND SUBJECT HIM TO HER

NOW, WHEN THE GIRL BEGINS TO SHOW HER LOVE BY OUTWARD signs and motions, as described in the last chapter, the lover should try to gain her over entirely by various ways and means, such as the following:

When engaged with her in any game or sport, he should intentionally hold her hand. He should practice upon her the various kinds of embraces, such as the touching embrace, and others already described in a preceding chapter (Part Two, Chapter II). He should show her a pair of human beings cut out of the leaf of a tree, and suchlike things, at intervals. When engaged in water sports, he should dive at a distance from her, and come up close to her. He should show an increased liking for the new foliage of trees and suchlike things. He should describe to her the pangs he suffers on her account. He should relate to her the beautiful dream that he has had with reference to other women. At parties and assemblies of his caste he should sit near her, and touch her under some pretense or other, and having placed his foot upon hers, he should slowly touch each of her toes, and press the ends of the nails; if successful in this, he should get hold of her foot with his hand and repeat the same thing. He should also press a finger of her hand between his toes when she happens to be washing his feet; and whenever he gives anything to her or takes anything from her, he should show her by his manner and looks how much he loves her.

He should sprinkle upon her the water brought for rinsing his mouth; and when alone with her in a lonely place, or in darkness, he should make love to her, and tell her the true state of his mind without distressing her in any way.

Whenever he sits with her on the same seat or bed he should say to her, "I have something to tell you in private," and then, when she comes to hear it in a quiet place, he should express his love to her more by manner and signs than by words. When he comes to know the state of her feelings toward him, he should pretend to be ill, and should make her come to his house to speak to him. There he should intentionally hold her hand and place it on his eyes and forehead, and under the pretense of preparing some medicine for him he should ask her to do the work for his sake in the following words: "This work must be done by you, and by nobody else." When she wants to go away he should let her go, with an earnest request to come and see him again. This device of illness should be continued for three days and three nights. After this, when she begins coming to see him frequently, he should carry on long conversations with her, for, says Ghotakamukha, "though a man loves a girl ever so much, he never succeeds in winning her without a great deal of talking." At last, when the man finds the girl completely won over, he may then begin to enjoy her. As for the saying that women grow less timid than usual during the evening, at night, and in darkness, and are desirous of congress at those times, and do not oppose men then, and should only be enjoyed at these hours, it is a matter of talk only.

When it is impossible for the man to carry on his endeavors alone, he should, by means of the daughter of her nurse, or of a female friend in whom she confides, cause the girl to be brought to him without making known to her his design, and he should then proceed with her in the manner above described. Or he should in the beginning send his own female servant to live with the girl as her friend, and should then gain her over by her means.

At last, when he knows the state of her feeling by her outward manner and conduct toward him at religious ceremonies, marriage ceremonies, fairs, festivals, theaters, public assemblies, and suchlike occasions, he should begin to enjoy her when she is alone, for Vatsyayana lays it down that women, when resorted to at proper times and in proper places, do not turn away from their lovers.

When a girl, possessed of good qualities and well bred, though born of a humble family, or destitute of wealth, and not therefore desired by her equals, or an orphan girl, or one deprived of her parents but observing the rules of her family and caste, wishes to bring about her own marriage when she comes of age, such a girl should endeavor to gain over a strong and good-looking young man or a person whom she thinks would marry her on account of the weakness of his mind, and even without the consent of his parents. She should do this by such means as would endear her to the said person, as well as by frequently seeing and meeting him. Her mother also should constantly cause them to meet by means of her female friends, and the daughter of her nurse. The girl herself should try to get alone with her beloved in some quiet place, and at odd times should give him flowers, betel nut, betel leaves, and perfumes. She should also show her skill in the practice of the arts, in shampooing, in scratching and in pressing with the nails. She should also talk to him on the subjects he likes best, and discuss with him the ways and means of gaining over and winning the affections of a girl.

But old authors say that although the girl loves the man ever so much, she should not offer herself, or make the first overtures, for a girl who does this loses her dignity, and is liable to be scorned and rejected. But when the man shows his wish to enjoy her, she should be favorable to him, and should show no change in her demeanor when he embraces her, and should receive all the manifestations of his love as if she were ignorant of the state of his mind. But when he tries to kiss her she should oppose him; when he begs to be allowed to have sexual intercourse with her she should let him touch her private parts only and with considerable difficulty; and though importuned by him, she should not yield herself up to him as if of her own accord, but should resist his attempts to have her. Moreover, it is only when she is certain that she is truly loved and that her lover is indeed devoted to her, and will not change his mind, that she should then give herself up to him, and persuade him to marry her quickly. After losing her virginity she should tell her confidential friends about it.

Here ends discourse of the efforts of a girl to gain over a man.

There are also some verses on the subject, as follows:

"A girl who is much sought after should marry the man she likes, and whom she thinks would be obedient to her, and capable of giving her pleasure. But when from the desire of wealth a girl is married by her parents to a rich man without taking into consideration the character or looks of the bridegroom, or when given to a man who has several wives, she never becomes attached to the man, even though he be endowed with good qualities, obedient to her will, active, strong, and healthy, and anxious to please her in every way. A husband who is obedient but yet master of himself, though he be poor and not good looking, is better than one who is common to many women, even though he be handsome and attractive. The wives of rich men, where there are many wives, are not generally attached to their husbands, and are not confidential with them, and even though they possess all the external enjoyments of life, still have recourse to other men. A man who is of a low mind, who has fallen from his social position, and who is much given to traveling, does not deserve to be married; neither does one who has many wives and children, or one who is devoted to sport and gambling, and who comes to his wife only when he likes. Of all the lovers of a girl, he only is her true husband who possesses the qualities that are liked by her, and such a husband enjoys real superiority over her only because he is the husband of love."

→ CHAPTER FIVE ←

# ON CERTAIN FORMS
# OF MARRIAGE[1]

WHEN A GIRL CANNOT MEET HER LOVER FREQUENTLY IN PRIVATE, she should send the daughter of her nurse to him, it being understood that she has confidence in her, and had previously gained her over to her interests. On seeing the man, the daughter of the nurse should, in the course of conversation, describe to him the noble birth, the good disposition, the beauty, talent, skill, knowledge of human nature, and affection of the girl in such a way as not to let him suppose that she had been sent by the girl, and should thus create affection for the girl in the heart of the man. To the girl also she should speak about the excellent qualities of the man, especially of those qualities which she knows are pleasing to the girl. She should, moreover, speak with disparagement of the other lovers of the girl, and talk about the avarice and indiscretion of their parents, and the fickleness of their relations. She should also quote samples of many girls of ancient times, such as Sakuntala and others who, having united themselves with lovers of their own caste and their own choice, were happy ever afterward in their society. She should also tell of other girls who married into great families, and being troubled by rival wives became wretched and miserable, and were finally abandoned. She should further speak of the good fortune, the continual happiness, the chastity, obedience, and affection of the man; and if the girl gets amorous about him, she should endeavor to allay her shame and her fear, as well as her suspicions about any disaster that might result from her marriage. In a word, she should act the whole part of a female messenger by telling the girl all about the man's affection for her, the places he frequented, and the endeavors he made to meet her, and by frequently repeating, "It will be all right if the man takes you away forcibly and unexpectedly."

## The Forms of Marriage

When the girl is gained over, and acts openly with the man as his wife, he should cause fire to be brought from the house of a Brahman, and having spread the Kusha grass upon the ground, and offered an oblation to the fire, he should marry her according to the precepts of the religious law. After this he should inform his parents of the fact, because it is the opinion of ancient authors that a marriage solemnly contracted in the presence of fire cannot afterward be set aside.

After the consummation of the marriage, the relations of the man should gradually be made acquainted with the affair, and the relations of the girl should also be apprised of it in such a way that they may consent to the marriage, and overlook the manner in which it was brought about, and when this is done they should afterward be reconciled by affectionate presents and favorable conduct. In this manner the man should marry the girl according to the Gandharva form of marriage.

When the girl cannot make up her mind, or will not express her readiness to marry, the man should obtain her in any one of the following ways:

1. On a fitting occasion, and under some excuse, he should, by means of a female friend with whom he is well acquainted and whom he can trust, and who also is well known to the girl's

family, get the girl brought unexpectedly to his house, and he should then bring fire from the house of a Brahman, and proceed as before described.

2. When the marriage of the girl with some other person draws near, the man should disparage the future husband to the utmost in the mind of the mother of the girl, and then, having got the girl to come with her mother's consent to a neighboring house, he should bring fire from the house of a Brahman, and proceed as above.

3. The man should become a great friend of the brother of the girl, the said brother being of the same age as himself, and addicted to courtesans and to intrigues with the wives of other people, and should give him assistance in such matters, and also give him occasional presents. He should then tell him about his great love for his sister, as young men will sacrifice even their lives for the sake of those who may be of the same age, habits, and dispositions as themselves. After this the man should have the girl brought by means of her brother to some secure place, and, having brought fire from the house of a Brahman, should proceed as before.

4. The man should on the occasion of festivals get the daughter of the nurse to give the girl some intoxicating substance, and then cause her to be brought to some secure place under the pretense of some business, and there having enjoyed her before she recovers from her intoxication, should bring fire from the house of a Brahman, and proceed as before.

5. The man should, with the connivance of the daughter of the nurse, carry off the girl from her house while she is asleep, and then, having enjoyed her before she recovers from her sleep, should bring fire from the house of a Brahman, and proceed as before.

6. When the girl goes to a garden, or to some village in the neighborhood, the man should, with his friends, fall on her

guards, and having killed them or frightened them away, forcibly carry her off, and proceed as before.

There are verses on this subject as follows:

"In all the forms of marriage given in this chapter of this work, the one that precedes is better than the one that follows it on account of its being more in accordance with the commands of religion, and therefore it is only when it is impossible to carry the former into practice that the latter should be resorted to. As the fruit of all good marriages is love, the Gandharva[2] form of marriage is respected, even though it is formed under unfavorable circumstances, because it fulfills the object sought for. Another cause of the respect accorded to the Gandharva form of marriage is that it brings forth happiness, causes less trouble in its performance than the other forms of marriage, and is above all the result of previous love."

# ABOUT A WIFE

## ❧ PART FOUR ❧

→ CHAPTER ONE ←

# ON THE MANNER OF LIVING OF A VIRTUOUS WOMAN, AND OF HER BEHAVIOR DURING THE ABSENCE OF HER HUSBAND

A VIRTUOUS WOMAN, WHO HAS AFFECTION FOR HER HUSBAND, should act in conformity with his wishes as if he were a divine being, and with his consent should take upon herself the whole care of his family. She should keep the whole house well cleaned, and arrange flowers of various kinds in different parts of it, and make the floor smooth and polished so as to give the whole a neat and becoming appearance. She should surround the house with a garden, and place ready in it all the materials required for the morning, noon, and evening sacrifices. Moreover, she should herself revere the sanctuary of the household gods, for, says Gonardiya, "Nothing so much attracts the heart of a householder to his wife as a careful observance of the things mentioned above."

Toward the parents, relations, friends, sisters, and servants of her husband she should behave as they deserve. In the garden she should plant beds of green vegetables, bunches of the sugar cane, and clumps of the fig tree, the mustard plant, the parsley plant, the fennel plant, and the *Xanthochymus pictorius*. Clusters of various flowers, such as the *Trapa bispinosa,* the jasmine, the *Jasminum grandiflorum,* the yellow amaranth, the wild jasmine, the *Tabernaemontana coronaria,* the nadyawort, the China rose, and others, should likewise be planted, together with the fragrant grass *Andropogon schœnanthus* and the fragrant root of the plant *Andropogon miricatus*. She should also have seats and arbors made in the garden, in the middle of which a well, tank, or pool should be dug.

The wife should always avoid the company of female beggars, female Buddhist mendicants, unchaste and roguish women, female fortunetellers and witches. As regards meals, she should aways consider what her husband likes and dislikes, and what things are good for him, and what are injurious to him. When she hears the sound of his footsteps coming home she should at once get up, and be ready to do whatever he may command her, and either order her female servant to wash his feet, or wash them herself. When going anywhere with her husband she should put on her ornaments, and without his consent she should neither give nor accept invitations, or attend marriages and sacrifices, or sit in the company of female friends, or visit the temples of the Gods. And if she wants to engage in any kind of games or sports, she should not do it against his will. In the same way she should always sit down after him, and get up before him, and should never awaken him when he is asleep. The kitchen should be situated in a quiet and retired place, so as not to be accessible to strangers, and should always look clean.

In the event of any misconduct on the part of her husband, she should not blame him excessively, though she be a little displeased. She should not use abusive language toward him, but rebuke him with conciliatory words, whether he be in the company of friends or alone. Moreover, she should not be a scold, for, says Gonardiya "There is no cause of dislike on the part of a husband so great as this characteristic in a wife." Lastly, she should avoid bad expressions, sulky looks, speaking aside, standing in the doorway, and looking at passers-by, conversing in pleasure groves, and remaining in a lonely place for a long time; and finally she should always keep her body, her teeth, her hair, and everything belonging to her tidy, sweet, and clean.

When the wife wants to approach her husband in private, her dress should consist of many ornaments, various kinds of flowers, and a cloth decorated with different colors, and some sweet-smelling ointments or unguents. But her everyday dress should be composed of a thin, close-textured cloth, a few ornaments and flowers, and a little scent, not too much. She should also observe the fasts and vows of her husband, and when he tries to prevent her doing this, she should persuade him to let her do it.

At appropriate times of the year, and when they happen to be cheap, she should buy earth, bamboos, firewood, skins, and iron pots, as well as salt and oil. Fragrant substances, vessels made of the fruit of the plant *Wrightea antidysenterica,* or oval-leaved *Wrightea,* medicines, and other things which are always wanted, should be obtained when required and kept in a secret place of the house. The seeds of the radish, the potato, the common beet, the Indian wormwood, the mango, the cucumber, the eggplant, the kushmanda, the pumpkin gourd, the surana, the *Bignonia indica,* the sandalwood, the *Premna spinosa,* the garlic plant, the onion, and other vegetables, should be bought and sown at the proper seasons.

The wife, moreover, should not tell to strangers the amount of her wealth, or the secrets which her husband has confided to her. She should surpass all the women of her own rank in life in her cleverness, her appearance, her knowledge of cookery, her pride, and her manner of serving her husband. The expenditure of the year should be regulated by the profits. The milk that remains after the meals should be turned into ghee, or clarified butter. Oil and sugar should be prepared at home: spinning and weaving should also be done there; and a store of ropes and cords, and barks of trees for twisting into ropes, should be kept. She should also attend to the pounding and cleaning of rice, using its small grain and chaff in some way or other. She should pay the salaries of the servants, look after the tilling of the fields, the keeping of the flocks and herds, superintend the making of vehicles, and take care of the rams, cocks, quails, parrots, starlings, cuckoos, peacocks, monkeys, and deer; and finally adjust the income and expenditure of the day. The worn-out clothes should be given to those servants who have done good work, in order to show them that their services have been appreciated, or they may be applied to some other use. The vessels in which wine is prepared, as well as those in which it is kept, should be carefully looked after, and put away at the proper time. All sales and purchases should also be well attended to. The friends of her husband she should welcome by presenting them with flowers, ointment, incense, betel leaves, and betel nut. Her father-in-law and mother-in-law she should treat as they deserve, always remaining dependent on their will, never contradicting them, speaking to them in few and not harsh words, not laughing loudly in their presence, and acting with their friends and enemies as with her own. In addition to the above she should not be vain, or too much taken up with her enjoyments. She should be liberal toward her servants, and reward them on holidays and festivals; and not give away anything without first making it known to her husband.

Thus ends discourse on the manner of a virtuous woman.

During the absence of her husband on a journey, the virtuous woman should wear only her auspicious ornaments, and observe the fasts in honor of the gods. While anxious to hear the news of her husband, she should still look after her household affairs. She should sleep near the elder women of the house, and make herself agreeable to them. She should look after and keep in repair the things that are liked by her husband, and continue the works that have been begun by him. To the abode of her relations she should not go except on occasions of joy and sorrow, and then she should go in her usual traveling dress, accompanied by her husband's servants, and not remain there for a long time. The fasts and feasts should be observed with the consent of the elders of the house. The resources should be increased by making purchases and sales according to the practice of the merchants, and by means of honest servants, superintended by herself. The income should be increased, and the expenditure diminished, as much as possible. And when her husband returns from his journey, she should receive him at first in her ordinary clothes, so that he may know in what way she has lived during his absence, and should bring to him some presents, as well as materials for the worship of the Deity.

Thus ends the part relating to the behavior of a wife during the absence of her husband on a journey.

There are also some verses on the subjects as follows: "The wife, whether she be a woman of noble family or a virgin widow[1] remarried or a concubine, should lead a chaste life, devoted to her husband, and doing everything for his welfare. Women acting thus acquire Dharma, Artha, and Kama, obtain a high position, and generally keep their husbands devoted to them.

# ON THE CONDUCT OF THE ELDER WIFE TOWARD THE OTHER WIVES OF HER HUSBAND, AND ON THAT OF A YOUNGER WIFE TOWARD THE ELDER ONES. ON THE CONDUCT OF A VIRGIN WIDOW REMARRIED. ON A WIFE DISLIKED BY HER HUSBAND. ON THE WOMEN IN THE KING'S HAREM. AND, LASTLY, ON THE CONDUCT OF A HUSBAND TOWARD MANY WIVES

THE CAUSES OF REMARRIAGE DURING THE LIFETIME OF THE WIFE are as follows:

1. The folly or ill temper of the wife
2. Her husband's dislike to her
3. The want of offspring
4. The continual birth of daughters
5. The incontinence of the husband

From the very beginning a wife should endeavor to attract the heart of her husband by showing to him continually her devotion, her good temper, and her wisdom. If, however, she bears him no children, she should herself tell her husband to marry another woman. And when the second wife is married, and brought to the house, the first wife should give her a position superior to her own, and look upon her as a sister. In the morning the elder wife should forcibly make the younger one decorate herself in the presence of their husband, and should not mind all the husband's favor being given to her. If the younger wife does anything to displease her husband, the elder one should not neglect her, but should always be ready to give her most careful advice, and should teach her to do various things in the presence of her husband. Her children she should treat as her own, her attendants she should look upon with more regard even than on her own servants, her friends she should cherish with love and kindness, and her relatives with great honor.

When there are many other wives besides herself, the elder wife should associate with the one who is immediately next to her in rank and age, and should instigate the wife who has recently enjoyed her husband's favor to quarrel with the present favorite. After this, she should sympathize with the former, and having collected all the other wives together, should get them to denounce the favorite as a scheming and wicked woman, without, however, committing herself in any way. If the favorite wife happens to quarrel with the husband, then the elder wife should take her part and give her false encouragement, and thus cause the quarrel to be increased. If there be only a little quarrel between the two, the elder wife should do all she can to work it up into a large quarrel. But if after all this she finds that her husband still continues to love his favorite wife, she should then change her tactics, and endeavor to bring about a reconciliation between them, so as to avoid her husband's displeasure.

Thus ends discourse on the conduct of the elder wife.

The younger wife should regard the elder wife of her husband as her mother, and should not give anything away, even to her own relations, without her knowledge. She should tell her everything about herself, and not approach her husband without her permission. Whatever is told to her by the elder wife she should not reveal to others, and she should take care of the children of the senior even more than of her own. When alone with her husband she should serve him well, but should not tell him of the pain she suffers from the existence of a rival wife. She may also obtain secretly from her husband some marks of his particular regard for her, and may tell him that she lives only for him and for the regard that he has for her. She should never reveal her love for her husband, or her husband's love for her to any person, either in pride or in anger, for a wife that reveals the secrets of her husband is despised by him. As for seeking to obtain the regard of her husband, Gonardiya says that it should always be done in private, for fear of the elder wife. If the elder wife be disliked by her husband, or be childless, she should sympathize with her, and should ask her husband to do the same, but should surpass her in leading the life of a chaste woman.

Thus ends discourse on the conduct of the younger wife toward the elder.

A widow in poor circumstances, or of a weak nature, who allies herself again to a man, is called a widow remarried.

The followers of Babhravya say that a virgin widow should not marry a person whom she may be obliged to leave because of his bad character, or of his being destitute of the excellent qualities of a man, or of his being obliged to have recourse to another person. Gonardiya is of opinion that as the cause of a widow's marrying again is her desire for happiness, and as happiness is secured by the possession of excellent qualities in her husband, joined to a love of enjoyment, it is therefore better to secure a person endowed with such qualities in the first instance. Vatsyayana, however, thinks that a widow may marry any person that she likes and that she thinks will suit her.

At the time of her marriage the widow should obtain from her husband the money to pay the cost of drinking parties, and picnics with her relations, and of giving them and her friends kindly gifts and presents; or she may do these things at her own cost if she likes. In the same way she may wear either her husband's ornaments or her own. As to the presents of affection mutually exchanged between the husband and herself there is no fixed rule about them. If she leaves her husband after marriage of her own accord, she should restore to him whatever he may have given her, with the exception of the mutual presents. If, however, she is driven out of the house by her husband she should not return anything to him.

After her marriage she should live in the house of her husband like one of the chief members of the family, but should treat the other ladies of the family with kindness, the servants with generosity, and all the friends of the house with familiarity and good temper. She should show that she is better acquainted with the sixty-four arts than the other ladies of the house, and in any quarrels with her husband she should not rebuke him severely, but in private do everything that he wishes, and make use of the sixty-four ways of enjoyment. She should be obliging to the other wives of her husband; and to their children she should give presents, behave as their mistress, and make ornaments and playthings for their use. In the friends and servants of her husband she should confide more than in his other wives, and finally she should have a liking for drinking parties, going to picnics, attending fairs and festivals, and for carrying out all kinds of games and amusements.

Thus ends discourse on the conduct of a virgin widow remarried.

A woman who is disliked by her husband, and annoyed and distressed by his other wives, should associate with the wife who is liked most by her husband and who serves him more than the others, and should teach her all the arts with which she is acquainted. She should act as the nurse of her husband's children, and having gained over his friends to her side, should through them make him acquainted of her devotion to him. She should be a leader in religious ceremonies and in vows and fasts, and should not hold too good an opinion of herself. When her husband is lying on his bed, she should go near him only when it is agreeable to him, and should never rebuke him, or show obstinacy in any way. If her husband happens to quarrel with any of his other wives, she should reconcile them to each other, and if he desires to see any woman secretly, she should manage to bring about the meeting between them. She should, moreover, make herself acquainted with the weak points of her husband's character, but always keep them secret, and on the whole behave herself in such a way as may lead him to look upon her as a good and devoted wife.

Here ends discourse on the conduct of a wife disliked by her husband.

The above sections will show how all the women of the king's seraglio are to behave, and therefore we shall now speak separately only about the king.

The female attendants in the harem (called severally Kanchukiyas,[1] Mahallarikas,[2] and Mahallikas[3]), should bring flowers, ointments, and clothes from the king's wives to the king; and he, having received these things, should give them as presents to the servants, along with the things worn by him the previous day. In the afternoon the king, having dressed and put on his ornaments, should interview the women of the harem, who should also be dressed and decorated with jewels. Then, having given to each of them such place and such respect as may suit the occasion and as they may deserve, he should carry on a cheerful conversation with them. After that, he should see such of his wives as may be virgin widows remarried, and after them the concubines and dancing girls. All these should be visited in their own private rooms.

When the king rises from his noonday sleep, the woman whose duty it is to inform the king regarding the wife who is to spend the night with him should come to him accompanied by the female attendants of that wife whose turn may have arrived in the regular course, and of her who may have been accidentally passed over as her turn arrived, and of her who may have been unwell at the time of her turn. These attendants should place before the king the ointments and unguents sent by each of these wives, marked with the seal of her ring; and their names and their reasons for sending the ointments should be told to the king. After this the king accepts the ointment of one of them, who then is informed that her ointment has been accepted and that her day has been settled.[4]

At festivals, singing parties, and exhibitions all the wives of the king should be treated with respect and served with drinks.

But the women of the harem should not be allowed to go out alone, nor should any women outside the harem be allowed to enter in except those whose character is well known. And, lastly, the work which the king's wives have to do should not be too fatiguing.

Thus ends discourse of the conduct of the king toward the women of the harem, and of their own conduct.

A man marrying many wives should act fairly toward them all. He should neither disregard nor pass over their faults, and should not reveal to one wife the love, passion, bodily blemishes, and confidential reproaches of the other. No opportunity should be given to any one of them of speaking to him about their rivals, and if one of them should begin to speak ill of another, he should chide her and tell her that she has exactly the same blemishes in her character. One of them he should please by secret confidence, another by secret respect, and another by secret flattery, and he should please them all by goings to gardens, by amusements, by presents, by honoring their relations, by telling them secrets, and lastly by loving unions. A young woman who is of a good temper and who conducts herself according to the precepts of the Holy Writ (Dharma Shastras) wins her husband's attachment, and obtains a superiority over her rivals.

Thus ends discourse of the conduct of a husband toward many wives.

# ABOUT THE WIVES
## OF OTHER MEN

⊰ PART FIVE ⊱

# ON THE CHARACTERISTICS OF MEN AND WOMEN. ON THE REASONS WHY WOMEN REJECT THE ADDRESSES OF MEN. ON MEN WHO HAVE SUCCESS WITH WOMEN; AND ON WOMEN WHO ARE EASILY GAINED OVER

THE WIVES OF OTHER PEOPLE MAY BE RESORTED TO ON THE occasions already described in Part One, Chapter V, of this work, but the possibility of their acquisition, their fitness for cohabitation, the danger to oneself in uniting with them, and the future effect of these unions, should first of all be examined. A man may resort to the wife of another, for the purpose of saving his own life, when he perceives that his love for her proceeds from one degree of intensity to another. These degrees are ten in number, and are distinguished by the following marks:

1. Love of the eye
2. Attachment of the mind
3. Constant reflection
4. Destruction of sleep
5. Emaciation of the body
6. Turning away from objects of enjoyment

7. Removal of shame
8. Madness
9. Fainting
10. Death

Ancient authors say that a man should know the disposition, truthfulness, purity, and will of a young woman, as also the intensity or weakness of her passions from the form of her body, and from her characteristic marks and signs. But Vatsyayana is of opinion that the forms of bodies and the characteristic marks or signs are but erring tests of character and that women should be judged by their conduct, by the outward expression of their thoughts, and by the movements of their bodies.

Now, as a general rule Gonikaputra says that a woman falls in love with every handsome man she sees, and so does every man at the sight of a beautiful woman, but frequently they do not take any further steps owing to various considerations. In love the following circumstances are peculiar to the woman. She loves without regard to right or wrong and does not try to gain over a man simply for the attainment of some particular purpose. Moreover, when a man first makes up to her she naturally shrinks from him, even though she may be willing to unite herself with him. But when the attempts to gain her are repeated and renewed, she at last consents. But with a man, even though he may have begun to love, he conquers his feelings from a regard for morality and wisdom, and although his thoughts are often on the woman, he does not yield, even though an attempt be made to gain him over. He sometimes makes an attempt or effort to win the object of his affections, and having failed, he leaves her alone for the future. In the same way, once a woman is gained, he often becomes indifferent about her. As for the saying that a man does not care for what is easily gained, and desires only a thing which cannot be obtained without difficulty, it is only a matter of talk.

The causes of a woman rejecting the addresses of a man are as follows:

1. Affection for her husband
2. Desire of lawful progeny
3. Want of opportunity
4. Anger at being addressed by the man too familiarly
5. Difference in rank of life
6. Want of certainty because of the man being devoted to traveling
7. Thinking that the man may be attached to some other person
8. Fear of the man's not keeping his intentions secret
9. Thinking that the man is too devoted to his friends, and has too great a regard for them
10. The apprehension that he is not in earnest
11. Bashfulness because of his being an illustrious man
12. Fear because of his being powerful, or possessed of too impetuous passion, in the case of the deer woman
13. Bashfulness because of his being too clever
14. The thought of having once lived with him on friendly terms only
15. Contempt of his want of knowledge of the world
16. Distrust of his low character
17. Disgust at his want of perception of her love for him
18. In the case of an elephant woman, the thought that he is a hare man, or a man of weak passion
19. Compassion lest any thing befall him because of his passion
20. Despair at her own imperfections
21. Fear of discovery
22. Disillusion at seeing his gray hair or shabby appearance
23. Fear that he may be employed by her husband to test her chastity
24. The thought that he has too much regard for morality

Whichever of the above causes a man may detect, he should endeavor to remove it from the very beginning. Thus, the bashfulness that may arise from his greatness or his ability he should remove by showing his great love and affection for her. The difficulty of the want of opportunity, or of his inaccessibility, he should remove by showing her some easy way of access. The excessive respect entertained by the woman for him should be removed by making himself very familiar. The difficulties that arise from his being thought a low character he should remove by showing his valor and his wisdom; those that come from neglect by extra attention, and those that arise from fear by giving her proper encouragement.

The following are the men who generally obtain success with women:

1. Men well versed in the science of love
2. Men skilled in telling stories
3. Men acquainted with women from their childhood
4. Men who have secured their confidence
5. Men who send presents to them
6. Men who talk well
7. Men who do things that they like
8. Men who have not loved other women previously
9. Men who act as messengers
10. Men who know their weak points
11. Men who are desired by good women
12. Men who are united with their female friends
13. Men who are good looking
14. Men who have been brought up with them
15. Men who are their neighbors
16. Men who are devoted to sexual pleasures, even though these be their own servants
17. The lovers of the daughters of their nurse

18. Men who have been lately married

19. Men who like picnics and pleasure parties

20. Men who are liberal

21. Men who are celebrated for being very strong (bull men)

22. Enterprising and brave men

23. Men who surpass their husbands in learning and good looks, in good qualities, and in liberality

24. Men whose dress and manner of living are magnificent

The following are the women who are easily gained over:

1. Women who stand at the door of their houses

2. Women who are always looking out on the street

3. Women who sit conversing in their neighbor's house

4. A woman who is always staring at you

5. A female messenger

6. A woman who looks sideways at you

7. A woman whose husband has taken another wife without any just cause

8. A woman who hates her husband, or who is hated by him

9. A woman who has nobody to look after her, or keep her in check

10. A woman who has not had any children

11. A woman whose family or caste is not well known

12. A woman whose children are dead

13. A woman who is very fond of society

14. A woman who is apparently very affectionate with her husband

15. The wife of an actor

16. A widow

17. A poor woman

18. A woman fond of enjoyments

19. The wife of a man with many younger brothers

20. A vain woman

21. A woman whose husband is inferior to her in rank or abilities

22. A woman who is proud of her skill in the arts

23. A woman disturbed in mind by the folly of her husband

24. A woman who has been married in her infancy to a rich man, and not liking him when she grows up, desires a man possessing a disposition, talents, and wisdom suitable to her own tastes

25. A woman who is slighted by her husband without any cause

26. A woman who is not respected by other women of the same rank or beauty as herself

27. A woman whose husband is devoted to traveling

28. The wife of a jeweler

29. A jealous woman

30. A covetous woman

31. An immoral woman

32. A barren woman

33. A lazy woman

34. A cowardly woman

35. A humpbacked woman

36. A dwarfish woman

37. A deformed woman

38. A vulgar woman

39. An ill-smelling woman

40. A sick woman

41. An old woman

There are also two verses on the subject, as follows:

"Desire, which springs from nature, and which is increased by art, and from which all danger is taken away by wisdom, becomes firm and secure. A clever man, depending on his own ability, and observing carefully the ideas and thoughts of women, and removing the causes of their turning away from men, is generally successful with them."

## CHAPTER TWO

# ON MAKING ACQUAINTANCE WITH THE WOMAN, AND ON EFFORTS TO GAIN HER OVER

ANCIENT AUTHORS ARE OF OPINION THAT GIRLS ARE NOT SO easily seduced by employing female messengers as by the efforts of the man himself but that the wives of others are more easily got at by the aid of female messengers than by the personal efforts of the man. But Vatsyayana lays it down that whenever it is possible a man should always act himself in these matters, and it is only when such is impracticable, or impossible, that female messengers should be employed. As for the saying that women who act and talk boldly and freely are to be won by the personal efforts of the man and that women who do not possess those qualities are to be got at by female messengers, it is only a matter of talk.

Now, when a man himself acts in the matter he should first of all make the acquaintance of the woman he loves in the following manner:

First, he should arrange to be seen by the woman either on a natural or on a special opportunity. A natural opportunity is when one of them goes to the house of the other, and a special opportunity is when they meet either at the house of a friend, or a caste-fellow, or a minister, or a physician, as well as on the occasion of marriage, ceremonies, sacrifices, festivals, funerals, and garden parties.

Second, whenever they do meet, the man should be careful to look at her in such a way as to cause the state of his mind to be known to her; he should pull about his moustache, make a sound with his nails, cause his own ornaments to tinkle, bite his lower lip, and make various other signs of that description. When she is looking at him he should speak to his friends about her and other women, and should show to her his liberality and his appreciation of enjoyments. When sitting by the side of a female friend he should yawn and twist his body, contract his eyebrows, speak very slowly as if he were weary, and listen to her indifferently. A conversation having two meanings should also be carried on with a child or some other person, apparently having regard to a third person, but really having reference to the woman he loves, and this way his love should be made manifest under the pretext of referring to others rather than to herself. He should make marks that have reference to her, on the earth with his nails, or which a stick, and should embrace and kiss a child in her presence, and give it the mixture of betel nut and betel leaves with his tongue, and press its chin with his fingers in a caressing way. All these things should be done at the proper time and in proper places.

Third, the man should fondle a child that may be sitting on her lap, and give it something to play with, and also take the same back again. Conversation with respect to the child may also be held with her, and in this manner he should gradually become well acquainted with her, and he should also make himself agreeable to her relations. Afterward, this acquaintance should be made a pretext for visiting her house frequently, and on such occasions he should converse on the subject of love in her absence, but within her hearing. As his intimacy with her increases, he should place in her charge some kind of deposit or trust, and take away from it a small portion at a time; or he may give her some fragrant substances, or betel nuts to be kept for him by her. After this, he should endeavor to make her well acquainted with his own wife, and get them to carry on confidential conversations, and to sit together in lonely places. In order to see her frequently he should arrange that the same goldsmith, the same jeweler, the same basket maker, the same dyer, and the same washerman be employed by the two families. And he should also pay her long visits openly under the pretense of being engaged with her on business, and one business should lead to another, so as to keep up the intercourse between them. Whenever she wants anything, or is in need of money, or wishes to acquire skill in one of the arts, he should cause her to understand that he is willing and able to do anything that she wants, to give her money, or teach her one of the arts, all these things being quite within his ability and power. In the same way he should hold discussions with her in company with other people, and they should talk of the doings and sayings of other persons, and examine different things like jewelry, precious stones, and so forth. On such occasions he should show her certain things with the values of which she may be unacquainted, and if she begins to dispute with him about the things or their value, he should not contradict her, but point out that he agrees with her in every way.

Thus ends discourse of the ways of making the acquaintance of the woman desired.

Now, after a girl has become acquainted with the man as above described, and has manifested her love to him by the various outward signs and by the motions of her body, the man should make every effort to gain her over. But as girls are not acquainted with sexual union, they should be treated with the greatest delicacy, and the man should proceed with considerable caution, though in the case of other women accustomed to sexual intercourse this is not necessary. When the intentions of the girl are known, and her bashfulness put aside, the man should begin to make use of her money, and an interchange of clothes, rings, and flowers should be made. In this, the man should take particular care that the things given by him are handsome and valuable. He should, moreover, receive from her a mixture of betel leaves, and when he is going to a party he should ask for the flower in her hair or the flower in her hand. If he himself gives her a flower, it should be a sweet-smelling one, marked with marks made by his nails or teeth. With increasing assiduity he should dispel her fears, and by degrees get her to go with him to some lonely place, and there he should embrace and kiss her. And finally, at the time of giving her some betel nut, or of receiving the same from her, or at the time of making an exchange of flowers, he should touch and press her private parts, thus bringing his efforts to a satisfactory conclusion.

When a man is endeavoring to seduce one woman, he should not attempt to seduce any other at the same time. But after he has succeeded with the first, and enjoyed her for a considerable time, he can keep her affections by giving her presents that she likes, and then commence making up to another woman. When a man sees the husband of a woman going to some place near his house, he should not enjoy the woman then, even though she may be easily gained over at that time. A wise man, having a regard for his reputation, should not think of seducing a woman who is apprehensive, timid, or not to be trusted, or one who is well guarded or possessed of a father-in-law or mother-in-law.

## CHAPTER THREE

# EXAMINATION OF THE STATE
# OF A WOMAN'S MIND

WHEN A MAN IS TRYING TO GAIN OVER A WOMAN, HE SHOULD examine the state of her mind, and act as follows.

If she listens to him, but does not manifest to him in any way her own intentions, he should then try to gain her over by means of a go-between.

If she meets him once, and again comes to meet him better dressed than before, or comes to him in some lonely place, he should be certain that she is capable of being enjoyed by the use of a little force. A woman who lets a man make up to her, but does not give herself up, even after a long time, should be considered a trifler in love; but owing to the fickleness of the human mind, even such a woman can be conquered by always keeping up a close acquaintance with her.

When a woman avoids the attentions of a man, and because of respect for him and pride in herself will not meet him or approach him, she can be gained over with difficulty, either by endeavoring to keep on familiar terms with her or else by an exceedingly clever go-between.

When a man makes up to a woman, and she reproaches him with harsh words, she should be abandoned at once.

When a woman reproaches a man, but at the same time acts affectionately toward him, she should be made love to in every way.

A woman who meets a man in lonely places, and puts up with the touch of his foot, but pretends, because of the indecision of her mind, not to be aware of it, should be conquered by patience, and by continued efforts as follows:

If she happens to go to sleep in his vicinity, he should put his left arm around her, and see when she awakes whether she repulses him in reality, or only as if she were desirous of the same thing being done to her again. And what is done by the arm can also be done by the foot. If the man succeeds in this point, he should embrace her more closely; and if she will not stand the embrace, and gets up, but behaves with him as usual the next day, he should consider then that she is not unwilling to be enjoyed by him. If, however, she does not appear again, the man should try to win her over by means of a go-between; and if, after having disappeared for some time she again appears, and behaves with him as usual, the man should then consider that she would not object to being united with him.

When a woman gives a man an opportunity, and makes her own love manifest to him, he should proceed to enjoy her. And the signs of a woman manifesting her love are these:

1. She calls out to a man without being addressed by him in the first instance.

2. She shows herself to him in secret places.

3. She speaks to him tremblingly and inarticulately.

4. The fingers of her hand and the toes of her feet are moistened with perspiration, and her face is blooming with delight.

5. She occupies herself with shampooing his body and pressing his head.

6. When shampooing him, she works with one hand only, and with the other she touches and embraces parts of his body.

7. She remains with both hands placed on his body motionless, as if she had been surprised by something or was overcome by fatigue.

8. She sometimes bends her face down upon his thighs, and when asked to shampoo them does not manifest any unwillingness to do so.

9. She places one of her hands quite motionless on his body, and even though the man should press it between two members of his body, she does not remove it for a long time.

10. Lastly, when she has resisted all the efforts of the man to gain her over, she returns to him the next day to shampoo his body as before.

When a woman neither gives encouragement to a man nor avoids him, but hides herself and remains in some lonely place, she must be got at by means of the female servant who may be near her. If when called by the man she acts in the same way, then she should be gained over by means of a skillful go-between. But if she will have nothing to say to the man, he should consider well before he begins any further attempts to gain her over.

Thus ends the examination of the state of a woman's mind.

A man should first get himself introduced to a woman, and then carry on a conversation with her. He should give her hints of his love for her, and if he finds from her replies that she receives these hints favorably, he should then set to work to gain her over without any fear. A woman who shows her love by outward signs to the man at his first interview should be gained over very easily. In the same way a lascivious woman, who when addressed in loving words replies openly in words expressive of her love, should be considered to have been gained over at that very moment. With regard to all women, whether they be wise, simple, or confiding, this rule is laid down that those who make an open manifestation of their love are easily gained over.

## → CHAPTER FOUR ←

# THE BUSINESS OF A GO-BETWEEN

IF A WOMAN HAS MANIFESTED HER LOVE OR DESIRE EITHER BY signs or by motions of the body, and is afterward rarely or never seen anywhere, or if a woman is met for the first time, the man should get a go-between to approach her.

Now the go-between, having wheedled herself into the confidence of the woman by acting according to her disposition, should try to make her hate or despise her husband by holding artful conversations with her, by telling about medicines for getting children, by talking to her about other people, by tales of various kinds, by stories about the wives of other men, and by praising her beauty, wisdom, generosity, and good nature, and by saying to her: "It is indeed a pity that you, who are so excellent a woman in every way, should be possessed of a husband of this kind. Beautiful lady, he is not fit even to serve you." The go-between should further talk to the woman about the weakness of the passion of her husband, his jealousy, his roguery, his ingratitude, his aversion to enjoyments, his dullness, his meanness, and all the other faults that he may have, and with which she may be acquainted. She should particularly harp upon that fault or failing by which the wife may appear to be most affected. If the wife be a deer woman, and the husband a hare man, then there would be no fault in that direction, but in the event of his being a hare man, and she a mare woman or elephant woman, then this fault should be pointed out to her.

Gonikaputra is of the opinion that when it is the first affair of the woman, or when her love has been only very secretly shown, the man should then secure and send to her a go-between with whom she may be already acquainted and in whom she confides.

But to return to our subject. The go-between should tell the woman about the obedience and love of the man, and as her confidence and affection increase, she should then explain to her the thing to be accomplished in the following way: "Hear this, O beautiful lady. This man, born of a good family, having seen you, has gone mad on your account. The poor young man, who is tender by nature, has never been distressed in such a way before, and it is highly probable that he will succumb under his present affliction, and experience the pains of death." If the woman listens with a favorable ear, then on the following day the go-between, having observed marks of good spirits in her face, in her eyes, and in her manner of conversation, should again converse with her on the subject of the man, and should tell her the stories of Ahalya[1] and Indra, of Shakuntala[2] and Dushyanti, and such others as may be fit for the occasion. She should also describe to her the strength of the man, his talents, his skill in the sixty-four sorts of enjoyments mentioned by Babhravya, his good looks, and his liaison with some praiseworthy woman, no matter whether this last ever took place or not.

In addition to this, the go-between should carefully note the behavior of the woman, which if favorable would be as follows: She would address her with a smiling look, would seat herself close beside her, and ask her, "Where have you been? What have you been doing? Where did you dine? Where did you sleep? Where have you been sitting?" Moreover, the woman would meet the go-between in lonely places and tell her stories there, would yawn contemplatively, draw long sighs, give her presents, remember her on occasions of festivities, dismiss her with a wish to see her again, and say to her jestingly, "O well-speaking woman, why do you speak these bad words to me?" She would discourse on the sin of her union with the man, would not tell her about any previous visits or conversations that she may have had with him, but would wish to be asked about these, and lastly would laugh at the man's desire, but would not reproach him in any way.

Thus ends the behavior of the woman with the go-between.

When the woman manifests her love in the manner above described, the go-between should increase it by bringing to her love tokens from the man. But if the woman be not acquainted with the man personally, the go-between should win her over by extolling and praising his good qualities, and by telling stories about his love for her. Here Auddalaka says that when a man and woman are not personally acquainted with each other, and have not shown each other any signs of affection, the employment of a go-between is useless.

The followers of Babhravya, on the other hand, affirm that even though they be personally unacquainted, but have shown each other signs of affection, there is an occasion for the employment of a go-between. Gonikaputra asserts that a go-between should be employed, provided they are acquainted with each other, even though no signs of affection may have passed between them. Vatsyayana, however, lays it down that even though they may not be personally acquainted with each other, and may not have shown each other any signs of affection, still they are both capable of placing confidence in a go-between.

Now the go-between should show to the woman the presents, such as the betel nut and the betel leaves, the perfumes, the flowers, and the rings the man may have given to her for the sake of the woman, and on these presents should be impressed the marks of the man's teeth and nails, and other signs. On the cloth that he may send he should draw with saffron both his hands joined together as if in earnest entreaty.

The go-between should also show to the woman ornamental figures of various kinds cut in leaves, together with ear ornaments, and chaplets made of flowers containing love letters expressive of the desire of the man, and she should cause her to send affectionate presents to the man in return. After they have mutually accepted each other's presents, a meeting should be arranged between them on the faith of the go-between.

The followers of Babhravya say that this meeting should take place at the time of going to the temple of a deity; or on occasions of fairs, garden parties, theatrical performances, marriages, sacrifices, festivals, and funerals, as well as at the time of going to the river to bathe, or at times of natural calamities,[3] during fear of robbers or of hostile invasions of the country.

Gonikaputra is of the opinion, however, that these meetings had better be brought about in the abodes of female friends, mendicants, astrologers, and ascetics. But Vatsyayana decides that only that place is well suited for the purpose which has proper means of ingress and egress, and where arrangements have been made to prevent any accidental occurrence, and where a man who has once entered the house can also leave it at the proper time without any disagreeable encounter.

Now, go-betweens or female messengers are of the following different kinds:

1. A go-between who takes upon herself the whole burden of the business.
2. A go-between who does only a limited part of the business.
3. A go-between who is the bearer of a letter only.
4. A go-between acting on her own account.
5. The go-between of an innocent young woman.

6. A wife serving as a go-between.

7. A mute go-between.

8. A go-between who acts the part of the wind.

(1). A woman who, having observed the mutual passion of a man and woman, brings them together and arranges it by the power of her own intellect, such a one is called a go-between who takes upon herself the whole burden of the business. This kind of go-between is chiefly employed when the man and the woman are already acquainted with each other, and have conversed together, and in such cases she is sent not only by the man (as is always done in all other cases) but by the woman also. The above name is also given to a go-between who, perceiving that the man and the woman are suited to each other, tries to bring about a union between them even though they are not acquainted with each other.

(2). A go-between who, perceiving that some part of the affair is already done, or that the advances on the part of the man are already made, completes the rest of the business is called a go-between who performs only a limited part of the business.

(3). A go-between who simply carries messages between a man and a woman who love each other but who cannot frequently meet is called the bearer of a letter or message.

This name is also given to one who is sent by either of the lovers to acquaint either the one or the other with the time and place of their meeting.

(4). A woman who goes herself to a man, and tells him of her having enjoyed sexual union with him in a dream, and expresses her anger at his wife having rebuked him for calling her by the name of her rival instead of by her own name, and gives him something bearing the marks of her teeth and nails, and informs him that she knew she was formerly desired by him, and asks him privately whether she or his wife is the better looking, such a person is called a woman who is a go-between for herself. Now, such a woman should be met and interviewed by the man in private and secretly.

The above name is also given to a woman who, having made an agreement with some other woman to act as her go-between, gains the man for herself by making him personally acquainted with herself, and thus causes the other woman to fail. The same applies to a man who, acting as a go-between for another, and having no previous connection with the woman, gains her for himself, and thus causes the failure of the other man.

(5). A woman who has gained the confidence of the innocent young wife of any man, and who has learned her secrets without exercising any pressure on her mind, and found out from her how her husband behaves to her, if this woman then teaches her the art of securing his favor, and decorates her so as to show her love, and instructs her how and when to be angry, or to pretend to be so, and then, having herself made marks of the nails and teeth on the body of the wife, gets the latter to send for her husband to show these marks to him, and thus excite him for enjoyment, such is called the go-between of an innocent young woman. In such cases the man should send replies to his wife through the same woman.

(6). When a man gets his wife to gain the confidence of a woman whom he wants to enjoy, and to call on her and talk to her about the wisdom and ability of her husband, that wife is called a wife serving as a go-between. In this case the feelings of the woman with regard to the man should also be made known through the wife.

(7). When any man sends a girl or a female servant to any woman under some pretext or other, and places a letter in her bouquet of flowers, or in her ear ornaments, or marks something about her with his teeth or nails, that girl or female servant is called a mute go-between. In this case the man should expect an answer from the woman through the same person.

(8). A person who carries a message to a woman which has a double meaning, or which relates to some past transactions, or which is unintelligible to other people, is called a go-between who acts the part of the wind. In this case the reply should be asked for through the same woman.

Thus ends the discourse of the different kinds of go-betweens.

A female astrologer, a female servant, a female beggar, or a female artist are well acquainted with the business of a go-between, and very soon gain the confidence of other women. Any one of them can raise enmity between any two persons if she wishes to do so, or extol the loveliness of any woman that she wishes to praise, or describe the arts practiced by other women in sexual union. They can also speak highly of the love of a man, of his skill in sexual enjoyment, and of the desire of other women, more beautiful even than the woman they are addressing, for him, and explain the restraint under which he may be at home.

Lastly, a go-between can by the artfulness of her conversation unite a woman with a man, even though he may not have been thought of by her, or though she may have been considered beyond his aspirations. She can also bring back a man to a woman who, owing to some cause or other, has separated himself from her.

➢ CHAPTER FIVE ➣

# ON THE LOVE OF PERSONS
# IN AUTHORITY FOR
# THE WIVES OF OTHER MEN

KINGS AND THEIR MINISTERS HAVE NO ACCESS TO THE ABODES of others; moreover, their mode of living is constantly watched and observed and imitated by the people at large, just as the animal world, seeing the sun rise, get up after him, and when he sets in the evening, lie down again in the same way. Therefore persons in authority should not do any improper act in public, since such are reprehensible for one in their position, and would be deserving of censure. But if they find that such an act is necessary to be done, they should make use of the proper means, as described in the following paragraphs.

The head man of the Village (Gramani), the king's officer employed there, and the man[1] whose business it is to glean corn, can gain over female villagers simply by asking them. It is on this account that this class of woman are called unchaste women by voluptuaries.

The union of the above-mentioned men with this class of woman takes place on the occasions of unpaid labor, of filling the granaries in their houses, of taking things in and out of the house, of cleaning the houses, of working in the fields, and of purchasing cotton, wool, flax, hemp, and thread, and at the season of the purchase, sale, and exchange of various other articles, as well as at the time of doing various other works. In the same way the superintendents of cow pens enjoy the women in the cow pens; and officers who have the superintendence of widows, of women who are without supporters, and of women who have left their husbands have sexual intercourse with these women. The intelligent accomplish their object by wandering at night in the village, while villagers also unite with the wives of their sons, being much alone with them. Lastly, the superintendents of markets have a great deal to do with female villagers at the time of their making purchases in the market.

(1). During the festival of the eighth moon, that is, during the bright half of the month of Nargashirsha, as also during the moonlight festival of the month of Kartika, and the spring festival of Chaitra, the women of cities and towns generally visit the women of the king's harem in the royal palace. These visitors go to the several apartments of the women of the harem, as they are acquainted with them, and pass the night in conversation, and in proper sports and amusement, and go away in the morning. On such occasions a female attendant of the king (previously acquainted with the woman whom the king desires), should loiter about, and accost this woman when she sets out to go home, and induce her to come and see the amusing things in the palace. Even before these festivals, the attendant should have caused it to be intimated to this woman that on the occasion of this festival she would show her all the interesting things in the royal palace. Accordingly she should show her the bower of the coral creeper, the garden house with its floor inlaid with precious stones, the bower of grapes, the building on the water, the secret passages in the walls of the palace, the pictures, the sporting animals, the machines, the birds, and the cages of the lions and the tigers. After this, when alone with her, she should tell her about the love of the king for her, and should describe to her the good fortune which would attend upon her union with the king, giving her at the time a strict promise of secrecy. If the woman does not accept the offer, the attendant should conciliate and please her with handsome presents befitting the position of the king, and having accompanied her for some distance should dismiss her with great affection.

(2). Or, having made the acquaintance of the husband of the woman whom the king desires, the wives of the king should get the wife to pay them a visit in the harem, and on this occasion a female attendant of the king, having been sent thither, should act as described above.

(3). Or one of the king's wives should get acquainted with the woman that the king desires, by sending one of the female attendants to her, who should, on their becoming more intimate, induce her to come and see the royal abode. Afterward, when she has visited the harem, and acquired confidence, a female confidante of the king, sent thither, should act as before described.

(4). Or the king's wife should invite the woman whom the king desires, to come to the royal palace, so that she might see the practice of the art in which the king's wife may be skilled, and after she has come to the harem, a female attendant of the king, sent thither, should act as before described.

(5). Or a female beggar, in league with the king's wife, should say to the woman desired by the king, and whose husband may have lost his wealth, or may have some cause for fear from the king: "This wife of the king has influence over him; she is, moreover, naturally kindhearted, and we must therefore go to her in this matter. I shall arrange for your entrance into the harem, and she will do away with all cause of danger and fear from the king." If the woman accepts this offer, the female beggar should take her two or three times to the harem, and the king's wife there should give her a promise of protection. After this, when the woman, delighted with her reception and promise of protection, again goes to the harem, then a female attendant of the king, sent thither, should act as directed.

(6). What has been said above regarding the wife of one who has some cause for fear from the king applies also to the wives of those who seek service under the king or who are oppressed by the king's ministers, or who are poor, or who are not satisfied with their position, or who are desirous of gaining the king's favor, or who wish to become famous among the people, or who are oppressed by the members of their own caste or who want to injure their caste fellows, or who are spies of the king, or who have any other object to attain.

(7). Lastly, if the woman desired by the king be living with some person who is not her husband, then the king should cause her to be arrested, and having made her a slave because of her crime, should place her in the harem. Or the king should cause his ambassador to quarrel with the husband of the woman desired by him, and should then imprison her as the wife of an enemy of the king, and by this means should place her in the harem.

Thus ends discourse of the means of gaining over the wives of others secretly.

The above-mentioned ways of gaining over the wives of other men are chiefly practiced in the palaces of kings. But a king should never enter the abode of another person, for Abhira[2] the King of the Kottas was killed by a washerman while in the house of another, and in the same way Jayasana the King of the Kashis was slain by the commandant of his cavalry (Senapati).

But according to the customs of some countries, there are facilities for kings to make love to the wives of other men. Thus in the country of the Andras the newly married daughters of the people thereof enter the king's harem with some presents on the tenth day of their marriage, and having been enjoyed by the king are then to serve him. In the country of the Vaidarbbas the wives of the chief ministers approach the king at night to serve him. In the country of the Vaidarbbas the beautiful wives of the inhabitants pass a month in the king's harem under the pretense of affection for the king. In the country of the Aparatakas the people gave their beautiful wives as presents to the ministers and the kings. And lastly, in the country of the Saurashtras the women of the city and the country enter the royal harem for the king's pleasure either together or separately.

There are also two verses on the subject, as follows:

"The above and other ways are the means employed in different countries by kings with regards to the wives of other persons. But a king who has the welfare of his people at heart should not on any account put them into practice."

"A king who has conquered the six[3] enemies of mankind becomes the master of the whole earth."

## CHAPTER SIX

# ABOUT THE WOMEN OF THE ROYAL HAREM; AND ON THE KEEPING OF ONE'S OWN WIFE

THE WOMEN OF THE ROYAL HAREM CANNOT SEE OR MEET ANY men because of their being strictly guarded, neither do they have their desires satisfied, because their only husband is common to many wives. For this reason, among themselves they give pleasure to each other in various ways as now described.

Having dressed the daughters of their nurses, or their female friends, or their female attendants, like men, they accomplish their object by means of bulbs, roots, and fruits having the form of the lingam, or they lie down upon the statue of a male figure, in which the lingam is visible and erect.

Some kings, who are compassionate, take or apply certain medicines to enable them to enjoy many wives in one night, simply for the purpose of satisfying the desire of their women, though they perhaps have no desire of their own. Others enjoy with great affection only those wives that they particularly like, while others take them only as the turn of each wife arrives, in due course. Such are the ways of enjoyment prevalent in Eastern countries, and what is said about the means of enjoyment of the female is also applicable to the male.

144

By means of their female attendants the ladies of the royal harem generally get men into their apartments in the disguise or dress of women. Their female attendants, and the daughters of their nurses, who are acquainted with their secrets, should exert themselves to get men to come to the harem in this way by telling them of the good fortune attending it, and by describing the facilities of entering and leaving the palace, the large size of the premises, the carelessness of the sentinels, and the irregularities of the attendants about the persons of the royal wives. But these women should never induce a man to enter the harem by telling him falsehoods, for that would probably lead to his destruction.

As for the man himself, he had better not enter a royal harem, even though it may be easily accessible, because of the numerous disasters to which he may be exposed there. If, however, he wants to enter it, he should first ascertain whether there is an easy way to get out, whether it is closely surrounded by the pleasure garden, whether it has separate enclosures belonging to it, whether the sentinels are careless, whether the king has gone abroad, and then, when he is called by the women of the harem, he should carefully observe the localities, and enter by the way pointed out by them. If he is able to manage it, he should hang about the harem every day, and, under some pretext or other, make friends with the sentinels, and show himself attached to the female attendants of the harem, who may have become acquainted with his design, and to whom he should express his regret at not being able to obtain the object of his desire. Lastly, he should cause the whole business of a go-between to be done by the woman who may have access to the harem, and he should be careful to be able to recognize the emissaries of the king.

When a go-between has no access to the harem, then the man should stand in some place where the lady whom he loves and whom he is anxious to enjoy can be seen.

If that place is occupied by the king's sentinels, he should then disguise himself as a female attendant of the lady who comes to the place, or passes by it. When she looks at him he should let her know his feeling by outward signs and gestures, and should show her pictures, things with double meanings, chaplets of flowers, and rings. He should carefully mark the answer she gives, whether by word or by sign or by gesture, and should then try and get into the harem. If he is certain of her coming to some particular place, he should conceal himself there, and at the appointed time should enter along with her as one of the guards. He may also go in and out, concealed in a folded bed, or bed covering, or with his body made invisible,[1] by means of external applications, a recipe for one of which is as follows:

The heart of an ichneumon, the fruit of the long gourd (Tumbaki), and the eyes of a serpent should all be burned without letting out the smoke; the ashes should then be ground and mixed in equal quantities with water. By putting this mixture upon the eyes a man can go about unseen.

Other means of invisibility are prescribed by Dhyana Brahmans and Yogashiras.

Again, the man may enter the harem during the festival of the eighth moon in the month of Nargashirsha, and during the moonlight festivals when the female attendants of the harem are all busily occupied, or in confusion.

The following principles are laid down on this subject:

The entrance of young men into harems, and their exit from them, generally take place when things are being brought into the palace, or when things are being taken out of it, or when drinking festivals are going on, or when the female attendants are in a hurry, or when the residence of some of the royal ladies is being changed, or when the king's wives go to gardens or to fairs, or when they enter the palace on their return from them, or lastly, when the king is absent on a long pilgrimage. The women of the royal harem know each other's secrets, and having but one object to attain, they give assistance to each other. A young man who enjoys all of them, and who is common to them all, can continue enjoying his union with them so long as it is kept quiet, and is not known abroad.

Now, in the country of the Aparatikas the royal ladies are not well protected, and consequently many young men are passed into the harem by the women who have access to the royal palace. The wives of the king of the Abhira country accomplish their objects with those sentinels in the harem who bear the name of Kshatriyas. The royal ladies in the country of the Vatsagulmas cause such men as are suitable to enter into the harem along with their female messengers. In the country of the Vaidarbhas the sons of the royal ladies enter the royal harem when they please, and enjoy the women, with the exception of their own mothers. In the Stri Rajya the wives of the king are enjoyed by his caste fellows and relations. In the Gandak country the royal wives are enjoyed by Brahmans, friends, servants, and slaves. In the Samdhava country, servants, foster children, and other persons like them enjoy the women of the harem. In the country of the Himalayas adventurous citizens bribe the sentinels and the harem. In the country of the Vanyas and the Kalmyas, Brahmans, with the knowledge of the king, enter the harem under the pretense of giving flowers to the ladies, and speak with them from behind a curtain, and from such conversation union afterward takes place. Lastly, the women in the harem of the king of the Prachyas conceal one young man in the harem for every batch of nine or ten of the women.

Thus act the wives of the others.

For these reasons a man should guard his own wife. Old authors say that a king should select for sentinels in his harem such men as have had their freedom from carnal desires well tested. But such men, though free themselves from carnal desire, by reason of their fear or avarice may cause other persons to enter the harem, and therefore Gonikaputra says that kings should place such men in the harem as may have had their freedom from carnal desires, their fears, and their avarice well tested. Lastly, Vatsyayana says that under the influence of Dharma[2] people might be admitted, and therefore men should be selected who are free from carnal desires, fear, avarice, and Dharma.

The followers of Babhravya say that a man should cause his wife to associate with a young woman who would tell him the secrets of other people, and thus find out from her about his wife's chastity. But Vatsyayana says that as wicked persons are always successful with women, a man should not cause his innocent wife to be corrupted by bringing her into the company of a deceitful woman.

The following are the causes of the destruction of a woman's chastity:

Always going into society, and sitting in company
Absence of restraint
The loose habits of her husband
Want of caution in her relations with other men
Continued and long absence of her husband
Living in a foreign country
Destruction of her love and feelings by her husband
The company of loose women
The jealousy of her husband

There are also the following verses on the subject:
"A clever man, learning from the Shastras the ways of winning over the wives of other people, is never deceived in the case of his own wives. No one, however, should make use of these ways for seducing the wives of others, because they do not

always succeed, and, moveover, often cause disasters, and the destruction of Dharma and Artha. This book, which is intended for the good of people, and to teach them the ways of guarding their own wives, should not be made use of merely for gaining over the wives of others."

# ABOUT COURTESANS

## ⊰ PART SIX ⊱

# → CHAPTER ONE ←

# ON THE CAUSES OF A COURTESAN RESORTING TO MEN; ON THE MEANS OF ATTACHING TO HERSELF THE MAN DESIRED; AND ON THE KIND OF MAN THAT IT IS DESIRABLE TO BE ACQUAINTED WITH

BY HAVING INTERCOURSE WITH MEN, COURTESANS OBTAIN SEXUAL pleasure, as well as their own maintenance. Now, when a courtesan takes up with a man from love, the action is natural; but when she resorts to him for the purpose of getting money, her action is artificial or forced. Even in this latter case, however, she should conduct herself as if her love were indeed natural, because men repose their confidence in those women who apparently love them. In making known her love to the man, she should show an entire freedom from avarice, and for the sake of her future credit she should abstain from acquiring money from him by unlawful means.

A courtesan, well dressed and wearing her ornaments, should sit or stand at the door of her house, and without exposing herself too much, should look on the public road so as to be seen by the passersby, she being like an object on view for sale. She should form friendships with such persons as would enable her to separate men from other women, and attach them to herself, to repair her own misfortunes, to acquire wealth, and to protect her from being bullied or set upon by persons with whom she may have dealings of some kind or another.

These persons are:

The guards of the town, or the police
The officers of the courts of justice
Astrologers
Powerful men, or men with interest
Learned men
Teachers of the sixty-four arts
Pithamardas or confidants
Vitas or parasites
Vidushakas or jesters
Flower sellers
Perfumers
Vendors of spirits
Washermen
Barbers
Beggars

And such other persons as may be found necessary for the particular object to be acquired.

The following kinds of men may be taken up with, simply for the purpose of getting their money:

Men of independent income
Young men
Men who are free from any ties
Men who hold places of authority under the king
Men who have secured their means of livelihood without difficulty

Men possessed of unfailing sources of income
Men who consider themselves handsome
Men who are always praising themselves
One who is a eunuch, but wishes to be thought a man
One who hates his equals
One who is naturally liberal
One who has influence with the king or his ministers
One who is always fortunate
One who is proud of his wealth
One who disobeys the orders of his elders
One upon whom the members of his caste keep an eye
An only son whose father is wealthy
An ascetic who is internally troubled with desire
A brave man
A physician of the king
Previous acquaintances

On the other hand, those who are possessed of excellent qualities are also to be resorted to for the sake of love and fame. Such men are as follows:

Men of high birth, learned, with a good knowledge of the world, and doing the proper things at the proper times; poets, good storytellers, eloquent men, energetic men skilled in various arts, farseeing into the future, possessed of great minds, full of perseverance, of a firm devotion, free from anger, liberal, affectionate to their parents, and with a liking for all social gatherings, skilled in completing verses begun by others and in various other sports, free from all disease, possessed of a perfect body, strong, and not addicted to drinking, powerful in sexual enjoyment, sociable, showing love toward woman and attracting their hearts to himself but not entirely devoted to them, possessed of independent means of livelihood, free from envy and, last of all, free from suspicion.

Such are the good qualities of a man.

The woman also should have the following characteristics:

She should be possessed of beauty and amiability, with auspicious body marks. She should have a liking for good qualities in other people, as well as a liking for wealth. She should take delight in sexual unions resulting from love, and should be of firm mind, and of the same class as the man with regard to sexual enjoyment.

She should always be anxious to acquire and obtain experience and knowledge, be free from avarice, and always have a liking for social gatherings, and for the arts.

The following are the ordinary qualities of all women:

To be possessed of intelligence, good disposition, and good manners; to be straightforward in behavior, and to be grateful; to consider well the future before doing anything; to possess activity, to be of consistent behavior, and to have a knowledge of the proper times and places for doing things; to speak always without meanness, loud laughter, malignity, anger, avarice, dullness, or stupidity, to have a knowledge of the *Kama Sutra*, and to be skilled in all the arts connected with it.

The faults of the women are to be known by the absence of any of the above-mentioned good qualities.

The following kinds of men are not fit to be resorted to by courtesans:

One who is consumptive; one who is sickly; one whose mouth contains worms; one whose breath smells like human excrement; one whose wife is dear to him; one who speaks harshly; one who is always suspicious; one who is avaricious; one who is pitiless; one who is a thief; one who is self-conceited; one who has a liking for sorcery; one who does not care for respect or disrespect; one who can be gained over even by his enemies by means of money; and lastly, one who is extremely bashful.

Ancient authors are of the opinion that the causes of a courtesan resorting to men are: love, fear, money, pleasure, returning some act of enmity, curiosity, sorrow, constant intercourse, Dharma, celebrity, compassion, the desire of having a friend, shame, the likeness of the man to some beloved person, the search after good fortune, getting rid of the love of somebody else, being of the same class as the man with respect to sexual union, living in the same place, constancy, and poverty. But Vatsyayana decides that desire of wealth, freedom from misfortune, and love are the only causes that affect the union of courtesans with men.

Now, a courtesan should not sacrifice money to her love, because money is the chief thing to be attended to. But in cases of fear, and so on, she should pay regard to strength and other qualities. Moreover, even though she be invited by any man to join him, she should not at once consent to a union, because men are apt to despise things which are easily acquired. On such occasions she should first send the shampooers and the singers and the jesters who may be in her service, or in their absence the Pithamadras, or confidants, and others, to find out the state of his feelings and the condition of his mind. By means of these persons she should ascertain whether the man is pure or impure, affected or unaffected, capable of attachment, or indifferent, liberal or niggardly; and if she finds him to her liking, she should then employ the Vita and others to attach his mind to her.

Accordingly, the Pithamarda should bring the man to her house, under the pretense of seeing the fights of quails, cocks, and rams, of hearing the myna (a kind of starling) talk, or of seeing some other spectacle, or the practice of some art; or he may take the woman to the abode of the man. After this, when the man comes to her house, the woman should give him something capable of producing curiosity and love in his heart, such as an affectionate present, telling him that it was specially designed for his use. She should also amuse him for a long time by telling him such stories and doing such things as he may take most delight in. When he goes away she should frequently send to him a female attendant, skilled in carrying on a jesting conversation, and also a small present at the same time. She should also sometimes go to him herself under the pretense of some business, and accompanied by the Pithamarda.

Thus ends discourse of the means of attaching to herself the man desired.

There are also some verses on the subject, as follows:

"When a lover comes to her abode, a courtesan should give him a mixture of betel leaves and betel nut, garlands of flowers, and perfumed ointments, and, showing her skill in arts, should entertain him with a long conversation. She should also give him some loving presents, and make an exchange of her own things with him, and at the same time should show him her skill in sexual enjoyment. When a courtesan is thus united with her lover, she should always delight him by affectionate gifts, by conversation, and by the application of tender means of enjoyment."

# → CHAPTER TWO ←

# ON A COURTESAN LIVING
# LIKE A WIFE

WHEN A COURTESAN IS LIVING AS A WIFE WITH HER LOVER, SHE should behave like a chaste woman, and do everything to his satisfaction. Her duty in this respect, in short, is that she should give him pleasure but should not become attached to him, though behaving as if she were really attached.

Now, the following is the manner in which she is to conduct herself so as to accomplish the above-mentioned purpose. She should have a mother dependent on her, one who is represented as very harsh, and who looks upon money as her chief object in life. If there is no mother, then an old and confidential nurse should play the same role. The mother, or nurse, on her part, should appear to be displeased with the lover, and forcibly take the courtesan away from him. The woman herself should always show pretended anger, dejection, fear, and shame on this account, but should not disobey the mother or nurse at any time.

She should pretend to the mother or nurse that the man is suffering from bad health; and, making this a pretext for going to see him, she should go on that account. She is, moreover, to practice the following things for the purpose of gaining the man's favor:

Sending her female attendant to bring the flowers used by him on the previous day, in order that she may use them herself as a mark of affection; asking for the mixture of betel nut and leaves that have remained uneaten by him; expressing wonder at his knowledge of sexual intercourse, and the several means of enjoyment used by him; learning from him the sixty-four kinds of pleasure mentioned by Babhravya; continually practicing the ways of enjoyment as taught by him and according to his liking; keeping his secrets; telling him her own desires and secrets; concealing her anger; never neglecting him on the bed when he turns his face toward her; touching any parts of his body according to his wish; kissing and embracing him when he is asleep; looking at him with apparent anxiety when he is rapt in thought or thinking of some other subject than herself; showing neither complete shamelessness nor excessive bashfulness when he meets her or sees her standing on the terrace of her house from the public road; hating his enemies; loving those who are dear to him; showing a liking for that which he likes; being in high or low spirits according to the state that he is in himself; expressing a curiosity to see his wives; not continuing her anger for a long time; suspecting even the marks and wounds made by herself with her nails and teeth on his body to have been made by some other woman; keeping her love for him unexpressed by words but showing it by deeds and signs and hints; remaining silent when he is asleep, intoxicated, or sick; being very attentive when he describes his good actions, and reciting them afterward to his praise and benefit; giving witty replies to him if he be sufficiently attached to her; listening to all his stories except those that relate to her rivals; expressing feelings of dejection and sorrow if he sighs, yawns, or falls down; pronouncing the words "live long" when he sneezes; pretending to be ill or to having the desire of pregnancy when he feels dejected; abstaining from praising the good qualities of anybody else and from censuring those who possess the same faults as her own man; wearing anything that may have been given to her by him; abstaining from putting on her ornaments, and from taking food when he is in pain, sick, low-spirited, or suffering from misfortune, and condoling and lamenting with him over the same; wishing to accompany him if he happens to leave the country himself or if he be banished from it by the king; expressing a desire not to live after him; telling him that the whole object and desire of her life was to be united with him; offering previously promised sacrifices to the Deity when he acquires wealth or has some desire fulfilled or when he has recovered from some illness or disease; putting on ornaments every day; not acting too freely with him; reciting his name and the name of his family in her songs; placing his hand on her loins, bosom, and forehead, and falling asleep after feeling the pleasure of his touch; sitting on his lap and falling asleep there; wishing to have a child by him; desiring not to live longer than he does; abstaining from revealing his secrets to others; dissuading him from vows and fasts by saying "let the sin fall upon me"; keeping vows and fasts along with him when it is impossible to change his mind on the subject; telling him that vows and fasts are difficult to be observed, even by herself, when she has any dispute with him about them; looking on her own wealth and his without any distinction; abstaining from going to public assemblies without him, and accompanying him when he desires her to do so; taking delight in using things previously used by him, and in eating food that he has left uneaten; venerating his family, his disposition, his skill in the arts, his learning, his caste, his complexion, his native country, his friends, his good qualities, his age, and his sweet temper; asking him to sing, and to do other suchlike things, if able to do them; going to him without paying any regard to fear, to cold, to heat, or to rain; saying with regard to the next world that he should be her lover even there; adapting her tastes, disposition, and actions to his liking; abstaining from sorcery; disputing continually with her mother on the subject of going to him, and when forcibly taken by her mother to some other place, expressing her desire to die by taking poison, by starving herself to death, by stabbing herself with some weapon, or by hanging herself; and, lastly, practice assuring the man of her constancy and love by means of her agents, and receiving money herself, but abstaining from any dispute with her mother with regard to pecuniary matters.

When the man sets out on a journey, she should make him swear that he will return quickly, and in his absence should put aside her vows of worshiping the Deity, and should wear no ornaments except those that are lucky. If the time fixed for his return has passed, she should endeavor to ascertain the real time of his return from omens, from the reports of the people, and from the position of the planets, the moon, and the stars. On occasions of amusement and of auspicious dreams she should wear no ornaments except those that are lucky. If, moreover, she feels melancholy, or sees any inauspicious omen, she should perform some rite to appease the Deity.

When the man does return home she should worship the god Kama (that is, the Indian Cupid), and offer oblations to other deities, and having caused a pot filled with water to be brought by her friends, she should perform the worship in honor of the crow who eats the offerings which we make to the manes of deceased relations. After the first visit is over, she should ask her lover also to perform certain rites, and this he will do if he is sufficiently attached to her.

Now, a man is said to be sufficiently attached to a woman when his love is disinterested; when he has the same object in view as his beloved one; when he is quite free from any suspicions on her account; and when he is indifferent to money with regard to her.

Such is the manner of a courtesan living with a man like a wife, and it is set forth here for the sake of guidance from the rules of Dattaka. What is not laid down here should be practiced according to the custom of the people and the nature of each individual man.

There are also two verses on the subject, as follows:

"The extent of the love of women is not known, even to those who are the objects of their affection, on account of its subtlety, and on account of the avarice, and natural intelligence of womankind."

"Women are hardly ever known in their true light, though they may love men, or become indifferent toward them; may give them delight, or abandon them; or may extract from them all the wealth that they may possess."

# ON THE MEANS OF GETTING MONEY. ON THE SIGNS OF CHANGE OF A LOVER'S FEELINGS, AND ON THE WAY TO GET RID OF HIM

MONEY IS GOT OUT OF A LOVER IN TWO WAYS:

By natural or lawful means, and by artifices. Old authors are of the opinion that when a courtesan can get as much money as she wants from her lover, she should not make use of artifice. But Vatsyayana lays down that though she may get some money from him by natural means, yet when she makes use of artifice he gives her doubly more, and therefore artifice should be resorted to for the purpose of extorting money from him at all events.

Now, the artifices to be used for getting money from the lover are as follows:

1. Taking money from him on different occasions, for the purpose of purchasing various articles such as ornaments, food, drink, flowers, perfumes, and clothes, and either not buying them or getting from him more than their cost.

2. Praising his intelligence to his face.

3. Pretending to be obliged to make gifts on occasions of festivals connected with vows, trees, gardens, temples, or tanks.

4. Pretending that at the time of going to his house, her jewels have been stolen either by the king's guards or by robbers.

5. Alleging that her property has been destroyed by fire, by the falling of her house, or by the carelessness of the servants.

6. Pretending to have lost the ornaments of her lover along with her own.

7. Causing him to hear through other people of the expenses incurred by her in coming to see him.

8. Contracting debts for the sake of her lover.

9. Disputing with her mother on account of some expense, incurred by her for the lover, which was not approved of by her mother.

10. Not going to parties and festivities in the houses of her friends for the want of presents to make to them, she having previously informed her lover of the valuable presents given to her by these very friends.

11. Not performing certain festive rites under the pretense that she has no money to perform them with.

12. Engaging artists to do something for her lover.

13. Entertaining physicians and ministers for the purpose of attaining some object.

14. Assisting friends and benefactors both on festive occasions and in misfortune.

15. Performing household rites.

16. Having to pay the expenses of the ceremony of marriage of the son of a female friend.

17. Having to satisfy curious wishes during her state of pregnancy.

18. Pretending to be ill, and charging her cost of treatment.

19. Having to remove the troubles of a friend.

20. Selling some of her ornaments, so as to give her lover a present.

21. Pretending to sell some of her ornaments, furniture, or cooking utensils to a trader, who has already been tutored how to behave in the matter.

22. Having to buy cooking utensils of greater value than those of other people, so that they might be more easily distinguished, and not changed for others of an inferior description.

23. Remembering the former favors of her lover, and causing them always to be spoken of by her friends and followers.

24. Informing her lover of the great gains of other courtesans.

25. Describing before them, and in the presence of her lover, her own great gains, and making them out to be greater even than theirs, though such may not have been really the case.

26. Openly opposing her mother when she endeavors to persuade her to take up with men with whom she had been formerly acquainted, on account of the great gains to be got from them.

27. Lastly, pointing out to her lover the liberality of his rivals.

Thus ends discourse of the ways and means of getting money.

A woman should always know the state of the mind, of the feelings, and of the disposition of her lover toward her, from the changes of his temper, his manner, and the color of his face.

The behavior of a waning lover is as follows:

1. He gives the woman either less than is wanted or something other than that which is asked for.

2. He keeps her in hopes by promises.

3. He pretends to do one thing, and does something else.

4. He does not fulfill her desires.

5. He forgets his promises, or does something other than that which he has promised.

6. He speaks with his own servants in a mysterious way.

7. He sleeps in some other house under the pretense of having to do something for a friend.

8. Lastly, he speaks in private with the attendants of a woman with whom he was formerly acquainted.

Now, when a courtesan finds that her lover's disposition toward her is changing, she should get possession of all his best things before he becomes aware of her intentions, and allow a supposed creditor to take them away forcibly from her in satisfaction of some pretended debt. After this, if the lover is rich, and has always behaved well toward her, she should ever treat him with respect; but if he is poor and destitute she should get rid of him as if she had never been acquainted with him in any way before.

The means of getting rid of a lover are as follows:

1. Describing the habits and vices of the lover as disagreeable and censurable, with a sneer of the lip and a stamp of the foot.

2. Speaking on a subject with which he is not acquainted.

3. Showing no admiration for his learning, and passing a censure upon it.

4. Putting down his pride.

5. Seeking the company of men who are superior to him in learning and wisdom.

6. Showing a disregard for him on all occasions.

7. Censuring men possessed of the same faults as her lover.

8. Expressing dissatisfaction at the ways and means of enjoyment used by him.

9. Not giving him her mouth to kiss.

10. Refusing access to her jaghana, that is, the part of the body between the navel and the thighs.

11. Showing a dislike for the wounds made by his nails and teeth.

12. Not pressing close up against him at the time when he embraces her.

13. Keeping her limbs without movement at the time of congress.

14. Desiring him to enjoy her when he is fatigued.

15. Laughing at his attachment to her.

16. Not responding to his embraces.

17. Turning away from him when he begins to embrace her.

18. Pretending to be sleepy.

19. Going out visiting, or into company, when she perceives his desire to enjoy her during the daytime.

20. Misconstruing his words.

21. Laughing without any joke; or, at the time of any joke made by him, laughing under some other pretense.

22. Looking with side glances at her own attendants, and clapping her hands when he says anything.

23. Interrupting him in the middle of his stories, and beginning to tell other stories herself.

24. Reciting his faults and his vices, and declaring them to be incurable.

25. Saying words to her female attendants calculated to cut the heart of her lover to the quick.

26. Taking care not to look at him when he comes to her.

27. Asking from him what cannot be granted.

28. And, after all, finally dismissing him.

There are also two verses on this subject, as follows:

"The duty of a courtesan consists in forming connections with suitable men after due and full consideration, and attaching the person with whom she is united to herself; in obtaining wealth from the person who is attached to her; and then dismissing him after she has taken away all his possessions."

"A courtesan leading in this manner the life of a wife is not troubled with too many lovers, and yet obtains abundance of wealth."

# → CHAPTER FOUR ←

# ON REUNION WITH
# A FORMER LOVER

WHEN A COURTESAN ABANDONS HER PRESENT LOVER AFTER ALL his wealth is exhausted, she may then consider about her reunion with a former lover. But she should return to him only if he has acquired fresh wealth, or is still wealthy, and if he is still attached to her. And if this man be living at the time with some other woman, she should consider well before she acts.

Now, such a man can be in only one of the six following conditions:

1. He may have left the first woman of his own accord, and may even have left another woman since then.

2. He may have been driven away from both women.

3. He may have left the one woman of his own accord, and been driven away by the other.

4. He may have left the one woman of his own accord and be living with another woman.

5. He may have been driven away from the one woman, and left the other of his own accord.

6. He may have been driven away by the one woman, and may be living with another.

(1). Now, if the man has left both women of his own accord, he should not be resorted to, because of the fickleness of his mind and his indifference to the excellences of both of them.

(2). As regards the man who may have been driven away from both women, if he has been driven away from the last one because the woman could get more money from some other man, then he should be resorted to, for if attached to the first woman he would give her more money through vanity and emulation to spite the other woman. But if he has been driven away by the woman on account of his poverty, or stinginess, he should not then be resorted to.

(3). In the case of the man who may have left the one woman of his own accord, and been driven away by the other, if he agrees to return to the former and give her plenty of money beforehand, then he should be resorted to.

(4). In the case of the man who may have left the one woman of his own accord, and be living with another woman, the former (wishing to take up with him again) should first ascertain if he left her in the first instance in the hope of finding some particular excellence in the other woman, and that not having found any such excellence, he was willing to come back to her, and to give her much money because of his conduct and because of his affection still existing for her.

Or whether, having discovered many faults in the other woman, he would now see even more excellences in herself than actually exist, and would be prepared to give her much money for these qualities.

Or, lastly, to consider whether he was a weak man, or a man fond of enjoying many women, or one who liked a poor woman, or one who never did anything for the woman that he was with. After maturely considering all these things, she should resort to him or not, according to circumstances.

(5). As regards the man who may have been driven away from the one woman, and left the other of his own accord, the former woman (wishing to reunite with him) should first ascertain whether he still has any affection for her, and would consequently spend much money upon her; or whether, being attached to her excellent qualities, he did not take delight in any other women; or whether, being driven away from her formerly before completely satisfying his sexual desires, he wished to get back to her so as to be revenged for the injury done to him; or whether he wished to create confidence in her mind, and then take back from her the wealth which she formerly took from him, and finally destroy her; or, lastly, whether he wished first to separate her from her present lover, and then to break away from her himself. If, after considering all these things, she is of opinion that his intentions are really pure and honest, she can reunite herself with him. But if his mind be at all tainted with evil intentions, he should be avoided.

(6). In the case of the man who may have been driven away by one woman, and be living with another, if the man makes overtures to return to the first one, the courtesan should consider well before she acts, and while the other woman is engaged in attracting him to herself, she should try in her turn (though keeping herself behind the scenes) to gain him over, on the grounds of any of the following considerations:

1. That he was driven away unjustly and for no proper reason, and now that he has gone to another woman, every effort must be used to bring him back to myself.

2. That if he were once to consort with me again, he would break away from the other woman.

3. That the pride of my present lover would be put down by means of the former one.

4. That he has become wealthy, has secured a higher position, and holds a place of authority under the king.

5. That he is separate from his wife.

6. That he is now independent.

7. That he lives apart from his father or brother.

8. That by making peace with him, I shall be able to get hold of a very rich man, who is now prevented from coming to me by my present lover.

9. That as he is not respected by his wife, I shall now be able to separate him from her.

10. That the friend of this man loves my rival, who hates me cordially. I shall therefore by this means separate the friend from his mistress.

11. And, lastly, I shall bring discredit upon him by bringing him back to me, thus showing the fickleness of his mind.

When a courtesan is resolved to take up again with a former lover, her Pithamarda and other servants should tell him that his former expulsion from the woman's house was caused by the wickedness of her mother; that the woman loved him just as much as ever at that time, but could not help the occurrence because of her deference to her mother's will; that she hated the union of her present lover, and disliked him excessively. In addition to this, they should create confidence in his mind by speaking to him of her former love for him, and should allude to the mark of that love that she has ever remembered. This mark of her love should be connected with some kind of pleasure that may have been practiced by him, such as his way of kissing her, or manner of having connection with her.

Thus ends discourse of the ways of bringing about a reunion with a former lover.

When a woman has to choose between two lovers, one of whom was formerly united with her, while the other is a stranger, the Acharyas (sages) are of the opinion that the first one is preferable because, his disposition and character being already known by previous careful observation, he can be easily pleased and satisfied; but Vatsyayana thinks that a former lover, having already spent a great deal of his wealth, is not able or willing to give much money again, and is not therefore to be relied upon so much as a stranger. Particular cases differing from this general rule may, however, arise because of the different natures of men.

There are also verses on these subjects, as follows:

"Reunion with a former lover may be desirable so as to separate some particular woman from some particular man, or some particular man from some particular woman, or to have a certain effect upon the present lover."

"When a man is excessively attached to a woman, he is afraid of her coming into contact with other men; he does not then regard or notice her faults; and he gives her much wealth through fear of her leaving him."

"A courtesan should be agreeable to the man who is attached to her, and despise the man who does not care for her. If while she is living with one man, a messenger comes to her from some other man, she may either refuse to listen to any negotiations on his part, or appoint a fixed time for him to visit her, but she should not leave the man who may be living with her and who may be attached to her."

"A wise woman should renew her connection with a former lover only if she is satisfied that good fortune, gain, love, and friendship are likely to be the result of such a reunion."

# → CHAPTER FIVE ←

# ON DIFFERENT KINDS OF GAIN

WHEN A COURTESAN IS ABLE TO REALIZE MUCH MONEY EVERY day, by reason of many customers, she should not confine herself to a single lover; under such circumstances she should fix her rate for one night, after considering the place, the season, and the condition of the people, also having regard to her own good qualities and good looks, and after comparing her rates with those of other courtesans. She can inform her lovers and friends and acquaintances about these charges. If, however, she can obtain great gain from a single lover, she may resort to him alone, and live with him like a wife.

Now, the sages are of the opinion that when a courtesan has the chance of equal gain from two lovers at the same time, a preference should be given to the one who would give her the kind of thing she wants. But Vatsyayana says that the preference should be given to the one who gives her gold, because it cannot be taken back like some other things, it can be easily received, and it is also the means of procuring anything that may be wished for. Of such things as gold, silver, copper, bell metal, iron, pots, furniture, beds, upper garments, undervestments, fragrant substances, vessels made of gourds, ghee, oil, corn, cattle, and other things of like nature, the first, namely, gold, is superior to all the others.

When the same labor is required to gain any two lovers or when the same kind of thing is to be got from each of them, the choice should be made by the advice of a friend, or it may be made from the lovers' personal qualities, or from the signs of good or bad fortune that may be connected with them.

When there are two lovers, one of whom is attached to the courtesan, and the other is simply very generous, the sages say that a preference should be given to the generous lover; but Vatsyayana is of the opinion that the one who is really attached to the courtesan should be preferred, because he can be made to be generous, even as a miser gives money if he becomes fond of a woman, but a man who is simply generous cannot be made to love with real attachment. But among those who are attached to her, if there is one who is poor, and one who is rich, the preference is of course to be given to the latter.

When there are two lovers, one of whom is generous, and the other ready to do any service for the courtesan, some sages say that the one who is ready to do the service should be preferred; but Vatsyayana is of the opinion that a man who does a service thinks that he has gained his object when he has done something once, but a generous man does not care for what he has given before. Even here the choice should be guided by the likelihood of the future good to be derived from her union with either of them.

When one of two lovers is grateful, and the other liberal, some sages say that the liberal one should be preferred; but Vatsyayana is of the opinion that the former should be chosen, because liberal men are generally haughty, plain-spoken, and wanting in consideration toward others. Even though these liberal men have been on friendly terms for a long time, yet if they see any fault in the courtesan, or are told lies about her by some other woman, they do not care for past services, but leave abruptly. On the other hand, the grateful man does not at once break off from her, because of a regard for the pains she may have taken to please him. In this case also, the choice is to be guided with regard to what may happen in the future.

When an occasion for complying with the request of a friend, and a chance of getting money come together, the sages say that the chance of getting money should be preferred. But Vatsyayana thinks that money can be obtained tomorrow as well as today, but if the request of a friend be not at once complied with, he may become disaffected. Even here, in making the choice, regard must be paid to future good fortune.

On such an occasion, however, the courtesan might pacify her friend by pretending to have some work to do, and telling him that his request will be complied with next day, and in this way secure the chance of getting the money that has been offered her.

When the chance of getting money, and the chance of avoiding some disaster come at the same time, the sages are of the opinion that the chance of getting money should be preferred, but Vatsyayana says that money has only a limited importance, while a disaster that is once averted may never occur again. Here, however, the choice should be guided by the greatness or smallness of the disaster.

The gains of the wealthiest and best kind of courtesans are to be spent as follows:

Building temples, tanks, and gardens; giving a thousand cows to different Brahmans; carrying on the worship of the gods, and celebrating festivals in their honor; and, lastly, performing such vows as may be within their means.

The gains of other courtesans are to be spent as follows:

Having a white dress to wear every day; getting sufficient food and drink to satisfy hunger and thirst; eating daily a perfumed tambula, that is, a mixture of betel nut and betel leaves; and wearing ornaments gilt with gold. The sages say that these represent the gains of all the middle and lower classes of courtesans, but Vatsyayana is of the opinion that their gains cannot be calculated, or fixed in any way, as these depend on the influences of the place, the customs of the people, their own appearance, and many other things.

When a courtesan wants to keep some particular man from some other woman, or wishes to get him away from some woman to whom he may be attached, or to deprive some woman of the gains realized by her from him; or if she thinks that she would raise her position, or enjoy some great good fortune, or become desirable to all men by uniting herself with this man; or if she wishes to get his assistance in averting some misfortune, or is really attached to him and loves him, or wishes to injure somebody through this means, or has regard to some former favor conferred upon her by him, or wishes to be united with him merely from desire—for any of the above reasons she should agree to take from him only a small sum of money in a friendly way.

When a courtesan intends to abandon a particular lover and take up with another one; or when she has reason to believe that her lover will shortly leave her, and return to his wives; or that having squandered all his money, and become penniless, his guardian or master or father would come and take him away; or that her lover is about to lose his position; or, lastly, that he is of a very fickle mind; she should, under any of these circumstances, endeavor to get as much money as she can from him as soon as possible.

On the other hand, when the courtesan thinks that her lover is about to receive valuable presents, or get a place of authority from the king, or be near the time of inheriting a fortune, or that his ship will soon arrive laden with merchandise, or that he has large stocks of corn and other commodities, or that if anything was done for him it would not be done in vain, or that he is always true to his word, then should she have regard to her future welfare, and live with the man like a wife.

There are also verses on these subjects, as follows:

"In considering her present gains, and her future welfare, a courtesan should avoid such persons as have gained their means of subsistence with very great difficulty, as well as those who have become selfish and hardhearted by becoming the favorites of kings."

"She should make every endeavor to unite herself with prosperous and well-to-do people and with those whom it is dangerous to avoid or to slight in any way. Even at some cost to herself she should become acquainted with energetic and liberal-minded men, who when pleased would give her a large sum of money, even for very little service, or for some small thing."

## ON GAINS AND LOSSES; ATTENDANT GAINS, LOSSES, AND DOUBTS. AND, LASTLY, ON THE DIFFERENT KINDS OF COURTESANS

IT SOMETIMES HAPPENS THAT WHILE GAINS ARE BEING SOUGHT for, or expected to be realized, only losses are the result of our efforts. The causes of these losses are:

> Weakness of intellect
> Excessive love
> Excessive pride
> Excessive self-conceit
> Excessive simplicity
> Excessive confidence
> Excessive anger
> Carelesness
> Recklesness
> Influence of evil genius
> Accidental circumstances

The results of these losses are:

> Expense incurred without any result
> Destruction of future good fortune
> Stoppage of gains about to be realized

> Loss of what is already obtained
> Acquisition of a sour temper
> Becoming unamiable to everybody
> Injury to head
> Loss of hair, and other accidents

Now, gain is of three kinds: gain of wealth, gain of religious merit, and gain of pleasure; and similarly, loss is of three kinds: loss of wealth, loss of religious merit, and loss of pleasure. At the time when gains are sought for, if other gains come along with them, these are called attendant gains. When gain is uncertain, the doubt of its being a gain is called a simple doubt. When there is a doubt whether either of two things will happen or not, it is called a mixed doubt. If while one thing is being done, two results take place, it is called a combination of two results; and if several results follow from the same action, it is called a combination of results on every side.

We shall now give examples of the above.

As already stated, gain is of three kinds; and loss, which is opposed to gain, is also of three kinds.

(*a*). When by living with a great man a courtesan acquires present wealth, and in addition to this becomes acquainted with other people, and thus obtains a chance of future fortune and an accession of wealth, and becomes desirable to all, this is called a gain of wealth attended by other gain.

(*b*). When by living with a man a courtesan simply gets money, this is called a gain of wealth not attended by any other gain.

(*c*). When a courtesan receives money from other people besides her lover, the results are: the chance of the loss of future good from her present lover; the chance of disaffection of a man securely attached to her; the hatred of all; and the chance of a union with some low person tending to destroy her future good. This gain is called a gain of wealth attended by losses.

(*d*). When a courtesan at her own expense, and without any results in the shape of gain, has connection with a great man, or with an avaricious minister, for the sake of diverting some misfortune or removing some cause that may be threatening the destruction of a great gain, this loss is said to be a loss of wealth attended by gains of the future good which it may bring about.

(*e*). When a courtesan is kind, even at her own expense, to a man who is very stingy, or to a man proud of his looks, or to an ungrateful man skilled in gaining the heart of others, without any good resulting from these connections to her in the end, this loss is called a loss of wealth not attended by any gain.

(*f*). When a courtesan is kind to any such men as described above, but who in addition are favorites of the king, and who, moreover, are cruel and powerful, without any good result in the end, and with a chance of her being turned away at any moment, this loss is called a loss of wealth attended by other losses.

In this way gains and losses, and attendant gains and losses in religious merit and in pleasures, may become known to the reader, and combinations of all of them may also be made.

Thus end the remarks on gains and losses, and attendant gains and losses.

In the next place we come to doubts, which are again of three kinds: doubts about wealth, doubts about religious merit, and doubts about pleasures.

The following are examples.

(*a*). When a courtesan is not certain how much a man may give her or spend upon her, this is called a doubt about wealth.

(*b*). When a courtesan feels doubtful whether she is right in entirely abandoning a lover from whom she is unable to get money, she having taken all his wealth from him in the first instance, this doubt is called a doubt about religious merit.

(*c*). When a courtesan is unable to get hold of a lover to her liking, and is uncertain whether she will derive any pleasure from a person surrounded by his family, or from a low person, this is called a doubt about pleasure.

(*d*). When a courtesan is uncertain whether some powerful but low-principled fellow would cause loss to her because of her being civil to him, this is called a doubt about the loss of wealth.

(*e*). When a courtesan feels doubtful whether she would lose religious merit by abandoning a man who is attached to her without giving him the slightest favor, and thereby causing him unhappiness in this world and the next,[1] this doubt is called a doubt about the loss of religious merit.

(*f*). When a courtesan is uncertain as to whether she might create disaffection by speaking out, and revealing her love, and thus not get her desire satisfied, this is called a doubt about the loss of pleasure.

Thus end the remarks on doubts.

*Mixed Doubts*

(*a*). The intercourse or connection with a stranger whose disposition is unknown, and who may have been introduced by a lover or by one who possessed authority, may be productive either of gain or loss, and therefore this is called a mixed doubt about the gain and loss of wealth.

(*b*). When a courtesan is requested by a friend, or is impelled by pity to have intercourse with a learned Brahman, a religious student, a sacrificer, a devotee, or an ascetic who may have all fallen in love with her, and who may be consequently at the point of death, by doing this she might either gain or lose religious merit, and therefore this is called a mixed doubt about the gain or loss of religious merit.

(*c*). If a courtesan relies solely upon the report of other people (hearsay) about a man, and goes to him without ascertaining herself whether he possesses good qualities or not, she may either gain or lose pleasure in proportion as he may be good or bad, and therefore this is called a mixed doubt about the gain and loss of pleasure.

Uddalika has described the gains and losses on both sides as follows:

(*a*). If, when living with a lover, a courtesan gets both wealth and pleasure from him, it is called a gain on both sides.

(*b*). When a courtesan lives with a lover at her own expense without getting any profit out of it, and the lover even takes back from her what he may have formerly given her, it is called a loss on both sides.

(*c*). When a courtesan is uncertain whether a new acquaintance would become attached to her, and, moreover, if he became attached to her, whether he would give her anything, it is called a doubt on both sides about gains.

(*d*). When a courtesan is uncertain whether a former enemy, if made up to by her at her own expense, would do her some injury because of his grudge against her; or, if becoming attached to her, would angrily take away from her anything that he may have given to her, this is called a doubt on both sides about loss.

Babhravya has described the gains and losses on both sides as follows:

(*a*). When a courtesan can get money from a man whom she may go to see, and also money from a man whom she may not go to see, this is called a gain on both sides.

(*b*). When a courtesan has to incur further expense if she goes to see a man, and yet runs the risk of incurring an irremediable loss if she does not go to see him, this is called a loss on both sides.

(*c*). When a courtesan is uncertain whether a particular man would give her anything on her going to see him, without incurring expense on her part, or whether on her neglecting him another man would give her something, this is called a doubt on both sides about gain.

(*d*). When a courtesan is uncertain whether, on going at her own expense to see an old enemy, he would take back from her what he may have given her, or whether by her not going to see him he would cause some disaster to fall upon her, this is called a doubt on both sides about loss.

By combining the above, the following six kinds of mixed results are produced:

(*a*). Gain on one side, and loss on the other.
(*b*). Gain on one side, and doubt of gain on the other.
(*c*). Gain on one side, and doubt of loss on the other.
(*d*). Loss on one side, and doubt of gain on the other.
(*e*). Doubt of gain on one side, and doubt of loss on the other.
(*e*). Doubt of gain on one side, and doubt of loss on the other.
(*f*). Doubt of loss on one side, and loss on the other.

A courtesan, having considered all the above things and taken counsel with her friends, should act so as to acquire gain, the chances of great gain, and the warding off of any great disaster. Religious merit and pleasure should also be formed into separate combination like those of wealth, and then all should be combined with each other, so as to form new combinations.

When a courtesan consorts with men, she should cause each of them to give her money as well as pleasure. At particular times, such as the Spring Festivals, and so on, she should make her mother announce to the various men that on a certain day her daughter would remain with the man who would gratify such and such a desire of hers.

When young men approach her with delight, she should think of what she may accomplish through them.

The combination of gains and losses on all sides are: gain on one side, and loss on all others; loss on one side, and gain on all others; gain on all sides, loss on all sides.

A courtesan should also consider doubts about gain and doubts about loss with reference both to wealth, religious merit, and pleasure.

Thus ends the consideration of gain, loss, attendant gains, attendant losses, and doubts.

The different kinds of courtesans are:

> A bawd
> A female attendant
> An unchaste woman
> A dancing girl
> A female artisan
> A woman who has left her family
> A woman living on her beauty
> And, finally, a regular courtesan

All the above kinds of courtesans are acquainted with various kinds of men, and should consider the ways of getting money from them, of pleasing them, of separating themselves from them, and of reuniting with them. They should also take into consideration particular gains and losses, attendant gains and losses, and doubts in accordance with their several conditions.

Thus ends the consideration of courtesans.

There are also two verses on the subject, as follows:

"Men want pleasure, while women want money, and therefore this Part, which treats of the means of gaining wealth, should be studied."

"There are some women who seek for love, and there are others who seek for money; for the former the ways of love are told in previous portions of this work, while the ways of getting money, as practiced by courtesans, are described in this Part."

# On the Means of Attracting Others to Yourself

⊰ PART SEVEN ⊱

# ON PERSONAL ADORNMENT; ON SUBJUGATING THE HEARTS OF OTHERS; AND ON TONIC MEDICINES

WHEN A PERSON FAILS TO OBTAIN THE OBJECT OF HIS DESIRES BY any of the ways previously related, he should then have recourse to other ways of attracting others to himself.

Now, good looks, qualities, youth, and liberality are the chief and most natural means of making a person agreeable in the eyes of others. But in the absence of these, a man or woman must have resort to artificial means, or to art, and the following are some recipes that may be found useful:

(*a*). An ointment made of the *Tabernaemontana coronaria,* the *Costus speciosus* or arabicus, and the *Flacourtia Cataphracta,* can be used as an unguent of adornment.

(*b*). If a fine powder is made of the above plants, and applied to the wick of a lamp, which is made to burn with the oil of blue vitriol, the black pigment or lampblack produced there-from, when applied to the eyelashes, has the effect of making a person look lovely.

(*c*). The oil of the hogweed, the *Echites putescens,* the sarina plant, the yellow amaranth, and the leaf of the nymphæ, if applied to the body, has the same effect.

(*d*). A black pigment from the same plants produces a similar effect.

(*e*). By eating the powder of the *Nelumbium speciosum,* the blue lotus, and the *Mesna roxburghii,* with ghee and honey, a man becomes lovely in the eyes of others.

(*f*). The above things, together with the *Tabernaemontana coronaria,* and the *Xanthochymus pictorius,* if used as an ointment, produce the same results.

(*g*). If the bone of a peacock or of a hyena be covered with gold, and tied on the right hand, it makes a man lovely in the eyes of other people.

(*h*). In the same way, if a bead, made of the seed of the jujube, or of the conch shell, be enchanted by the incantations mentioned in the Arthava Veda, or by the incantations of those well skilled in the science of magic, and tied on the hand, it produces the same result as described above.

(*i*). When a female attendant arrives at the age of puberty, her master should keep her secluded, and when men ardently desire her because of her seclusion, and because of the difficulty of approaching her, he should then bestow her hand on such a person as may endow her with wealth and happiness.

This is a means of increasing the loveliness of a person in the eyes of others.

In the same way, when the daughter of a courtesan arrives at the age of puberty, the mother should get together a lot of young men of the same age, disposition, and knowledge as her daughter, and tell them that she would give her in marriage to the person who would give her presents of a particular kind.

After this, the daughter should be kept in seclusion as far as possible, and the mother should give her in marriage to the man who may be ready to give her the presents agreed upon. If the mother is unable to get so much out of the man, she should show some of her own things as having been given to the daughter by the bridegroom.

Or the mother may allow her daughter to be married to the man privately, as if she were ignorant of the whole affair, and then, pretending that it has come to her knowledge, she may give her consent to the union.

The daughter, too, should make herself attractive to the sons of wealthy citizens, unknown to her mother, and make them attached to her, and for this purpose should meet them at the time of learning to sing, and in places where music is played, and at the houses of other people, and then request her mother, through a female friend or servant, to be allowed to unite herself to the man who is most agreeable to her.[1]

When the daughter of a courtesan is thus given to a man, the ties of marriage should be observed for one year, and after that she may do what she likes. But even after the end of the year, when otherwise engaged, if she should be now and then invited by her first husband to come and see him, she should put aside her present gain, and go to him for the night.

Such is the mode of temporary marriage among courtesans, and of increasing their loveliness and their value in the eyes of others. What has been said about them should also be understood to apply to the daughters of dancing women, whose mothers should give them only to such persons as are likely to become useful to them in various ways.

Thus ends discourse of the ways of making oneself lovely in the eyes of others.

(*a*). If a man, after anointing his lingam with a mixture of the powders of the white thorn apple, the long pepper and the black pepper, and honey, engages in sexual union with a woman, he makes her subject to his will.

(*b*). The application of a mixture of the leaf of the plant vatodbhranta, of the flowers thrown on a human corpse when carried out to be burned, and of the powder of the bones of the peacock, and of the jiwanjiva bird produces the same effect.

(*c*). The remains of a kite who has died a natural death, ground into powder, and mixed with cowhage and honey, has also the same effect.

(*d*). Anointing oneself with an ointment made of the plant *Emblica myrobolans* has the power of subjecting women to one's will.

(*e*). If a man cuts into small pieces the sprouts of the vajnasunhi plant, and dips them into a mixture of red arsenic and sulphur, and then dries them seven times, and applies this powder mixed with honey to his lingam, he can subjugate a woman to his will directly he has had sexual union with her; or if by burning these very sprouts at night and looking at the smoke, he sees a golden moon behind, he will then be successful with any woman; or if he throws some of the powder of these same sprouts mixed with the excrement of a monkey upon a maiden, she will not be given in marriage to anybody else.

(*f*). If pieces of the orrisroot are dressed with the oil of the mango, and placed for six months in a hole made in the trunk of the sisu tree, and are then taken out and made up into an ointment, and applied to the lingam, this is said to serve as the means of subjugating women.

(*g*). If the bone of a camel is dipped into the juice of the plant *Eclipta prostata,* and then burned, and the black pigment produced from its ashes is placed in a box also made of the bone of a camel, and applied together with antimony to the eyelashes with a pencil also made of the bone of a camel, then that pigment is said to be very pure, and wholesome for the eyes, and serves as a means of subjugating others to the person who uses it. The same effect can be produced by black pigment made of the bones of hawks, vultures, and peacocks.

Thus ends discourse of the ways of subjugating others to one's own will.

Now, the means of increasing sexual vigor are as follows:

(*a*). A man obtains sexual vigor by drinking milk mixed with sugar, the root of the uchchata plant, the pipar chaba, and licorice.

(*b*). Drinking milk mixed with sugar, and having the testicle of a ram or a goat boiled in it, is also productive of vigor.

(*c*). The drinking of the juice of the *Hedysarum gangeticum,* the kuili, and the kshirika plant, mixed with milk, produces the same effect.

(*d*). The seed of long pepper, along with the seeds of the *Sansevieria roxburghiana,* and the *Hedysarum gangeticum* plant, all pounded together, and mixed with milk, is productive of a similar result.

(*e*). According to ancient authors, if a man pounds the seeds or roots of the *Trapa bispinosa,* the kasurika, the tuscan jasmine, and licorice, together with the kshirikapoli (a kind of onion), and puts the powder into milk mixed with sugar and ghee, and having boiled the whole mixture on a moderate fire, drinks the paste so formed, he will be able to enjoy innumerable women.

(*f*). In the same way, if a man mixes rice with the eggs of the sparrow, and having boiled this in milk, adds to it ghee and honey, and drinks as much of it as is necessary, this will produce the same effect.

(*g*). If a man takes the outer covering of sesame seeds, and soaks them with the eggs of sparrows, and then, having boiled them in milk, mixed with sugar and ghee, along with the fruits of the *Trapa bispinosa* and the kasurika plant, and adds to it the flour of wheat and beans, and then drinks this composition, he is said to be able to enjoy many women.

(*h*). If ghee, honey, sugar, and licorice in equal quantities, the juice of the fennel plant, and milk are mixed together, this nectar-like composition is said to be holy, and provocative of sexual vigor, a preservative of life, and sweet to the taste.

(*i*). The drinking of a paste composed of the *Asparagus racemosus*, the shvadaushtra plant, the guduchi plant, the long pepper, and licorice, boiled in milk, honey, and ghee, in the spring, is said to have the same effect as the above.

(*j*). Boiling the *Asparagus racemosus* and the shvadaushtra plant, along with the pounded fruits of the *Premna spinosa* in water, and drinking the same, is said to act in the same way.

(*k*). Drinking boiled ghee, or clarified butter, in the morning, during the spring season, is said to be beneficial to health and strength, and agreeable to the taste.

(*l*). If the powder of the seed of the shvadaushtra plant and the flour of barley are mixed together in equal parts, and a portion of it, two palas in weight, is eaten every morning on getting up, it has the same effect as the preceding recipe.

There are also verses on the subject, as follows:

"The means[2] of producing love and sexual vigor should be learned from the science of medicine, from the Vedas, from those who are learned in the arts of magic, and from confidential relatives. No means should be tried which are doubtful in their effects, which are likely to cause injury to the body, which involve the death of animals, or which bring us in contact with impure things. Only such means should be used as are holy, acknowledged to be good, and approved of by Brahmans and friends."

## CHAPTER TWO

# ON THE WAYS OF EXCITING DESIRE;
# AND ON MISCELLANEOUS
# EXPERIMENTS AND RECIPES

IF A MAN IS UNABLE TO SATISFY A HASTINI, OR ELEPHANT WOMAN, he should have recourse to various means to excite her passion. At the commencement he should rub her yoni with his hand or fingers, and not begin to have intercourse with her until she becomes excited, or experiences pleasure. This is one way of exciting a woman.

Or he may make use of certain Apadravyas, or things which are put on or around the lingam to supplement its length or its thickness, so as to fit it to the yoni. In the opinion of Babhravya, these Apadravyas should be made of gold, silver, copper, iron, ivory, buffalo's horn, various kinds of wood, tin, or lead, and should be soft, cool, provocative of sexual vigor, and well fitted to serve the intended purpose. Vatsyayana, however, says that they may be made according to the natural liking of each individual.

The following are the different kinds of Apadravyas:

1. "The armlet" (Valaya) should be of the same size as the lingam, and should have its outer surface made rough with globules.
2. "The couple" (Sanghati) is formed of two armlets.

196 THE KAMA SUTRA

3. "The bracelet" (Chudaka) is made by joining three or more armlets, until they come up to the required length of the lingam.

4. "The single bracelet" is formed by wrapping a single wire around the lingam, according to its dimensions.

5. The Kantuka or Jalaka is a tube open at both ends, with a hole through it, outwardly rough and studded with soft globules, and made to fit the size of the yoni, and tied to the waist.

When such a thing cannot be obtained, then a tube made of the wood apple, or tubular stalk of the bottle gourd, or a reed made soft with oil and extracts of plants, and tied to the waist with string, may be made use of, as well as a row of soft pieces of wood tied together.

The above are the things that can be used in connection with, or in the place of, the lingam.

The people of the southern countries think that true sexual pleasure cannot be obtained without perforating the lingam, and they therefore cause it to be pierced like the lobes of the ears of an infant pierced for earrings.

Now, when a young man perforates his lingam he should pierce it with a sharp instrument, and then stand in water as long as the blood continues to flow. At night he should engage in sexual intercourse, even with vigor, so as to clean the hole. After this he should continue to wash the hole with decoctions, and increase the size by putting into it small pieces of cane, and the *Wrightea antidysenterica,* thus gradually enlarging the orifice. It may also be washed with licorice mixed with honey, and the size of the hole increased by the fruit stalks of the simapatra plant. The hole should also be anointed with a small quantity of oil.

In the hole made in the lingam a man may put Apadravyas of various forms, such as the "round," the "round on one side," the "wooden mortar," the "flower," the "armlet," the "bone of the heron," the "goad of the elephant," the "collection of eight balls," the "lock of hair," the "place where four roads meet," and other things named according to their forms and means of using them. All these Apadravyas should be rough on the outside according to their requirements.

The ways of enlarging the lingam must now be related.

When a man wishes to enlarge his lingam, he should rub it with the bristles of certain insects that live in trees, and then, after rubbing it for ten nights with oils, he should again rub it with the bristles as before. By continuing to do this a swelling will be gradually produced in the lingam, and he should then lie on a cot, and cause his lingam to hang down through a hole in the cot. After this, he should take away all the pain from the swelling by using cool concoctions. The swelling, which is called "Suka," and is often brought about among the people of the Dravidian country, lasts for life.

If the lingam is rubbed with the following things, namely, the plant *Physalis flexuosa*, the shavara-kandaka plant, the jalasuka plant, the fruit of the eggplant, the butter of a she-buffalo, the hasti-charma plant, and the juice of the vajrarasna plant, a swelling lasting for one month will be produced.

By rubbing it with oil boiled in the concoctions of the above things, the same effect will be produced, but lasting for six months.

The enlargement of the lingam is also effected by rubbing it or moistening it with oil boiled on a moderate fire along with the seeds of the pomegranate, and the cucumber, the juices of the valuka plant, the hasti-charma plant, and the eggplant.

In addition to the above, other means may be learned from experience and confidential persons.

The miscellaneous experiments and recipes are as follows:

(*a*). If a man mixes the powder of the milk hedge plant and the kantaka plant with the excrement of a monkey and the powdered root of the lanjalika plant, and throws this mixture on a woman, she will not love anybody else afterward.

(b). If a man thickens the juice of the fruits of the *Cassia fistula* and the *Eugenia jambolana* by mixing them with the powder of the soma plant, the *Vernonia anthelmintica,* the *Eclipta prostata,* and the lohopa-jihirka, and applies this composition to the yoni of a woman, and then has sexual intercourse with her, his love for her will be destroyed.

(c). The same effect is produced if a man has connection with a woman who has bathed in the buttermilk of a she-buffalo mixed with the powders of gopalika plant, the banupadika plant, and the yellow amaranth.

(d). An ointment made of the flowers of the *Nauclea cadamba,* the hog plum, and the *Eugenia jambolana,* and used by a woman, causes her to be dislike by her husband.

(e). Garlands made of the above flowers, when worn by the woman, produce the same effect.

(f). An ointment made of the fruit of the *Asteracantha longifolia* (kokilaksha) will contract the yoni of a Hastini, or elephant woman, and this contraction lasts for one night.

(g). An ointment made by pounding the roots of the *Nelumbium speciosum* and of the blue lotus, and the powder of the plant *Physalis flexuosa* mixed with ghee and honey, will enlarge the yoni of the Mrigi, or deer woman.

(h). An ointment made of the fruit of the *Emblica myrobolans,* soaked in the milky juice of the milk hedge plant, of the soma plant, the *Calotropis gigantea,* and the juice of the fruit of the *Vernonia anthelmintica,* will make the hair white.

(i). The juice of the roots of the madayantika plant, the yellow amaranth, the anjanika plant, the *Clitoria ternatea,* and the shlakshnaparni plant, used as a lotion, will make the hair grow.

(*j*). An ointment made by boiling the above roots in oil, and rubbed in, will make the hair black, and will also gradually restore hair that has fallen off.

(*k*). If lac is saturated seven times in the sweat of the testicle of a white horse, and applied to a red lip, the lip will become white.

(*l*). The color of the lips can be regained by means of the madayantika and other plants mentioned above under (*i*).

(*m*). A woman who hears a man playing on a reed pipe which has been dressed with the juices of the bahupadika plant, the *Tabernaemontana coronaria,* the *Costus speciosus* or arabicus, the *Pinus deodora,* the *Euphorbia antiquorum,* the vajra and the kantaka plant, becomes his slave.

(*n*). If food be mixed with the fruit of the thorn apple (datura) it causes intoxication.

(*o*). If water be mixed with oil and the ashes of any kind of grass except the kusha grass, it becomes the color of milk.

(*p*). If yellow myrobolans, the hog plum, the shrawana plant, and the priyangu plant be all pounded together, and applied to iron pots, these pots become red.

(*q*). If a lamp, trimmed with oil extracted from the shrawana and priyangu plants (its wick being made of cloth and the slough of the skins of snakes), is lighted, and long pieces of wood placed near it, those pieces of wood will resemble so many snakes.

(*r*). Drinking the milk of a white cow who has a white calf at her foot is auspicious, produces fame, and preserves life.

(*s*). The blessings of venerable Brahmans, well propitiated, have the same effect.

There are also some verses in conclusion:

"Thus have I written in a few words these *Aphorisms on Love,* after reading the texts of ancient authors, and following the ways of enjoyment mentioned in them.

"He who is acquainted with the true principles of this science pays regard to Dharma, Artha, Kama, and to his own experiences, as well as to the teachings of others, and does not act simply on the dictates of his own desire. As for the errors in the science of love which I have mentioned in this work, on my own authority as an author, I have, immediately after mentioning them, carefully censured and prohibited them.

"An act is never looked upon with indulgence for the simple reason that it is authorized by the science, because it ought to be remembered that it is the intention of the science that the rules which it contains should be acted upon only in particular cases. After reading and considering the works of Babhravya and other ancient authors, and thinking over the meaning of the rules given by them, the *Kama Sutra* was composed, according to the precepts of Holy Writ, for the benefit of the world, by Vatsyayana, while leading the life of a religious student, and wholly engaged in the contemplation of the Deity.

"This work is not intended to be used merely as an instrument for satisfying our desires. A person acquainted with the true principles of this science, and who preserves his Dharma, Artha, and Kama, and has regard for the practices of the people, is sure to obtain the mastery over his senses.

"In short, an intelligent and prudent person, attending to Dharma and Artha, and attending to Kama also, without becoming the slave of his passions, obtains success in everything that he may undertake."

# ANANGA RANGA

# PREFACE

THE FOLLOWING PAGES CONTAIN A HINDU "ART OF LOVE," WHICH may fairly be pronounced unique. From the days of Sotades and Ovid to our time, western authors have treated the subject either jocularly or with a tendency to hymn the joys of immorality, and the gospel of debauchery. The Indian author has taken the opposite view, and it is impossible not to admire the delicacy with which he has handled an exceedingly delicate theme. As he assures his readers before parting, the object of the book, which opens with praises of the gods, is not to encourage chambering and wantonness, but simply and in all sincerity to prevent the separation of husband and wife. Feeling convinced that monogamy is a happier state than polygamy, he would save the married couple from the monotony and satiety which follow possession, by varying their pleasures in every conceivable way, and by supplying them with the means of being psychically pure and physically pleasant to each other. He recognizes, fully as Balzac does, the host of evils which result from conjugal infidelity; and, if he allow adultery in order to save life, he does only what was done by the most civilized of pagan nations, who had the same opinions upon the subject: witness the liberality of Socrates in lending his wife to a friend, and the generosity of Seleucus quoted in the following pages.

Nor is it a small merit to the author, that he has been able to say so much of novelty and of interest upon the congress of the sexes, a subject which has been worked since the remotest ages, which is supposed to have been exhausted long ago, and yet which no one has treated as it is treated in this treatise. The originality is everywhere mixed up, it is true, with a peculiar quaintness, resulting from the language and from the peculiarities of Hindu thought, yet it is not the less original. Nothing can be more characteristic of the Indian than this laboured and mechanical style of love; when kisses are divided into so many kinds; when there are rules for patting with the palm and the back of the hand, and regulations for the several expirations of breath. Regarded in this light, the book becomes an ethnological treasure, which tells us as much of Hindu human nature as the "Thousand Nights and a Night" of Arab manners and customs in the *cinquecento*.

The author informs us that the treatise was composed by the Arch-poet Kalyána Mall (himself), and unfortunately we know little of him. A biography of the poets, the Kavi-Charika, states that he was a native of Kalinga, by caste a Brahman, who flourished during the reign of Anangabhima, alias Ladadiva, the King of that country; and an inscription in the Sanctuary of Jagannath proves that the Rajah built a temple in the Shaka, or year of Shalivana, 1094 = A. D. 1172.

On the other hand all MSS. of the Ananga-Ranga have a verse distinctly stating that the author Kalyána Mall, wrote the book for the amusement of Lada Khan, son of Ahmed, of the Lodi House. Hence the suggestion that the patron was Ahmad Chan, Subahdár or Viceroy of Gujarat (Guzerat) whom, with Eastern flattery and exaggeration, the poet crowns King of the Realm. This Officer was a servant of the Lodi or Pathán dynasty, who according to Elphinstone appointed many of their kinsmen to high office. Three Lodi kings (Bahlúl, Sikandar and Abrahim, who ruled between A. D. 1450 and 1526) immediately preceded the Taymur house in the person of Baber Shah. The work, which is not written in classical style and belongs to late Sanskrit literature, is an analysis of and a compilation from treatises of much earlier date, such as the Kama Sutra of Vatsyáyana (for which see Chapt. vi.) the Ratirahasya, the Panchasáyaka, the Smarapradipa, the Ratimanjari and, to quote no other, the Mánasolása or Abhilashitachintamani—the "Description of the King's Diversion," *le Roi s'amuse.*

The treatise, originally in Sanskrit, has been translated into every language of the East which boasts a literature, however humble. In Sanskrit and Prakrit (Marathi, Gujarati, Bengáli, etc.) it is called "Ananga-Ranga," Stage or form of the Bodiless one, Kama Deva (Kamadeva), the Hindu Cupid who was reduced to ashes by the fiery eye of Shiva and presently restored to life. The legend runs thus in Moore's "Hindu Pantheon:"—

"Mahadeva, *i. e.* Shiva, and Parvati his wife, playing with dice at the game of Chaturanga, disputed and parted in wrath; and severally performing rigid acts of devotion to the Supreme Being, kindled thereby such vehement fires as threatened a general conflagration. The Devas, in great alarm, hastened to Brahma, who led them to Mahadeva and supplicated him to recall his consort; but the wrathful god answered, that she must return to him of her own free choice. They accordingly deputed Ganga, the river-goddess, who prevailed on Parvati to return to her husband, on the condition that his love for her should be restored. The celestial mediators then employed Kamadeva, who wounded Shiva with one of his flowery arrows, but the angry deity reduced the God of Love to ashes. Parvati, soon after presenting herself before Shiva in the semblance of a Kerati, or daughter of a mountaineer, and seeing him enamoured of her, assumed her own shape and effected a re-union. The relenting Shiva consoled the afflicted Rati, the widow of Kama, by assuring her that she should rejoin her husband, when she should be born again in the form of Pradyamna, son of Krishna, and put Sambará Asura to death. This favourable prediction was in due time accomplished, and Pradyamna was seized by the demon Sambara, who placed him in a chest and threw it into the sea. The chest was swallowed by a large fish, which was caught and carried to the palace of the giant, where the unfortunate Rati had been compelled to perform manual service; it fell to her lot to open the fish, and finding the chest and its contents, she nursed the infant in private, and educated him until he had sufficient strength to destroy the malignant Sambara. He had before considered Rati as his mother; but their minds being now irradiated, the prophetic promise of Mahadeva was remembered, and the god of Love was re-united to the goddess of Pleasure."

In Arabic, Hindostani and the Moslem dialects, the Ananga-Ranga becomes Lizzat al-Nisá, or the Pleasures of Women; and it appears with little change in Persian and Turkish. Generally it is known in India as the Kamá Shástra, the Scripture of Káma or Lila Shástra, the Scripture of Play or amorous Sport—τò παίζειν. The vulgar call it "Koka Pandit," from the supposed author, concerning whom the following tale is told. A woman who was burning with love and could find none to satisfy her inordinate desires, threw off her clothes and swore she would wander the world naked till she met with her match. In this condition she entered the levee-hall of the Rajah upon whom Koka Pandit was attending; and, when asked if she were not ashamed of herself, looked insolently at the crowd of courtiers around her and scornfully declared that there was not a man in the room. The King and his company were sore abashed; but the Sage joining his hands, applied with due humility for royal permission to tame the shrew. He then led her home and worked so persuasively that wellnigh fainting from fatigue and from repeated orgasms she cried for quarter. Thereupon the virile Pandit inserted gold pins into her arms and legs; and, leading her before his Rajah, made her confess her defeat and solemnly veil herself in the presence. The Rajah was, as might be expected, anxious to learn how the victory had been won, and commanded Koka Pandit to tell his tale, and to add much useful knowledge on the subject of coition. In popular pictures the Sage appears sitting before and lecturing the Rajah who duly throned and shaded by the Chatri, or royal canopy, with his harem fanning him and forming tail, lends an attentive ear to the words of wisdom.

In these days the Ananga-Ranga enjoys deserved celebrity. Lithographed copies have been printed by hundreds of thousands, and the book is in the hands of both sexes and all ages throughout the nearer East, and possibly it may extend to China and Japan. It has become a part of natural life, and even the "Fables of Pilpay," to use a neutral term for a volume whose names are manifold, has not a wider circulation.

The Kama Sutra of Vatsyáyana, concerning which more presently, and Ananga-Ranga must be regarded as two valuable and interesting works on Social Science: they bear repeated readings and seem ever to present a something of novelty. Eastern students often apply to them the well-known lines of Hafiz:—

Oh songster sweet, begin the lay,
Ever fresh and ever gay;
For us once more the tale renew,
Ever old but ever new.

It was at first our intention, after rendering the "Káma Shastra" from Sanskrit into English, to dress it up in Latin, that it might not fall into the hands of the vulgar. But further considerations satisfied us that it contains nothing essentially immoral, and much matter deserving of more consideration than it receives at present. The generation which prints and reads literal English translations of the debauched Petronius Arbiter, and the witty indecencies of Rabelais, can hardly be prudish enough to complain of the devout and highly moral Kalyána Malla. At least, so think

THE TRANSLATORS.

# INTRODUCTION

MAY YOU BE PURIFIED BY PARVATI[1] WHO COLOURED THE NAILS of her hands which were white like the waters of Ganges, with lac after seeing the fire on the forehead of Shambu; who painted her eyes with collyrium after seeing the dark hues of Shambhu's neck and whose body-hair stood erect (with desire) after seeing in a mirror the ashes on Shambhu's body.

I invoke thee, O Kámadeva! thee the sportive; thee, the wanton one, who dwellest in the hearts of all created beings;

Thou instillest courage in time of war; thou destroyedst Sambar' A'sura and the Rákshasas; thou sufficest unto Rati,[2] and to the loves and pleasures of the world;

Thou art ever cheerful, removing uneasiness and over activity, and thou givest comfort and happiness to the mind of man.

King Ahmad was the ornament of the Lodí House. He was a Sea, having for waters the tears shed by the widows of his slaughtered foes, and he rose to just renown and wide-spread fame. May his son Láda Khan, versed in the Kama Shastra, or Scripture of Love, and having his feet rubbed with the diadems of other kings, be ever victorious!

The great princely sage and arch-poet, Kalyána Malla, versed in all the arts, after consulting many wise and holy men, and having examined the opinions of many poets, and extracted the essence of their wisdom, composed, with a view of pleasing his sovereign, a work which was called Ananga-Ranga.[3] May it ever be appreciated by the discerning, for it hath been dedicated to those who are desirous of studying the art and mystery of man's highest enjoyment, and to those who are best acquainted with the science and practice of dalliance and love-delight.

It is true that no joy in the world of mortals can compare with that derived from the knowledge of the Creator. Second, however, and subordinate only to this, are the satisfaction and pleasure arising from the possession of a beautiful woman. Men, it is true, marry for the sake of undisturbed congress, as well as for love and comfort, and often they obtain handsome and attractive wives. But they do not give them plenary contentment, nor do they themselves thoroughly enjoy their charms. The reason of which is, that they are purely ignorant of the Scripture of Cupid, the Káma Shastra; and, despising the difference between the several kinds of women, they regard them only in an animal point of view. Such men must be looked upon as foolish and unintelligent; and this book is composed with the object of preventing lives and loves being wasted in similar manner, and the benefits to be derived from its study are set forth in the following verses:—

"The man who knoweth the Art of Love, and who understandeth the thorough and varied enjoyment of woman;

"As advancing age cooleth his passions, he learneth to think of his Creator, to study religious subjects, and to acquire divine knowledge:

"Hence he is freed from further transmigration of souls; and when the tale of his days is duly told, he goeth direct with his wife to the Svarga (heaven)."

And thus all you who read this book shall know how delicious an instrument is woman, when artfully played upon; how capable she is of producing the most exquisite harmony; of executing the most complicated variations and of giving the divinest pleasures.

Finally, let it be understood that every Shloka (stanza) of this work has a double signification, after the fashion of the Vedanta, and may be interpreted in two ways, either mystical or amatory.

# → CHAPTER ONE ←

# ANANGA-RANGA; OR,
# THE HINDU ART OF LOVE

### SECTION I.

*Of the Four Orders of Women.*

FIRST, LET IT BE UNDERSTOOD, THAT WOMEN MUST BE DIVIDED
into four classes of temperament. These are:—

> 1. Padminí;
> 2. Chitriní;
> 3. Shankhiní; and
> 4. Hastiní.

The same correspond with the four different phases of
Moksha, or Release from further Transmigration. The first is
Sáyujyatá, or absorption into the essence of the Deity; the second
is Sámípyatá, nearness to the Deity, the being born in the
Divine Presence; the third is Sarúpatá, or resemblance to the
Deity in limbs and material body; the fourth and last is Salokatá,
or residence in the heaven of some especial god.

For the name of woman is Nárí, which, being interpreted,
means "No A'rí," or foe; and such is Moksha, or absorption,
because all love it and it loves all mankind.

Padminí, then means Sáyujyatá, also called Khadginí-
Moksha (Sword-release) the absorption of man into the
Náráyan (godhead), who lives in the Khshírábdí, or Milksea,

213

one of the Seven Oceans, and from whose navel sprang the Padma, or Lotus-flower.

Chitriní is Sámípyatá-Moksha, like those who, having been incarnated as gods, perform manifold and wonderful works. Shankhiní is Sarúpatá-Moksha, even as the man who takes the form of Vishnú, bears upon his body the Shankha (conch-shell), the Chakra or discus, and other emblems of that god. The Hastiní is Salokatá-Moksha, for she is what residence in Vishnu's heaven is to those of the fourth class who have attributes and properties, shape and form, hands and feet.

## SECTION II.

### *Personal Peculiarities of the Four Classes.*

AND NOW LEARN YE BY THESE WORDS TO DISTINGUISH FROM ONE another the four orders of woman-kind.

She in whom the following signs and symptoms appear, is called Padminí, or Lotus-woman.[1] Her face is pleasing as the full moon; her body, well clothed with flesh, is soft as the Shiras[2] or mustard-flower; her skin is fine, tender and fair as the yellow lotus, never dark-coloured, though resembling, in the effervescence and purple light of her youth, the cloud about to burst. Her eyes are bright and beautiful as the orbs of the fawn, well-cut, and with reddish corners. Her bosom is hard, full and high; her neck is goodly shaped as the conch-shell, so delicate that the saliva can be seen through it; her nose is straight and lovely, and three folds or wrinkles cross her middle, about the umbilical region. Her Yoni[3] resembles the opening lotus-bud, and her Love-seed (Káma-salila, the water of life)[4] is perfumed like the lily which has newly burst. She walks with swan-like gait, and her voice is low and musical as the note of the Kokila-bird[5]; she delights in white raiment, in fine jewels, and in rich dresses. She eats little, sleeps lighly and, being as respectable and religious as she is clever and courteous, she is ever anxious to worship the gods, and to enjoy the conversation of Brahmans. Such, then, is the Padminí, or Lotus-woman.

The Chitriní, or Art-woman,[6] is of middle size, neither short nor tall, with bee-black hair, thin, round, shell-like neck; tender body; waist lean-girthed as the lion's; hard, full breasts; well-turned thighs and heavily made hips. The hair is thin about the Yoni, the Mons Veneris being soft, raised and round. The Káma-salila (love-seed) is hot, and has the perfume of honey, producing from its abundance a sound during the venereal rite. Her eyes roll, and her walk is coquettish, like the swing of an elephant, whilst her voice is that of the peacock.[7] She is fond of pleasure and variety; she delights in singing and in every kind of accomplishment, especially the arts manual; her carnal desires are not strong, and she loves her "pets," parrots, Mamas and other birds. Such is the Chitriní, or Art-woman.

The Shankhiní,[8] or Conch-woman, is of bilious temperament, her skin being always hot and tawny, or dark yellow-brown; her body is large, her waist thick, and her breasts small; her head, hands, and feet are thin and long, and she looks out of the corners of her eyes. Her Yoni is ever moist with Káma-salila, which is distinctly salt, and the cleft is covered with thick hair. Her voice is hoarse and harsh, of the bass or contralto type; her gait is precipitate; she eats with moderation and she delights in clothes, flowers and ornaments of red colour. She is subject to fits of amorous passion, which makes her head hot and her brain confused, and at the moment of enjoyment, she thrusts her nails into her husband's flesh.[9] She is of choleric constitution, hard-hearted, insolent and vicious; irascible, rude and ever addicted to finding fault. Such is the Shankhiní, or Conch-woman.

The Hastiní is short of stature; she has a stout, coarse body, and her skin, if fair, is of dead white: her hair is tawny, her lips are large; her voice is harsh, choked, and throaty (*voix de gorge*) and her neck is bent. Her gait is slow, and she walks in a slouching manner: often the toes of one foot are crooked. Her Káma-salila has the savour of the juice which flows in spring from the elephant's temples. She is tardy in the art of Love, and can be satisfied only by prolonged congress, in fact, the longer the better, but it will never suffice her. She is gluttonous, shameless, and irascible. Such is the Hastiní, or elephant-woman.[10]

### SECTION III.

*The days of greatest enjoyment for the Four Classes.*

HAVING THUS LAID DOWN THE FOUR CLASSES OF WOMAN-KIND, Kalyana Malla, the arch-poet, proceeds to give a table of the times in which each order derives the greatest amount of pleasure from the venereal rite. These periods must be learnt by heart, and students will remember that on the other days not specified, no amount of congress will satisfy passions. Read, then, and master the elements.

TABLE.[11]

| Pratipadá<br>1st day | Dvitiyá<br>2nd day | Chaturthí<br>4th day | Panchamí<br>5th day | Satisfy the<br>Padminí |
|---|---|---|---|---|
| Shashatí<br>6th day | Ashtamí<br>8th day | Dashamí<br>10th day | Dwadashí<br>12th day | Satisfy the<br>Chatriní |
| Tritiyá<br>3rd day | Saptamí<br>7th day | Ekádashí<br>11th day | Trayodasí<br>13th day | Satisfy the<br>Shankhiní |
| Navamí<br>9th day | Chaturdashí<br>14th day | Purnima<br>Full Moon | Amávásyá<br>New Moon | Satisfy the<br>Hastiní |

## SECTION IV.

### *Of the hours which give the highest enjoyment.*

WOMEN, BE IT OBSERVED, DIFFER GREATLY IN THE SEASONS WHICH they prefer for enjoyment, according to their classes and temperaments. The Padminí, for instance, takes no satisfaction in night congress; indeed, she is thoroughly averse to it. Like the Súrya Camala (day lotus) which opens its eyes to the sun light, so she is satisfied even by a boy-husband in the bright hours. The Chitriní and the Shankhiní are like the Chandra Kamala, or night-lotus, that expands to the rays of the moon; and the Hastiní, who is the coarsest, ignores all these delicate distinctions.

### TABLE I.

*Regulating the Night Hours.*

| 1st Pahar 6—9 p. m. | 2nd Pahar 9—12 p. m. | 3rd Pahar 12—3 a. m. | 4th Pahar 3—6 a. m. |
|---|---|---|---|
| " | " | " | The Padminí |
| The Chitriní | " | " | " |
| " | " | The Shankhiní | " |
| The Hastiní | The Hastiní | The Hastiní | The Hastiní |

### TABLE II.

*Regulating the Day Hours.*

| 1st Pahar 6—9 a. m. | 2nd Pahar 9—12 a. m. | 3rd Pahar 12—3 p. m. | 4th Pahar 3—6 p. m. |
|---|---|---|---|
| The Padminí | The Padminí | The Padminí | The Padminí |
| " | The Hastiní | The Hastiní | " |

The above tables, then, show the Pahar,[12] or watch of the sight and day, during which the four classes of women derive the greatest pleasure.

And here it will be observed that the Chitriní and the Shankhiní derive no satisfaction from day-congress.

Thus did the arch-poet, Kalyana Malla, relate unto Ladkhan Rajah how women are divided into four classes, each of which has its own peculiarity of body and mind, and its several times of enjoyments, according to the state of the moon and the hour of the day or night.

# ❯ CHAPTER TWO ❮

## OF THE VARIOUS SEATS
## OF PASSION IN WOMEN

AND, FURTHER, LET MEN KNOW THAT PASSION RESIDES IN different parts and members of the woman's person, and that by applying to these the necessary Chandrakalá,[1] or preparatory *attouchements,* great comfort and pleasure are experienced by both husband and wife. On the other hand, if the process placed in the table opposite the respective days of the lunar fortnight be not performed, neither sex will be thoroughly satisfied; indeed, both will be disposed to lust after strange embraces, and thus they will be led by adultery into quarrels, murders, and other deadly sins, all of which may be avoided by studying and bearing in mind the Chandrakalá.

Passion resides in the woman's right side during the Shuklapkshá, the first or light fortnight of the lunar month, from new moon to full, including the fifteenth day. The reverse is the case on the dark fortnight, including its first day, and lasting from the full to the new moon. The shifting is supposed to take place by the action of light and darkness, otherwise the site of passion would be one and the same.

Now from generals, Kalyana-Malla, the poet, proceeds to particulars, and supplies details concerning the four different classes of women. He begins with the Padminí, and shows, firstly, in what limb or member passion resides; and, secondly, by what process it can be satisfied. The husband must continue his

## GENERAL TABLE III.

| Shuklapakshá or light fortnight; right side. | | The touches by which passion is satisfied | Krishnapakshá or dark fortnight; left side. | |
|---|---|---|---|---|
| Day | Place | | Place | Day |
| 15th | Head and hair | Hold hair, and caress the head and finger-tips | Head and hair | 1st |
| 14th | Right eye | Kiss and fondle | Left eye | 2nd |
| 13th | Lower lip | Kiss, bite and chew softly | Upper lip | 3rd |
| 12th | Right cheek | Do. | Left cheek | 4th |
| 11th | Throat | Scratch gently with nails | Throat | 5th |
| 10th | Side | Do. | Side | 6th |
| 9th | Breasts | Hold in hands and gently knead | Breasts | 7th |
| 8th | All bosom | Tap softly with base of fist | All bosom | 8th |
| 7th | Navel | Pat softly with open palm | Navel | 9th |
| 6th | Nates | Hold, squeeze and tap with fist | Nates | 10th |
| 5th | Yoní | Work with friction of Linga | Yoní | 11th |
| 4th | Knee | Press with application of knee and fillip with finger | Knee | 12th |
| 3rd | Calf of leg | Press with application of calf and fillip with finger | Calf and leg | 13th |
| 2nd | Foot | Press with toe, and thrust the latter | Foot | 14th |
| 1st | Big toe | Do. | Big toe | 15th |

action till he sees the body-hair bristle, and hears the Sítkára[2]—the inarticulate sound produced by drawing in the air between closed teeth. Thus he will know that the paroxysm has taken place, and the beloved one is thoroughly satisfied.

TABLE IV.

*Showing the Manipulations of the Padimí.*

| Member | Pratipadá 1st day | Dvitiyá. 2nd day | Chaturthí 4th day | Panchamí 5th day |
|---|---|---|---|---|
| Throat | Hug with force | ,, | ,, | ,, |
| Cheek | Kiss and scratch | Kiss and scratch | ,, | ,, |
| Hair | ,, | ,, | ,, | Stroke slowly with right hand |
| Waist | Apply nails and scratch | ,, | ,, | ,, |
| Breast | ,, | ,, | Scratch gently | ,, |
| Back | Scratch and tap with fist | ,, | ,, | ,, |
| Bosom | ,, | Press with nails | Squeeze and knead | Press and rub |
| Side | Scratch and press with nails | ,, | ,, | ,, |
| Thigh | ,, | Scratch and press with nails | ,, | ,, |
| Belly | Scratch and press with nails | ,, | ,, | ,, |
| Arm | ,, | ,, | Jerk suddenly and twitch | ,, |
| Lip | Bite softly | Kiss | Bite softly and suck | Bite softly |
| Nipple | ,, | ,, | ,, | Kiss, pinch softly and rub with thumb and forefinger |
| Space between eyes | Kiss | ,, | ,, | ,, |
| Foot | ,, | Scratch and press with nails | ,, | ,, |

## TABLE V.

*Showing the Manipulation of the Chritriní.*

| Member | Shastí 6th day | Ashtamí 8th day | Dashamí 15th day | Dwádashí 12th day |
|---|---|---|---|---|
| Yoní | ,, | Insert Linga | Rub and scratch with left hand | ,, |
| Lower lip | Kiss | ,, | ,, | Bite gently |
| Throat | Embrace | Clasp firmly with hands | Scratch, and pass fingers over it | Embrace firmly |
| Waist | Scratch and press with nails | ,, | Pass left hand over it and rub | ,, |
| Navel | ,, | Pinch with nails and fingers | ,, | ,, |
| Lip | ,, | Bite quickly & repeatedly | ,, | ,, |
| Breast | ,, | Hold in hand | Pass left hand over it and rub | ,, |
| Ear | ,, | ,, | Caress with left hand | Set nails upon it |
| Thigh | ,, | ,, | Rub with left hand | ,, |
| Middle of body | ,, | ,, | Pass left hand over it and rub | ,, |
| Back | ,, | ,, | Rub with left hand and tap with fist | ,, |
| Nates | ,, | ,, | ,, | ,, |
| Forehead | ,, | ,, | Kiss strongly | ,, |
| Chest | ,, | ,, | ,, | Kiss and pat |
| Eye | ,, | ,, | ,, | Do something to make the eyes close rapidly |
| Hair | ,, | ,, | ,, | Pull gently |

## TABLE VI.

### Showing the Manipulation of the Shankhiní.

| Member | Tritiyá 3rd day | Saptamí 7th day | Ekadashí 11th day | Trayodashí 13th day |
|---|---|---|---|---|
| Body generally | Twist it about | Embrace firmly | Clasp with force | ,, |
| Lower lip | Bite | ,, | ,, | ,, |
| Arm | ? | ,, | ,, | ‿ |
| Breasts | Scratch roughly till marks are left | ,, | ,, | Squeeze till she makes the sound of Sítkára |
| Belly | ,, | Scratch and press with nails | ,, | ,, |
| Chest | ,, | Press with nails and caress | ,, | ,, |
| Throat | ,, | Scratch and press with nails | ,, | ,, |
| Ear | ,, | Press with nails | ,, | ,, |
| Foot | ,, | Press so as to leave nailmarks | ,, | ,, |
| Mouth or face | ,, | Kiss | ,, | ,, |
| Yoní | ,, | Apply Linga with force | Apply Linga as it were with a blow[3] | ,, |
| Lip | ,, | ,, | Kiss and suck | ,, |
| Inch below head | ,, | ,, | ,, | Write upon it, as it were, with nails |
| Lower edge of Yoní | ,, | ,, | ,, | ,, |

*Ravola dum Rhodopes udâ terit inguina barbâ.*

TABLE VII.

*Showing the Manipulation of the Hastiní.*

| Member | Navamí 9th day | Chaturdashí 14th day | Púrnimá Full Moon | Amávásyá New Moon |
|---|---|---|---|---|
| Yoní | Thrust violently with Linga or even rub hard with hand | Scratch, press in member till her waist bends | ,, | Manipulate & pull open like a flower |
| Navel | Rub and frequently pass hand over | ,, | ,, | ,, |
| lip | Kiss and suck | ,, | Kiss in various ways[4] | Kiss in various ways |
| Side | Press with fingers and scratch very softly | ,, | ,, | ,, |
| Breast | Rub, twist squeeze, & make it very small | ,, | Pull hard | Scratch till it bears nail-marks |
| Chest | ,, | ,, | Scratch and leave marks | Scratch and leave marks |
| Nipple | ,, | ,, | Kiss and rub with thumb & fore-finger | Pass hand over it & rub with thumb & fore-finger |
| Body generally | ,, | ,, | Embrace in various ways | Embrace in various ways and press |
| Eye | ,, | Kiss | Kiss | Kiss |
| Armpit | ,, | ,, | Scratch and tickle | Scratch and tickle |

Here end the tables of the Chandrakalá, by the proper study of which men may satisfy women, and thereby subject the most strong-minded to their will.

## CHAPTER THREE

# OF THE DIFFERENT KINDS OF
# MEN AND WOMEN

### SECTION I.

#### *Men.*

THERE ARE THREE KINDS OF MEN, NAMELY, THE SHASHA, OR THE Hare-man; the Vrishabha, or Bull-man, and the Ashwa, or Horse-man.[1] These may be described by explanation of their nature, and by enumeration of their accidents.

The Shasha is known by a Linga which in erection does not exceed six finger-breadths, or about three inches. His figure is short and spare, but well-proportioned in shape and make; he has small hands, knees, feet, loins and thighs, the latter being darker than the rest of the skin. His features are clear and well proportioned; his face is round, his teeth are short and fine, his hair is silky, and his eyes are large and well-opened. He is of a quiet disposition; he does good for virtue's sake; he looks forward to making a name; he is humble in demeanor; his appetite for food is small, and he is moderate in carnal desires. Finally, there is nothing offensive in his Káma-salila or semen.

The Vrishabha is known by a Linga of nine fingers in length, or four inches and a-half. His body is robust and tough, like that of a tortoise; his chest is fleshy, his belly is hard, and the frogs of the upper arms are turned so as to be

225

brought in front. His forehead is high, his eyes large and long, with pink corners, and the palms of his hands are red. His disposition is cruel and violent, restless and irascible, and his Káma-salila is ever ready.

The Ashwa is known by a Linga of twelve fingers, or about six inches long. He is tall and large-framed, but not fleshy, and his delight is in big and robust women, never in those of delicate form. His body is hard as iron, his chest is broad, full, and muscular; his body below the hips is long, and the same is the case with his mouth and teeth, his neck and ears; whilst his hands and fingers are remarkably so. His knees are somewhat crooked, and this distortion may also be observed in the nails of his toes. His hair is long, coarse and thick. His look is fixed and hard, without changing form, and his voice is deep like that of a bull. He is reckless in spirit, passionate and covetuous, gluttonous, volatile, lazy, and full of sleep. He walks slowly, placing one foot in front of the other. He cares little for the venereal rite, except when the spasm approaches. His Káma-salila is copious, salt, and goat-like.

## SECTION II.

### *Women.*

AND AS MEN ARE DIVIDED INTO THREE CLASSES BY THE LENGTH of the Linga, so the four orders of women, Padminí, Chitriní, Shankhiní, and Hastiní, may be subdivided into three kinds, according to the depth and extent of the Yoní. These are the Mrigi, also called Hariní, the Deer-woman; the Vadavá or Ashviní, Mare-woman; and the Kariní, or Elephant-woman.

The Mrigi has a Yoní six fingers deep. Her body is delicate, with girlish aspect, soft and tender. Her head is small and well-proportioned; her bosom stands up well; her stomach is thin and drawn in; her thighs and Mons Veneris are fleshy, and her build below the hips is solid, whilst her arms from the shoulder downwards are large and rounded. Her hair is thick and curly; her eyes are black as the dark lotus-flower; her nostrils are fine; her cheeks and ears are large; her hands, feet, and lower lip are ruddy, and her fingers are straight. Her voice is that of the Kokila bird, and her gait the rolling of the elephant. She eats moderately, but is much addicted to the pleasures of love; she is affectionate but jealous, and she is active in mind when not subdued by her passions. Her Káma-salila has the pleasant perfume of the lotus-flower.

The Vadvá or Ashviní numbers nine fingers depth. Her body is delicate; her arms are thick from the shoulders downwards; her breasts and hips are broad and fleshy, and her umbilical region is high-raised, but without protuberant stomach. Her hands and feet are red like flowers, and well-proportioned. Her head slopes forwards and is covered with long and straight hair; her forehead is retreating; her neck is long and much bent; her throat, eyes, and mouth are broad, and her eyes are like the petals of the dark lotus. She has a graceful walk, and she loves sleep and good living. Though choleric and versatile, she is affectionate to her husband; she does not easily arrive at the venereal spasm, and her Káma-salila is perfumed like the lotus.

The Kariní has a Yoní twelve fingers in depth. Unclean in her person, she has large breasts; her nose, ears, and throat are long and thick; her cheeks are blown or expanded; her lips are long and bent outwards (bordés); her eyes are fierce and yellow-tinged; her face is broad; her hair is thick and somewhat blackish; her feet, hands, and arms are short and fat; and her teeth are large and sharp as a dog's. She is noisy when eating; her voice is hard and harsh; she is gluttonous in the extreme, and her joints crack with every movement. Of a wicked and utterly shameless disposition, she never hesitates to commit sin. Excited and disquieted by carnal desires, she is not easily satisfied, and requires congress unusually protracted. Her Káma-salila is very abundant, and it suggests the juice which flows from the elephant's temples.

The wise man will bear in mind that all these characteristics are not equally well defined, and their proportions can be known only by experience. Mostly the temperaments are mixed; often we find a combination of two and in some cases even of three. Great study, therefore, is required in judging by the absence or presence of the signs and symptoms, to choose the Chandrakalá and other manipulations proper to the several differences, as without such judgment the consequences of congress are not satisfactory. Thus the student is warned that the several distinctions of Padmaní, Chitriní, Shankhiní and Hastiní; of Shastra, Vrishabha, and Ashva, and of Mrigí (Hariní) Vadvá (Ashviní), and Kariní are seldom found pure, and that it is his duty to learn the proportions in which they combine.

Before proceeding to the various acts of congress, the symptoms of the orgasm in women must be laid down. As soon as she commences to enjoy pleasure, the eyes are half closed and watery; the body waxes cold; the breath after being hard and jerky, is expired in sobs or sighs; the lower limbs are limply stretched out after a period of rigidity; a rising and outflow of love and affection appear, with kisses and sportive gestures; and, finally, she seems as if about to swoon. At such time, a distaste for further embraces and blandishments becomes manifest: then the wise know that, the paroxysm having taken place, the woman has enjoyed plenary satisfaction; consequently, they refrain from further congress.

## SECTION III.

### *Of Congress.*

MEN AND WOMEN, BEING, ACCORDING TO THE ABOVE MEASUREMENTS, of three several divisions, it results that there are nine conditions under which congress takes place. Of these, however, four, being unusual, may be neglected, and attention is required only for the five following:

1. Samána is when the proportions of both lovers are alike and equal; hence there is plenary satisfaction to both.

2. Uchha is that excess of proportion in the man which renders congress hard and difficult and therefore does not content the woman.

3. Nichha, meaning literally *hollow* or *low,* and metaphorically when the man is deficient in size, gives but little contentment to either lover.

4. Anti-uchha is an exaggeration of Uchha; and

5. Anti-nichha is an exaggeration of Nichha.

The following table divides the congress of the several dimensions into three categories, which are respectively entitled Uttama, the best; Madhyama, the middling; and Kanishtha, the worst.

TABLE VIII.

*Applicable to the Shasha, or Hare-man.*

| Dimensional names. | | Actual dimensions of members. | Category. |
|---|---|---|---|
| Shasha Mrigí | } | 6 fingers long 6 fingers deep | Uttama |
| Shasha Vadvá or Ashviní | } | 6 fingers long 9 fingers deep | Madhyama |
| Shasha Karini | } | 6 fingers long 12 fingers deep | Kanishtha |

TABLE IX.

*Applicable to the Vrishabha, or Bull-man.*

| Dimensional Names. | Actual dimensions of members. | Category. |
|---|---|---|
| Vrishabha <br> Ashviní | 9 fingers long <br> 9 fingers long | Uttama |
| Vrishabha <br> Hariní | 9 fingers long <br> 6 fingers deep | Madhyama |
| Vrishabha <br> Hariní | 9 fingers long <br> 12 fingers deep | Kanishtha |

TABLE X.

*Applicable to the Ashva, or Horse-man.*

| Dimensional Names. | Actual dimensions of members. | Category. |
|---|---|---|
| Ashva <br> Kariní | 12 fingers long <br> 12 fingers deep | Uttama |
| Ashva <br> Ashviní | 12 fingers long <br> 9 fingers deep | Madhyama |
| Ashva <br> Hariní | 12 fingers long <br> 6 fingers deep | Kanishtha |

From an inspection of these tables, it is abundantly evident that the greatest happiness consists in the correspondence of dimensions, and that the discomfort increases with the ratio of difference. And of this fact the reason is palpable.

There are three species of vermicules bred by blood in the Yoní,[2] and these are either Sŭkshma (small), Madhyama (middling), or Adhikabala (large). In their several proportions they produce a prurience and a titillation, wherefrom springs that carnal desire which is caused to cease only by congress. And thus it is that a Linga of small dimensions fails to satisfy. On the other hand, excess of length offends the delicacy of the parts, and produces pain rather than pleasure.

But the proportion of enjoyment arises from the exact adaption of the Linga, especially when the diameter agrees with the extension, and when the vigour of tension enables the husband to turn his mind towards the usual arts which bring women under subjection.

### SECTION IV.

*Of other minor distinctions in Congress.*

EACH OF THE FOREGOING NINE FORMS OF CONGRESS IS SUBDIVIDED into nine other classes, which will now be noticed.

There are three forms of Vissrishtí, or the emission of Káma-salila, both in men and women, viewed with respect to length or shortness of time,—

1. Chirasambhava-vissrishtí is that which occupies a great length of time.

2. Madhyasambhava-vissrishtí is that which is accomplished within a moderate period.

3. Shíghrasambhava-vissrishtí is that which takes a short time to finish.

Again, there are three degrees of Vega, that is to say, force of carnal desire, resulting from mental or vital energy and acting upon men and women. In order to make this clear, a comparison may be instituted. Hunger for instance, is felt by all human beings, but it affects them differently. Some must satisfy it at once, without which they are ready to lose their senses; others can endure it for a moderate extent, whilst others suffer from it but little. The Vega, or capacities of enjoyment, are—

1. Chanda-vega, furious appetite or impulse; the highest capacity.

2. Madhyama-vega, or moderate desires.

3. Manda-vega, slow or cold concupiscence; the lowest capacity.

The woman who possesses Chanda-vega, may be known by her ever seeking carnal enjoyment; she must enjoy it frequently and she will not be satisfied with a single orgasm. If deprived of it, she will appear like one out of her senses. The reverse is she who has Manda-verga, and who seems to find in it so little enjoyment that she always denies herself to her husband. And the owner of Madhyana-vega is the most fortunate, as she is free from either excess.

Again, there are three Kriyás, acts or processes which brings on the orgasm in men and women; these are,—

1. Chirodaya-kriyá, is applied to the efforts which continue long before they bear any result.

2. Madhyodaya-kriyá, those which act in a moderate time.

3. Laghŭdaya-kriyá, the shortest.

Thus we may observe there are nine several forms of congress, according to the length and depth of the organs. There are also nine, determined by the longer or shorter period required to induce the orgasm, and there are nine which arise from the Kriyás or processes which lead to the conclusion. Altogether we have twenty-seven kinds of congress, which, by multiplying the nine species and the three periods, give a grand total of two hundred and forty-three (9x9 = 81x3 = 243).

# DESCRIPTION OF THE GENERAL QUALITIES, CHARACTERISTICS, TEMPERAMENTS, ETC., OF WOMEN

THE FOLLOWING TABLE WILL SHOW THE PECULIARITIES OF WOMEN according to the four periods of life during which she is open to love. It may be premised that she is called Kanyá from birth to the age of eight years, which is the time of Bályavasthá, or childhood; and Gaurí, after the white goddess Parvati, from that period to her eleventh year; Tarŭnyavastha, when she becomes marriageable: then follow Yavavastha, young-womanhood, and Vreuddhavastha, old-womanhood.

TABLE XI.

*Showing qualities attached to the several Ages.*

| Age | Name | Regarding art of love | Kind of Congress preferred | How subjected |
|---|---|---|---|---|
| 11—16 years | Bálá | Fit | In darkness | By flowers, small presents, gifts of betel, and so forth |
| 16—30 years | Taruní | Do. | In light | By gifts of dresses, pearls and ornaments |
| 30—55 years | Praudhá | Fit (?) | Both in darkness and light | By attention, politeness, kindness and love |
| Beyond 55 years | Viddhá | Unfit | Becomes sick and infirm | By flattery |

And further observe that there are three temperaments of women, as shown by the following characteristics:—

The signs of Kapha (lymphatic or phlegmatic diathesis) are bright eyes, teeth and nails; the body is well preserved, and the limbs do not lose their youthful form. The Yoní is cool and hard, fleshy, yet delicate; and there is love and regard for the husband. Such is the lympathic, or the highest temperament.[1]

The next is the Pitta, or bilious diathesis. The woman whose bosom and nates are flaccid and pendant, not orbiculate; whose skin is white, whilst her eyes and nails are red; whose perspiration is sour, and whose Yoní is hot and relaxed; who is well versed in the arts of congress, but who cannot endure it for a long time, and whose temper is alternately and suddenly angry and joyous, such a one is held to be of the Pitta or bilious temperament.

She whose body is dark, hard, and coarse; whose eyes and finger nails are blackish, and whose Yoní, instead of being smooth, is rough as the tongue of a cow; she whose laugh is harsh; whose mind is set on gluttony; who is volatile and loquacious, whilst in congress she can hardly be satisfied, that woman is of the Váta or windy temperament, the worst of all.

Furthermore, women require to be considered in connection with the previous state of their existence; the Satva, or disposition inherited from a former life, and which influences their wordly natures.

The Devasatva-strí, who belongs to the Gods, is cheerful and lively, pure-bodied and clean, with perspiration perfumed like the lotus-flower; she is clever, wealthy and industrious, of sweet speech and benevolent, always delighting in good works; her mind is sound as her body, nor is she ever tired of or displeased by her friends.

The Gandharvasarva-strí, who derives a name from the Gandharvas, or heavenly minstrels, is beautiful of shape, patient in mind, delighting in purity; wholly given to perfumes, fragrant substances and flowers, to singing and playing, to rich dress and fair ornaments, to sport and amorous play, especially to the Vilása, one of the classes of feminine actions which indicate the passion of love.

The Yakshasatva-strí, who derives a name from the demi-god presiding over the gardens and treasures of Kuvera,[2] has large and fleshy breasts, with a skin fair as the white champa-flower (*michelia champac*); she is fond of flesh and liquor; devoid of shame and decency; passionate and irascible, and at all hours greedy for congress.

The Munushyasatva-strí, who belongs essentially to humanity, delights in the pleasures of friendship and hospitality. She is respectable and honest; her mind is free from guile, and she is never wearied of religious actions, vows, and penances.

The Pisáchasatva-strí, who is concerned with that class of demons, has a short body, very dark and hot, with a forehead ever wrinkled; she is unclean in her person, greedy, fond of flesh and forbidden things, and, however much enjoyed she is ever eager of congress, like a harlot.

The Nágasatva-strí, or snake-woman, is always in hurry and confusion; her eyes look drowsy; she yawns over and over again, and she sighs with deep-drawn respiration; her mind is forgetful and she lives in doubt and suspicion.

The Kákasatva-strí, who retains the characteristics of the crow, ever rolls her eyes about as if in pain; throughout the day she wants food; she is silly, unhappy and unreasonable, spoiling everything that she touches.

The Vánarasatva-strí, or monkey-woman, rubs her eyes throughout the day, grinds and chatters with her teeth, and is very lively, active, and mercurial.

The Kharasatva-strí, who preserves the characteristics of the ass,[3] is unclean in her person, and aviods bathing, washing, and pure raiment; she cannot give a direct answer, and she speaks awkwardly and without reason, because her mind is crooked. Therefore she pleases no one.

The subject of the Satvas is one requiring careful study, for the characteristics are ever varying, and only experience can determine the class to which women belonged in the former life, and which has coloured their bodies and minds in this state of existence.

The woman whose bosom is hard and fleshy, who appears short from the fullness of her frame, and looks bright and light-coloured, such an one is known to enjoy daily congress with her husband.

The woman who, being thin, appears very tall and somewhat dark, whose limbs and body are unenergetic and languid, the effect of involuntary chastity, such an one is "Virahiní," who suffers from long separation from her husband and from the want of conjugal embraces.

A woman who eats twice as much as a man, is four times more reckless and wicked, six times more resolute and obstinate, and eight times more violent in carnal desire. She can hardly control her lust of congress, despite the shame which is natural to the sex.

The following are the signs by which the wise know that woman is amorous:—She rubs and repeatedly smoothes her hair (so that it may look well). She scratches her head (that notice may be drawn to it). She strokes her own cheeks (so as to entice her husband). She draws her dress over her bosom, apparently to readjust it, but leaves her breasts partly exposed. She bites her lower lip, chewing it, as it were. At times she looks ashamed without a cause (the result of her own warm fancies), and she sits quietly in the corner (engrossed by concupiscence). She embraces her female friends, laughing loudly and speaking sweet words, with jokes and jests, to which she desires a return in kind. She kisses and hugs young children, especially boys. She smiles with one cheek, loiters in her gait, and unnecessarily stretches herself under some pretence or other. At times she looks at her shoulders and under her arms. She stammers, and does not speak clearly and distinctly. She sighs and sobs without reason, and she yawns whenever she wants tobacco, food, or sleep. She even throws herself in her husband's way and will not readily get out of his path.

The following are the eight signs of indifference to be noted in womankind:—When worldly passion begins to subside, the wife does not look straight between her husband's eyes. If anything be asked of her, she shows unwillingness to reply. If the man draw near her, and looks happy, she feels pained. If he departs from her she shows symptoms of satisfaction. When seated upon the bedstead, she avoids amatory blandishments and lies down quietly to sleep. When kissed or toyed with she jerks away her face or her form. She cherishes malicious feelings towards her husband's friends; and finally, she has no respect nor reverence for his family. When these signs are seen, let it be known that the wife is already weaned from conjugal desires.

The following are the principal causes which drive women to deviate from the right way, and to fall into the society of profligates:—1. Remaining, when grown up, in her Máher, or mother's house, as opposed to that of her husband's parents. 2. Evil communication with the depraved of her own sex. 3. The prolonged absence of her husband. 4. Living in the society of vile and licentious men. 5. Poverty and the want of good food and dress. 6. Mental trouble, affliction, and unhappiness, causing her to become discontented and reckless.

The following are the fifteen principal causes which make women unhappy:—1. The parsimony of parents and husbands, because the youth are naturally generous. 2. Receiving too much respect or reverence when they are light-hearted; also being kept in awe by those with whom they would be familiar, and too strict restraint as regards orderly and guarded deportment. 3. Trouble of disease and sickness. 4. Separation from the husband and the want of natural enjoyment. 5. Being made to work too hard. 6. Violence, inhumanity, and cruelty, such as beating. 7. Rough language and abuse. 8. Suspicion that they are inclined to evil. 9. Intimidation and threats of punishment for going astray. 10. Calumny, accusing of ill deeds, and using evil words about them. 11. Want of cleanliness in person or dress. 12. Poverty. 13. Grief and sorrow. 14. Impotence of the husband. 15. Disregard of time and place in the act of love.

The following are the twelve periods when women have the greatest desire for congress, and at the same time are most easily satisfied:—1. When tired by walking and exhausted with bodily exercise. 2. After a long want of intercourse with the husband, such as in the case of the Virahiní. 3. When a month after childbirth has elapsed. 4. During the earlier stages of pregnancy. 5. When dull, idle and sleepy. 6. If recently cured of fever. 7. When showing signs of wantoness or bashfulness. 8. When feeling unusually merry and happy. 9. The Ritu-snátá, immediately before and after the monthly ailment.[4] 10. Maidens enjoyed for the first time. 11. Throughout the spring season. 12. During thunder, lightning and rain. At such times women are easily subjected to men.

And, furthermore, learn that there are four kinds of the Príti, or love-tie connecting men and women:—

1. Naisargikí-príti is that natural affection by which husband and wife cleave to each other like the links of an iron chain. It is a friendship amongst the good of both sexes.

2. Vishaya-príti is the fondness born in the woman, and increased by means of gifts, such as sweetmeats and delicacies, flowers, perfumery, and preparations of sandal-wood, musk, saffron, and so forth. It partakes, therefore, of gluttony, sensuality and luxury.

3. Sama-príti is also so far sensual, as it arises from the equally urgent desires of both husband and wife.

4. 'Abhyásiki-príti is the habitual love bred by mutual socitey: it is shown by walking in fields, gardens and similar places; by attending together at worship, penances and self-imposed religious observances; and by frequenting sportive assemblies, plays and dances, where music and similar arts are practised.

And, moreover, let it be noted, that the desires of the woman being colder,[5] and slower to rouse than those of the man, she is not easily satisfied by a single act of congress; her lower powers of excitement demand prolonged embraces, and if these be denied her, she feels aggrieved. At the second act, however, her passions being thoroughly aroused, she finds the orgasm more violent, and then she is thoroughly contented. This state of things is clean reversed in the case of the man, who approaches the first act burning with love-heat, which cools during the second, and which leaves him languid and disinclined for a third. But the wise do not argue therefrom, that the desires of the woman, as long as she is young and strong, are not the full as real and urgent as those of the man. The custom of society and the shame of the sex may compel her to conceal them and even to boast that they do not exist; yet the man who has studied the Art of Love is never deceived by this cunning.

And here it is necessary to offer some description of the Yoní; it being of four kinds.

1. That which is soft inside as the filaments (pollen?) of the lotus-flower; this is the best.

2. That whose surface is studded with tender flesh-knots and similar rises.

3. That which abounds in rolls, wrinkles, and corrugations; and,

4. That which is rough as the cow's tongue; this is the worst.

Moreover, in the Yoní there is an artery called Saspanda; which corresponds with that of the linga, and which, when excited by the presence and energetic action of the latter, causes Káma-salila to flow. It is inside and towards the navel, and it is attached to certain roughnesses (thorns), which are peculiarly liable to induce the paroxysm when subjected to friction. The Madanachatra (the clitoris)[6] in the upper part of the Yoní, is that portion which projects like the plantain-shoot sprouting from the ground; it is connected with the Mada-váhi (sperm-flowing) artery, and causes the latter to overflow. Finally, there is an artery, termed Pŭrna-chandra, which is full of the Káma-salila, and to this the learned men of old attribute the monthly ailment.

## CHAPTER FIVE

# CHARACTERISTICS OF THE
# WOMEN OF VARIOUS LANDS

FURTHERMORE, AFTER DIVIDING WOMEN INTO MANY DIFFERENT classes, it will be desirable to consider them with reference to the countries in which they dwell. The remarks will be confined to the Arya-varttá, the Land of Men, bounded by the Himálaya (snow-house) and Vindhya Mountains, the Kuru-Kshetra and Allahabad. And first of the woman of the Madhya-desha, the country between the Konkan and the Desha proper, whose chief cities are Puna (Poona), Nasik and Kolhapǔr.

The woman of the Middle Region has red nails, but her body is still redder. She dresses well and in various sorts of apparel. She is an excellent housekeeper, perfectly broken to manual labour and other works, and much given to religious ceremonies. Though wonderfully fond of, and skilful in, amatory dalliance, she is averse to the tricks of teeth and nails (biting and scratching).

The Maru (Malwa) woman likes to be enjoyed every day, and is well fitted for those who prefer the act of congress when long protracted. She is satisfied only by enduring embraces, which she greatly covets and desires, and the paroxysm must sometimes be induced by the touch of the fingers.

The woman of Mathrá, Krishná's country, also called Abhira-deshra, the Cow-herds' Land, is fascinated by various forms of kissing. She delights in the closest embraces, and even in attouch-ments; but she has no tricks of tooth and nail.

The woman of Láta-desha (Lar or Larice of the Classics) the northern part of the Dakhan (Deccan), is delicate and handsome. She will dance with joy at the prospect of congress, and during the act, her movements of pleasure are frequent and violent. She is prompt in her embraces, and the venereal orgasm may readily be introduced by gentle insertion, by striking with the hand, and by softly biting her lips.

The woman of Andhra-desha (Telangana) is so fascinating that she charms the stranger at first sight, and she is sweet in voice as she is beautiful of body. She delights in jests and dalliance, yet she is an utter stranger to shame, and she is one of the most wicked of her sex.

The woman of Koshalaráshtra-desha (Audh or Oude) is very clever in the art of congress. She suffers much from prurience and titillation of the Yoní, and she desires lengthened embraces, which satisfy her only when the Linga is of unusual vigour.

The woman of Maháráshtra (the Maratha country) and Pátalaputa-desha is fond of giving amorous side-glances, of dress and ornaments, of junketting and garden trips. Ever smiling gently, airy and gay, full of jest and sport and amorous dalliance, she is yet somewhat destitute of shame. Affectionate and coquettish, she is a proficient in the toying of love.

The woman of Vanga (Bengal) and Gaura has a body soft and delicate as a flower; she is coquettish and volatile; she delights in kissing and embracing, at the same time that she hates being roughly or cruelly handled, and she has little desire for congress.

The woman of Utkala-desha (Orissa) is so beautiful that man is attracted to her at first sight, and her voice is soft as her body is delicate. She is loose and licentious, caring very little for decency in her devotion to love, at which time she becomes violent, disquieted and excessively inflamed; she delights in different postures to vary enjoyment, especially in the contrary form, that is, when the lover is under the beloved, and she is easily satisfied, even by passing the fingers over her breasts.

The woman of Kámarŭpa-desha (Western Assam) has a soft body and sweet voice; her affections are warm, and she is well skilled in all the arts of love. During congress she abounds in the Káma-salila.

The Vana-strí, or forest woman (of the Bhills and other hill tribes), have stout bodies and healthy constitutions. They delight, while concealing their own defects and blemishes, their faults and follies, in exposing those of others.

The woman of Gurjara-desha (Gujrát, or Guzerat), is wise and sensible. She has beautiful features, and eyes proportioned as they ought to be; she delights in handsome dresses and ornaments, and though warm and devoted to the pleasures of love, she is easily satisfied by short congress.

The woman of Sindhu-desha (Sind), of Avanti-desha (Panjáb or Oujeín), and of Balhíka-desha (Baháwalpŭr), has lively eyes, casting sidelong and amorous glances. She is volatile, irascible, and wicked, and the fierceness, violence, and heat of her desires are very hard to be satisfied.

The woman of Tirotpatna (or Tira-desha, Tirhoot, in Central India,) has eyes blooming like the flowers of the lake; she loves her husband fondly and her passion is inflamed by a single look; she is especially skilful in congress; she enjoys various ways and postures; and, by reason of her delicacy, she cannot endure rough or protracted embraces.

The woman of Pushpapura, of Madda-desha (the north-western part of Hindostan Proper), and Tailanga-desha (Southern India), though a proficient in the art of love, is modest, and enjoys only her husband. Her form of passion is the Chanda-vega, and her amorousness is excessive; she communicates delight by "Nakhara," scratching, biting, and other signs of hot desire.

The woman of Dravia-desha (the Coromandel country, from Madras to Cape Comorin), of Sauvíra, and of Malaya-desha (Malayalim) is well-proportioned in body and limbs, soft and delicate in make, and sweet of voice; she delights in clean raiment and fine dresses, and she is satisfied with short congress, although fearless, shameless, and headlong in wickedness.

The woman of Kámbój (Camboge) and Paundra-desha is tall, robust, and gross in body, and of wicked disposition; she is ignorant of the acts of congress accompanied by tricks of nail and tooth, and she is satisfied only by the violent application of a solid Linga.

The woman of the Mlenchchhas (mixed races, or those not speaking Sanskrit like the Hindus), of Parvata, of Gandhára and of Káshm'r (Cashmere), are distinguished by evil savour of body. They are wholly ignorant of toying and dalliance, of kissing and embracing, they care little for congress, and they are easily satisfied by short embraces.

It is only by study and experience of women in different countries that the wise man learns to classify them according to their characteristics: to discern the Chandrakalás, or preparatory attouchments, which best suit races as well as individuals, and thus to endear himself to womankind.

# ON USEFUL MEDICINES, PRAYOGAS (EXTERNAL APPLICATIONS), PRESCRIPTIONS, RECIPES, REMEDIES, COSMETICS, CHARMS, MAGIC, UNGUENTS AND SPELLS

THE FOLLOWING ARE THE MOST USEFUL DRUGS AND SIMPLES, the receipts and prescriptions which have been handed down by learned men for the comfort of the married, and for the benefit of the world. Also the ignorant, whose coarse understandings cannot enter into the delicacies and intricacies of classes and temperaments, of Chandrakalás, and other excitants, are many, and they will do well to put themselves under the guidance of the wise. This history is intended for their pleasure and profit. It is for instance, dearly evident that unless by some act of artifice the venereal orgasm of the female, who is colder in blood and less easily excited, distinctly precede that of the male, the congress has been vain, the labour of the latter has done no good, and the former has enjoyed no satisfaction. Hence it results that one of man's chief duties in this life is to learn to withhold himself as much as possible, and, at the same time, to hasten the enjoyment of his partner.

245

## FIRST PRAYOGA (EXTERNAL APPLICATION).[1]

Take Shopa, or aniseed (in Hindostani, "Sanv," *anethum sowa or Pimpinella anisium*), reduced to impalpable powder; strain and make it into an electuary with honey. This being so applied to the Linga before congress that it may reach as far inside as possible, will induce venereal paroxysm in the woman, and subject her to the power of man.

## SECOND PRAYOGA.

Take cleansed seed of the Rui[2] (gigantic swallow-wort, *Asclepias* or *Callotropis gigantea,*) pound and rub in mortar with leaves of the Jai tree (*Jasminum auriculatum*, large flowered double jasmine,) till the juice is expressed; strain, and apply as before.

## THIRD PRAYOGA.

Take fruit of the Tamarind (*Tamarinda Indica*), pound in a mortar, together with honey and Sindura (red lead, minium, cinnabar, or red sulphuret of mercury), and apply as before.

## FOURTH PRAYOGA.

Take equal parts (Sama-bhága) of camphor, Tankan (Tincal, or brute borax, vulgarly called Tankan-khár), and purified quicksilver,[3] pound them with honey, and apply them as before.

## FIFTH PRAYOGA.

Take equal parts of honey, Ghí (melted or clarified butter), brute borax, as above, and juice of the leaves of the Agastá-tree (*Æschynomene grandiflora*); pound, and apply as before.

### SIXTH PRAYOGA.

Take equal parts of old Gur (also called Jagri, molasses, or sugar juice, inspissated by boiling), the bean of the Tamarind-pod, and powder of aniseed; levigate with honey and apply as before.

### SEVENTH PRAYOGA.

Take black pepper-corns, the seed of the thorn-apple (Dhatura or Dhotarà, *datura stramonium*), the pod of the long pepper plant (Pinpallí, the *Piper longum,* also applied to the pod of the betel pepper,) and bark of Lodhora (the *symplocos racemosa* (?), the *morinda citrifolia,* used in dyeing?) pound in white honey, and use as before. This medicine is of sovereign virtue.

Here end the prescriptions for hastening the paroxysm of the woman, and begin those which delay the orgasm of the man. In cases where this comes on too fast, the desire of congress remains unsatisfied; therefore, pitying the frailty of human nature, the following recipes have been recommended by the wise:

### FIRST PRAYOGA.

Take root of the Lajjálŭ or sensitive plant (*mimosa pudica*), and levigate with milk of the cow, or if none be found, with the thick juice of the Panja-dhari-nivarung, the fine-edged milk-plant (*euphorbia pentagonia*). If this be applied before congress to the soles of the man's feet, his embraces will be greatly prolonged by the retention of the water of life.[4]

### SECOND PRAYOGA.

Take powdered root of Rúí (gigantic swallow root), levigate it in oil of safflower-seed (Kardai *carthamus tinctorius*), and apply as above.

### THIRD PRAYOGA.

Take root of Káng or white panic (*P. italicum*), and the filaments (pollen?) of lotus flowers, levigate in honey, and apply as above.

### FOURTH PRAYOGA.

Take equal parts of Sishu bark (the blackwood tree, *dalbergia sissoo*), camphor, and purified quicksilver; levigate as above, and apply to the (man's) navel.

### FIFTH PRAYOGA.

If the seeds of the White Tál-makháná (*barleria longifolia*, a medicinal herb), be gathered upon the Pushya-nakshatra, or eighth lunar mansion[5] (corresponding with part of December and January, and be bound round the waist with a twist of red thread, it will have the desired effect.

### SIXTH PRAYOGA.

Having invited (addressed with prayer), on Saturday, the Saptaparna (*echides scholaris*, or the seven-leaved Scholaris), let it be taken on Sunday, and placed in the mouth; it will have the desired effect.

### SEVENTH PRAYOGA.

Let a person gather the seeds of the white Anvalli (emblic myrobalan) in the Pushya-nakshatra, when it happens to fall on a Sunday, and tie them round the waist with a thread spun by a virgin; it will have the desired effect.

### EIGHTH PRAYOGA.

Take the seeds of the white Tal-makháná that have been levigated in the sap of the Banyan tree (*ficus indica*), and, mixing them with the seeds of the Karanj (*galedupa arborea*), place them in the mouth, when the wished for effect will be observed.

Here end the prescriptions for delaying the orgasm of the man, and begin the Vájíkarna[6] (aphrodisiacs), which the wise of old have discovered, with a view of restoring physical strength and vigour. It is evident that the recipes given above are of no use to an impotent or to a very weak person: it is, therefore; necessary also to know the remedies which comfort the heart and excite desire, at the same time giving a power of satisfying them.[7]

### FIRST VÁJIKARANA.

Having exposed the juice of the Bhúya-Kohali (the *solanum Jacquini,* a prickly plant), to the sun till dried, mix it with clarified butter, sugar-candy, and honey. This prescription gives the strength of ten men, and enables the patient to conquer ten women.

### SECOND VÁJIKARANA.

Take the bark of the Anvallí (the emblic myrobalm, an astringent nut; *phyllanthus emblica*), extract the sap, expose to the sun till dried, mix with powder of the same tree, and before congress eat this powder with clarified butter, sugar-candy, and honey; a wonderful development will be the result; even an old man will become a young man.

### THIRD VÁJIKARANA.

Take powder of the Kuili (Cow-itch, or *dolichos pruriens*), of the Kanta-gokhru (Caltrops, the *tribulus lanuginosus*), of the Kákri, or cucumber, of the Chikana *hedysarum lagopodioides,* of the Lechí, and of the Laghushatávarí (*asparagus racemosus*), and mix them in equal parts with milk; the patient will at once recover flesh and vigour.

### FOURTH VÁJIKARANA.

Steep the grains of Uríd (the well-known pulse Mung, or *phaseolus radiata or P. mungo*) in milk and sugar, and expose for three days to the sun; grind it to powder, knead into a cake, fry in clarified butter, and eat every morning; the patient, though smitten with years, will gain enormous vigour, and enjoy a hundred women.

### FIFTH VÁJIKARANA.

Take ten máshás (150 grains) of inner bark of the Moh tree (*bassia latifolia,* whose flowers yield a well-known spirituous liquor), rub down in a mortar, eat, and drink cow's milk upon it; the effect will be that of the preceding.

### SIXTH VÁJIKARANA.

Take seeds of the White Tal-makháná and of Devabhat (wild rice, growing near tanks and swamps), of each ten máshás, mix with equal weight of honey, and eat at night; the effect will be the same as above.

### SEVENTH VÁJIKARANA.

Mix equal parts of the juice of the Kante-shevatí (*rosa glandulifera*) expressed from the leaves, and clarified butter, boil with ten parts of milk, sugar and honey, drink habitually, and great strength of back will be the result.

### EIGHTH VÁJIKARANA.

Take Loha-bhasma (a preparation from oxide of iron) powder of Triphalá (literally "the three myrobalans," *i. e.,* the yellow or chebulic myrobalan, *terminalia chébula,* the beleric myrobalan, or *terminalia belerica,* and the emblic myrobalan or *phyllanthus emblica*) and juice of liquorice (Jyestha-madh, *glycorrhiza glabra*): mix with clarified butter and honey, and take every day at sunset; the result will be the salacity of a sparrow, a bird which enjoys the females some ten or twenty times in succession.

Here end the remedies which comfort the heart and which excite desire. But when the linga is soft or small, it is quite incapable of satisfying the wife, and of inducing her to love and to be subject to the husband. Hence it is necessary to offer recipes for thickening and enlarging that member, making it sound and strong, hard and lusty.

### FIRST PRAYOGA.

Take equal quantities of Chikana (*hedysarum lagopodioides*), of Lechí, of Kosht (*costus specicosus* or *Arabicus*) of Vekhand (orris root), of Gajapimpalí (*pothos officinalis*), of Askhand (*physalis flexuosa*) in sticks, and of Kanher-root (oleander, *nerium odorum*), pound and levigate with butter, apply the result to the part, and after two ghari (48 minutes) it will assume an equine magnitude.[8]

### SECOND PRAYOGA.

Take equal parts of powdered Rakta-bol (myrrh, so called because it increases the blood),[9] of Manashíl (red sulphurate of arsenic), of Costus arabicus, of aniseed[10] and of borax; levigate in oil of sesamum orientate, anoint the member, and the desired erethrism will follow.

### THIRD PRAYOGA.

Take equal parts of Saindhava (rock salt), of pepper, of costus, of the Ringani-root (prickly nightshade), of Aghárá-filaments (*achyranthes aspera*) of Askhand (*physalisflexuosa*), of barley, of Urid (*phaselus mungo*) of the long pepper, of white Shiras (a kind of mustard), and of Til (Jingilee or *sesamum*), pound them, rub them with honey, and apply to the outer border of the ear. This medicament produces enormous growth, and, if done to a woman, it will cause the breasts to swell.

### FOURTH PRAYOGA.

Take Bibvá or marking nuts (*semicarpus anacardium*), black salt,[11] and leaves of the lotus-flower, reduce to ashes, and wet these with the juice of the prickly nightshade (*solanum Jacquini*), then anoint the Linga with the egesta of the Mahishi or she-buffalo, and apply the ashes. It will immediately become larger, and strong as the wooden pestle used for pounding rice. This is considered the most efficacious prescription.

### FIFTH PRAYOGA.

Mix Lodra-bark (*symplocos racemosa? morinda, citrifolia?*) Hirákas (copperas, green vitrol or sulphate of iron); Gajapimpilí (*pothos officinalis*), and Chikaná (*hedysarum lagopodioides*) with Til or sesamum oil, and apply to the Linga, when it will wax great. If done to a woman it will cause the labiæ to swell.

### SIXTH PRAYOGA.

Mix Dorlí fruit (*solanum macrorrhizon*), marking-nuts, and rind of the pomegranate (fruit) with bitter oil (of the mustard, *sinapis dichotoma,* used chiefly for burning,) and apply to the part, which will be greatly enlarged.

Here end the recipes for increasing the length and breadth of the Linga, and they are followed by the inverse process of narrowing and closing the Yoní. As women advance in years, and especially after childbirth, a certain enlargement takes place, followed by softness and flaccidity of the part. Hence it is necessary to give prescriptions for rendering it small and hard, thereby increasing the enjoyment of the husband, especially when he is in the flower of life.

### FIRST PRESCRIPTION.

Take the lotus, stalk as well as blossom, pound in milk, knead into small balls, and place inside the Yoní, when even a woman of fifty will become like a virgin.

### SECOND PRESCRIPTION.

Take a bit of fir bark (*pinus deodaru*), and pound it with turmeric, with (Dáru-halad) (zedoary), and with the filaments (pollen?) of the lotus flower; apply internally, the result will be great constriction of the tissues.

### THIRD PRESCRIPTION.

Take the pounded seed of Tal-makhaná, with the juice of the same seed, and apply inside and outside the Yoní. The effect will be instant induration.

### FOURTH PRESCRIPTION.

Pound together equal quantities of the Triphala (the three myrobalans specified above), of the Dhávátí-flower (*grislea tomentosa*), and of the inner body of the Jámbhulí (rose-apple tree), and the Sánvarí-tree (silk cotton-tree, *bombax heptaphyllum*) with honey; apply it inside the Yoní, and the effect will be a resemblance to that of an unmarried woman.

### FIFTH PRESCRIPTION.

Pound together the seeds of the Karu-bhonpalí (bitter white pompion, or pumpkin, *curcubita lagenaria*), and bark of the Lodhra-tree (*sympolocos racemosa? morinda citrofolia?*), apply them inside the Yoní and the hollowness which is felt after child birth will at once be filled up.

### SIXTH PRESCRIPTION.

Take 'Askhand-shoots, Chikaná, Onvá (or Ajvini, a kind of dill or bishop's weed), zedoary, blue lotus, costus and Válá, or Khaskhas (the grass whose roots are used as "Tatties," *andropogon muricata*); mix in equal parts, pound with water, and apply internally every day; the result will be very satisfactory constriction.

### SEVENTH PRESCRIPTION.

Take the salt made by boiling and evaporating the bark of the Moh-tree (*bassia latifolia*) mix with honey, and apply it as a suppository to the Yoní, filling the latter up to its lips every day; the effect will be that of tanning.[12]

Here end the recipes for contracting and hardening the Yoní; but this part requires further treatment, and it will be necessary to offer a variety of detached recipes. The result will be to remove certain inconveniences, and to supply their place by good qualities. And first of perfuming the member, which will be given in two recipes.[13]

### FIRST RECIPE.

Take oil of Shiras (a kind of mustard) and the extract from the Jáí, or Jasmine flower: let them be heated together over a slow fire, and be every day applied internally. There will be nothing unpleasant during or after the time of congress.

### SECOND RECIPE.

Take a piece of pine (*pinus deodaru*), sesamum oil, Shegwa, or tree horse-radish (*guilandina moringa*), pomegranate bark, bark of the bitter Ním-tree (the Persian lilac, Caloyer tree, *melia azadiracht indica*), and flowers of the yellow Champak (*michelia champaca*); extract the oil, and apply internally, with the same result.

The following three Recipes will be found useful in removing and destroying the body-pile (*poil amatoire*)[14]:

### FIRST RECIPE.

Place powdered oxide of lead in bitter oil; expose to sun for seven days, and apply to the "house of Smara,"[15] when all the hair will fall off.

### SECOND RECIPE.

Put calcined and powdered conch-shell[16] in the juice of the banana or plantain tree (*musa paradisiaco,* and *Sapientum*); keep in the sun for seven days, and mix with a little Haritál (orpiment, yellow arsenic, or salphuret of arsenic); then apply it to the Yoní, and all the hair will disappear.

### THIRD RECIPE.

If Hartál and the shades of Palásha wood (*butea frondosa*) be levigated in the juice of the plantain-tree, and applied to the part, no hair will ever grow again.[17]

When the monthly ailment is suddenly arrested, either by accident or disease, great evils result; and for their removal the following remedies are offered by the wise:—

### FIRST REMEDY.

The woman who will levigate in water the fallen leaves of the Pingaví, or Karad-kangoní (a scandent shrub, the heart-pea, *celastrus panicolata*), and the blossoms of the Jasvad (shoe-flower,) and continue to drink it, will presently be restored to her normal state.

### SECOND REMEDY.

Let a woman take equal parts of Tandul (rice),[18] Durva (Doob-grass, bent grass, or *agrestis linearis,* the well-known

gramen sacred to Ganesha), and pine-wood (*P. deodaru*), reduce
to powder, mix with water, and drink.

But if, on the other hand, it is judged necessary to abate the
immoderate appearance of the menses, the following remedies
will be found efficacious:—

### FIRST REMEDY.

Let a woman take equal parts of Hirada-dal (bark of yellow,
or chebulic myrobalans, of bitter Ním-bark,[19] and of Anwal-kathí
(dried myrobalans), pound, mix with water, and drink for six
successive days; the desired effect will be produced.

### SECOND REMEDY.

Let a woman take equal parts of the juice of the Kapitya-
fruit, (the elephant-apple, wood-apple or *feroni*), and of the Chivá
(small bamboo), and drink it mixed with honey; she will find
it equally efficacious.

The following prescriptions are invaluable for conceiving
and becoming gravid, but first the field (womb) must be duly
purified by the following:

### PRESCRIPTION. 20

Let a woman mix oxide of iron with calcined gold and copper,
and make it into an electuary with honey; she must then eat it from
the fourth (the time of bathing and purification) to the sixth day
after the monthly ailment, and the field will be duly cleansed.

When this is done, the following prescriptions will be
found efficacious:—

### FIRST PRESCRIPTION.

Let a woman take powdered Nága-kesar buds (a small Cassia,
*mesua ferrea*), mix with clarified butter, and eat for three consecu-
tive days after the fourth day, at the same time abstaining from

any food but "Dughdánu," that is to say, eating anything with milk; the result of the first congress will be evident.

### SECOND PRESCRIPTION.

Let a woman make a decoction of 'Askhand (*physalis flexuosa*) Gulvel (*menispermum glabrum? cocculus cordifolius?*), and of the resin called Laghu-Rál, and drink on the fourth day.

### THIRD PRESCRIPTION.

Let a woman take the root of the Játwand (shoe-flower), which has been pulled up by her husband in the Pushya Nakshatra; eat it with honey, and at the same time adhere to the milk diet.

### FOURTH PRESCRIPTION.

Let a woman rub down in milk the root of the Mahálung (common citron); boil it for a long time, and insert into it clarified butter; it must be drunk three days after the monthly ailment.

### FIFTH PRESCRIPTION.

Let a woman pound the root of white Chikaná, which has been gathered during the Pushya-Nakshatra, and mix with ten Máshás of the same root pounded, with an equal part of powdered liquorice root, and forty Máshás of sugar candy; this must be taken by the woman after the monthly impurity, in the milk of a cow which has brought forth a male calf of one colour. Nothing else must be eaten on the day of adhibiting this medicine; and, on the following day after congress with the husband at night, the woman must confine herself to rice and milk.

### SIXTH PRESCRIPTION.

The woman who will continue to drink in cow's milk equal parts of dry ginger powdered, of pepper, of the long pepper, of the prickly nightshade (*solanum Jacquinia* and of cassia buds, will conceive and bear a son, no matter how long she has been barren.

Here end the medicines which result in pregnancy. But it is not enough that the woman become gravid, she must also be protected from miscarriage and other accidents. The following are the recipes to be adopted by the mother that is about to be:—

### FIRST RECIPE.

Let a woman take of fine clay which adheres to the potter's hand, when he is fashioning his jar, and drink it in goat's milk. This will defend her from all injury.[21]

### SECOND RECIPE.

Take equal parts of powdered liquorice,[22] Lodhara-bark and dried emblic myrobalans; these must be drunk for seven days with milk in case of the fœtus becoming misplaced, a result of the falling of the womb.

### THIRD RECIPE.

Let a woman boil in milk, clarified butter, honey, and the root of the red lotus-flower; after long seething, the decoction must be allowed to cool, and it should be drunk for seven days. This medicine will prevent vomiting, irregular longings, and the vitiation of the three humours—bile, blood, and phlegm.

Here end the medicines which obviate miscarriage and accidents during pregnancy; the following are the prescriptions that ensure easy labour and easy deliverance:—

### FIRST PRESCRIPTION.

Let a woman take equal quantities of powdered citron, and the bark of the Bassia latifolia, mix with clarified butter and honey, and continue to use the electuary; her travail will be light.

### SECOND PRESCRIPTION.

Let a woman collect soot from the hearth or fire-place, and drink it in cold water which has been drawn the day before.

### THIRD PRESCRIPTION.

Invite the Gunj or Chanotí-tree (the *abrus precatorius*, whose red and black beads are the original "carat" of the goldsmith) on Saturday, pull up the root on the following Sunday, and bind it with a black thread to the woman's hair and waist.

### FOURTH PRESCRIPTION.

Let a holy man recite over water the following Mantra or charm:

अथ मक्षथ मथमथ वहिः ब्लिंबाब्बख्लोद्दर्ं मुंचमुंचबबघुबघु

with whose mysteries he is familiar, and give it to the woman to drink.

Here end the medicines for ensuring easy labour. On the other hand, it may be held desirable to limit the members of the family, in which case the following prescriptions will be found useful[23]:—

### FIRST PRESCRIPTION.

The woman who will eat every day for a fortnight forty Máshás of molasses (Jagri) which is three years old, will remain barren for the rest of her life.

### SECOND PRESCRIPTION.

Let a woman drink for three days after the fourth (purification day) a decoction of Chitraka (Ceylon leadwort, *plumbago zeylonica*) boiled with rice water.[24]

## THIRD PRESCRIPTION.

The woman who will drink for three days after the fourth a decoction of the Kallambha-plant (*nauclea cadamba* or *parvifolia*) and the feet of jungle-flies, will never have children.

## FOURTH PRESCRIPTION.

Levigate twenty Máshás of marking-nut (*semicarpus anacardium*), boil with Dhǔn or water in which rice has been washed, and drink for seven days, during which the monthly ailments last; the result will be life-long barrenness.

Here end the prescriptions for limiting a family. The following will be useful as cosmetics, and first of thickening and beautifying the hair:—

## FIRST RECIPE.

Take flowers of sesamum (the grain), and the fruit of caltrops (*tribulus lanuginosus*), levigate in cow's milk, and apply to the hair for seven days; however thin it may have been, it will become thick and long.

## SECOND RECIPE.

Levigate Croton seeds (*c. tiglium*) and Sambhar or elkhorn,[25] boil in sesamum oil and apply to the hair, which will so change its tawny colour for lamp black; and however weak and inclined to drop off it may be, it will lose all its infirmity.

## THIRD RECIPE.

Rub down finely powdered Gunj-beans (*abrus precatorius*) with honey, and apply to the head; this medicament will remove the disease called "Indra-lupta-roga," or baldness of the crown.[26]

### FOURTH RECIPE.

Burn ivory, pound it well, and apply it mixed with water to the head; the latter will recover hair.

Here end the prescriptions for thickening and beautifying the hair; the following are the recipes for obtaining a good black colour:—

### FIRST RECIPE.

Take blossoms of the Mango-tree: the fruits of the three myrobalans, the bark of Arjuna-vriksha (Arjuna-tree, or *pentaptera arjuna*), and the rind of the penduré shrub; grind them well and boil them in sesamum oil, which now gets the name of Nílá-tel, oil of indigo—*i. e.,* of dark colour. This medicament is by far the most potent for dyeing the hair—what need I say more, except that if the wing of the Hansa (wild white goose) be dipped into it, the hue will at once take the color of night?

### SECOND RECIPE.

Mix the powder of Persian gall-nut, long pepper, indigo leaves, and rock salt (the mordant) with sweet gruel of wheat, and the result will be a brilliant dark dye.[27]

### THIRD RECIPE.

Let a man drink every day for a month forty Máshás of Ním (Melim)-tree oil;[28] his hair will gradually change colour and become glaring black as the Bhramara's wing (the "bumble-bee" of India).

### FOURTH RECIPE.

Pound together Gorochana (Bezoar stones),[29] black sesamum seed, Kata-janghá (the heart pea, literally "crow's thigh") and

Shatávari (*asparagus racemosus*), and apply to the hair: it will soon turn black.

For the purpose of whitening and bleaching the hair, wise men propose the following:—

### PRESCRIPTION.

Wet the grain of sesamum with the juice of the Nivarung (*euphorbia pentagonia*), dry in the sun, and extract the oil; whatever part of the body is touched by this, the hair there growing will be white and bright as crystal.

For renewing the hair of the head, there is the following:—

### RECIPE.

Steep dried myrobolans in juice of the euphorbia (*pentagonia*), sun dry, pound, and apply to the hair.

It often happens that eruptions break out and leave black spots upon the face, greatly marring its comeliness. The following, therefore, are valuable prescriptions for clearing the skin:—

### FIRST.

If Vekhand (orris-root[30]), elk horn,[31] and coriander-seed be pounded together and applied to the face for three days, the exanthemata which break out upon the skin of young people of both sexes, presently disappear.

### SECOND.

Let a man reduce to powder the thorns of the silk-cotton-tree (*bombax heptaphyllum*), levigate it in milk, and apply it to the face: the effect will be all that he can desire.

### THIRD.

Take Lodhra, rock salt, white Shiras (mustard), and Vekhand, knead with water, and rub upon the skin.

The following two recipes will remove the black colour of the epidermis and restore it to its original lighter tint:—

### FIRST.

Levigate in milk, sesamum seed, coriander, Sháhá-jire (cummin; others say *nigella indica*), and Shiras-seed; if this be applied to the body for seven days it will make the aspect clean and brilliant as the moon.

### SECOND.

Take red Sanders (or sandal) wood, Tetví (the yellow wood of the *bignonia chelonoides*), root-bulbs of the sweet-smelling grass (*cyperus juncifolius*), liquorice, Tandulja (*amaranthus oleraceus*), turmeric, and zedoary; levigate with the sap drawn from crushed banana or plantain-stems, and apply to the body for seven days.

The two following are useful recipes for enlarging the breasts of women:—

### FIRST.

Take shoots of 'Askhand, Vekhand, Kosht, black cummin-seed (bitter fennel?) oleander-root and cloves; pound, levigate in a mortar with water and butter; and, lastly, apply to the breasts, which will rise firm and hard.

### SECOND.

Take equal parts of the kernels of the Badri (Ber, or jujube fruit, *zizyphus*), oleander-root, snake fat (?) Kankol (*myrtus pimenta*), and the heart of Jahád wood (the China cubeb tree?); pound, levigate, and use as the former prescription.

The following three recipes are invaluable for raising and hardening pendulous bosoms[32]:—

Boil the juice of the Narvel plant (*narwelia zeylonica*) in sesamum oil, and apply to the breasts; it will be efficacious, however flaccid they may have been.

### SECOND.

Boil powder of the pomegranate fruit-rind in mustard oil, and apply to the breasts of any woman; even though she be old, they will soon become fat, fair and round.

### THIRD.

Take equal parts of Rui juice (gigantic swallow-wort, *asclepias* or *callotropis gigantea*), levigate with Chikaná Tridhár (leaves of the indigo tree?), Onvá (dry ginger?), sensitive-plant, turmeric, and zedoary; and boil in sesamum oil, or in clarified butter of the cow, with great care, so that the contents of the pot may not remain raw nor be overboiled. If this ointment be placed in a woman's nostrils, the breasts will at once be drawn up. Moreover, if the same be mixed with water in which rice has been washed, and be drunk by a girl not older than sixteen, her breasts, will be enlarged and drawn up, and will never become pendulous in after-life.

It will now be right to describe the Angarág,[33] or unguents, which applied to the body after ablution, naturally breed love.

Let sandal-wood, Válá (*andropogon muricatum*, vulgarly, "Cuscus") Lodhra, and mango-bark be powdered very fine, and mixed with the water of Hardá (yellow, or chebulic myrobalans). This being rubbed on the skin, will give it a charming fragrance.

The following nine recipes are useful in removing the evil savour of too much perspiration, caused by the heat of the sun, and in arresting the secretion in warm weather:—

### FIRST.

Pound together, and apply leaves of the Nim and the Lodhra, with the rind of the pomegranate fruit, and bark of the Sátvani, mixed with Hardá-water.

### SECOND.

Pound together the seeds of the tamarind and the Karanj (*galedupa arborea,* Roxb.; *pomgamia glabra,* Grati.; *bonducilla,* nut-tree, Grey.), and the root of the Bel tree, mixed with Hardá-water. This is sovereign for the axillæ.

### THIRD.

Pound Nága-keshar, aloewood, Válá and sandal-wood, with the sap squeezed out of the inner bark of the Jujube tree.

### FOURTH.

Pound together parts of the fallen Sowers of the walnut tree,[34] and the fruit of the Janbali (rose apple); this arrests perspiration in warm weather.

### FIFTH.

Pound together Nim-leaves, Lodhra, lotus-root, and pomegranate-bark; it will have the same effect.

### SIXTH.

Pound the flower-filaments of the Shiras tree (*mimosa shirisa?*), Nágakesar, Válá, and Lodhra; this may either be applied to the body or eaten.

The following are sweet-smelling oils and unguents, to be used after bathing:—

### FIRST.

Place Bél-leaves in sweet oil (sesamum), and expose them to the sun till dry; add successively Bakul (the flowering tree, *mimusops elengi,*) Marvá (sweet Marjorum, *origanum marjorana*), Ashoka flowers (*Jonesia asoca*) and the flowers of the Kevadá (*pandanus odoratissimus*); moisten with oil, and keep in the shade. This preparation has a surpassing fragrance much affected by the voluptuous.

### SECOND.

Pound together the seeds of small cardamoms, Nágarmotha (a sweet-smelling grass) Nakhá (*unguis odoratus,* or black Byzantine), Sona-kevadá (yellow *pandamnus odoratissimus*), Jatámánsi (Indian spikenard), Kachorá (*salvia bengalensis*), and Tamál-patra (leaves of *laurus cassia,* or of *xanthochymus pictorius*); this medicament, applied to the body and hair, at bathing time, produces a delicious perfume.

### THIRD.

Pound together Anvalkathí, Sona-Kevadá, Nágarmothá, Válá, Haradá, Jatámánsí. This perfume, once applied, is capable of outlasting the fortnight.

### FOURTH.

Pound together equal parts of Sandal-wood, Elá-dáná cardamom seeds), Kachorá, Tamál-patra, Haradá, and seeds or beans of the Shegva (the horse-radish tree, or *guilandina moringa* seed, *hyperanthera moringa*), with Nágar-mothá and Válá; the result will be a most odorous unguent.

### FIFTH.

Pound together equal quantities of Kápŭrá (camphor), Kunkumágar (a kind of sandal wood),[35] Lodhra, Lohbán (frankincense) Válá, Nagar-motha and Kálá-válá (the dark variety of *andropogon muricatum*).

### SIXTH.

Apply to the body a composition of Tamál-patra, Válá, sandal-wood, Kálá-válá, and Krishná-graŭ (black aloe-wood, *aqualaria agellochum*).

### SEVENTH.

Reduce to fine powder Kastŭrí (musk), Nága-keshar, Shíla-ras (benzoin or olibanum supposed to ooze out of stone), Vishesha-dhŭp (a kind of incense, the sap of *boswellia serrata*), Ganeri-kápŭr (a kind of camphor), nutmegs and Lobhán; mix with the juice of betel leaves, and apply to the body. This perfume is fitted for Rajahs, and consequently for all other men.

### EIGHTH.

Take the following drugs in the following proportions— one part of Nágar-mothá, two parts of costus, Lehban and Kápŭr, four parts of Haradá, five parts of Shila-ras, and nine parts of Nakhlá (*unguis odoratus* or black Byzantine); this unguent is called Kástŭrí-dul (a bit of musk), and is perhaps the best fitted for Rajahs.

### NINTH.

Pound together one part of Nakhlá, Haradá, Vekhand, Nágarmothá, Jatimánsí, Shopá (aniseed), and Karanj-seed, two parts of Sona-kevadá, and three parts of camphor, black sanders, musk, nutmegs and Jatámánsí; this perfume is called Sugandha-garbha; the materials are difficult to procure, consequently it is the more prized.

To the above may be added five prescriptions causing the mouth to exhale a pleasant smell.

### FIRST.

Pound together Kalmí-dálchiní (a fine kind of cinnamon,) mace cardamon-grains, Nakhlá, Sona-kevadá and nutmegs; make into pills, and eat with betel leaf.[36]

### SECOND.

Pound together Kesar (saffron), Kankol (the *myrtus pimenia*) Lohbán, nutmegs and coriander-seed, made into pill and use as above.

### THIRD.

Take for a fortnight, every morning and evening, a powder composed of Ekangí-mura (marjoram), Nágakesa and costus.

### FOURTH.

If carats (abrus-beans) and costus, both reduced to powder, be mixed with honey, and be taken for a fortnight, morning and evening, the breath will be as the perfume of the Pandanus odoratissimus.

### FIFTH.

Pound the ashes of the Apámárga-vriksh (*acepranthes aspera*), and steep in the juice of Mango-leaves; dry in the sun and eat every morning a little of this Kshára (alkali) with areca-nuts and betel-leaf. It is the best of all prescriptions for purifying the breath after food.

# → CHAPTER SEVEN ←

# TREATING OF VASHÍKARANA

VASHIKARANA IS THE ART BY WHICH MAN OR WOMAN IS rendered submissive and obedient to the fascinator, who for that purpose uses certain drugs and charms. And first the magic "Talaka".[1]

### FIRST PRESCRIPTION.

The holy sage Vátsyáyana Muni[2] hath declared that whosoever will take the powder of sensitive plant, the root of green lotus-flowers, the Bassia latifolia, and barley-flower; and, after mixing it up with some of his own Kama salila, will apply it as a sectarian mark to his forehead, such an one will subdue the world of women, and she who looks upon his brow cannot fail to feel for him the most eager desire.

### SECOND PRESCRIPTION.

The man who will levigate the root of the giant Asclepias, the Jatámánsí, or spikenard (*valeriana Jatâmánsî*), Vekhand, the sweet-smelling grass Nágar-motha (*cyperus pertenuis* or *juncifolius*), and costus with the blood from a woman's Yoní, and apply it to his forehead, shall ever be successful in the affairs of love, and shall enjoy a long course of happiness.

### THIRD PRESCRIPTION.

The man who will take equal parts of Tagar (a flowering plant, *taberna montana* or *coronaria asarobacca*), of Pimpalimull (the root of *piper dichotomum,* or long pepper), of Mendha-shinghi (a plant whose fruit is compared with goat-horns or crab-claws), and of Indian spikenard; mix them together and knead them with honey, to which is added his Káma salila, or with any of the other five Mala (secretions of the body); that man will find that such a mixture applied to his forehead will enable him to overcome and subdue the women of the world.

The following recipe will enable a woman to attract and preserve her husband's love:—

Moisten Gorochana in the blood which appears every month, and apply it to the forehead as a "Tilak"; as long as it is there and the man looks upon it, so long shall he be in her power.

The following are "Anjan", or magical collyriums for winning love and friendship:—

#### FIRST.

Take a human skull from the cemetery or burning ground on the eighth day of the moonlit fortnight of the seventh month Ashviní (September–October), expose it to fire, and collect the soot upon a plate held over it; let this be drawn over the inner surface of the eye-lids, instead of the usual antimony, and the effect will be to fascinate every one.[3]

#### SECOND.

Take bamboo-manna, Nága-keshar (*messua ferrea*),[4] Korphad (*aloe perfoliata*) and Manshíla (red sulphuret of arsenic); reduce them to powder, sift, and use as collyrium; the wearer's eyes will attract the hearts of all.

### THIRD.

Take wood of the Tad-palm (toddy-tree), costus, and Tagar-root, levigate in water, and with the latter moisten a piece of silk stuff; convert this into wicks with Shiras-oil, light them and take the soot formed upon a human skull in a cemetery, when held above the lamp; this is a collyrium which will make every one who looks upon it the servant or slave of the wearer.

### FOURTH.

Take Manshíl, Nága-keshar, Kálá-umbar, (the fruit of *ficus glomerosa*) and bamboo-sugar, and make a collyrium when the Pushya-asterism falls upon a Sunday; its effect will be greatly to increase the mutual love of husband and wife.

The following three prescriptions are powerful in reducing other persons to submission:—

### FIRST.

If a powder made of the Káng, or white panic (*p. italicum*), white Nishottar (*thomea turpethum*), the wing of the Bhramra-bee, costus, lotus flower, and Tagar-root, be thrown upon a man, it will at once have the effect of fascination.

### SECOND.

If a powder, made of Vatálu leaves, of Soma-vallí (the moon-plant, *asclepias acida*, or *sarcostema viminalis*), and of a garland or rosary placed upon a dead body, and mingled with a little of the man's own Káma-salila, be thrown upon a person, the latter will be surely subdued.

### THIRD.

If a powder, made with equal quantities of the Sátavina Vrisksha (the "seven-flowered tree," *astonia scholaris,* or *echites*), of the Rudrasha *eleocarpus lanceolatus,* or Ganitrus, a tree sacred to

Shiva), and of the seeds of San (Bengal "sun"), be used as before, it will will have even a greater effect. This is perhaps the most potent compound for fascinating others.

### A PHILTER-PILL (VATIKA).

On any Tuesday, take out the bowels of the blue jay (*coracias indica*), and let some of the fascinator's own Káma-salila be placed inside the body; put the latter into an earthen pot, cover it with a second pot whose bottom must be turned upwards, lute with cloth and day, and keep in a solitary place for seven days; then take out the contents[5], pound, reduce to fine powder, make pellets, or pills, and dry them. If one of these be given to a woman, she will be subject to a man, and *vice versa*.

### ANOTHER CHARM.

The man who, after enjoying his wife, catches some of his own Káma-salila in his left hand, and applies it to her left foot, will find her entirely submissive to his will.

### ANOTHER CHARM.

The woman who before congress will touch with her left foot the Linga of her husband, and will make a practice of this, undoubtedly subdues him, and makes him her slave for life.

### ANOTHER CHARM.

Let a man take the egesta of the spotted-necked pigeon; rock-salt, and the leaves of the Bassia latifolia in equal parts, powder them, and rub the powder upon his Linga before congress, he will become the woman's master.

### ANOTHER CHARM.

Let a man levigate together Kásturí (common musk, also applied to a kind of camphor) and wood of the yellow Tetu-tree;

mix them with honey two months old, and apply the substance to his Linga before congress, it will have the same effect.

### A FASCINATING INCENSE, OR FUMIGATION.

Pound well together sandal-wood, Kunku (red powder prepared from turmeric and alum coloured with lemon-juice and other matters), costus, Krishna-guru (black sanders), Suvásika-pushpa (perfumed flowers?), white válá (the fragrant *andropogon muricatum*) and the bark of the Deodaru pine; and, after reducing them to fine powder, mix it with honey and thoroughly dry. It is now known as Chinta-mani-Dhupa, the "thought-mastering incense." If a little of this be used according to the ceremonies prescribed, he who employs it will snake all the world submissive to him.

### ANOTHER INCENSE.

Pound and mix together equal quantities of cardamom-seeds, Olibanum (or gum benzoin), the plant Garur-wel Moon-seed, *monispermum glabrum,* or *cocculus cardifolius,* sandal-wood, the flowers of the eared jasmine, and Bengal madder. This incense is powerful as that above.

The following are the Mantras, or magical versets which have the power of fascination:—

### 1. KAMESHWAR MANTRA[6]

श्रीमेश्वर अमुका आनय आजय वग्यतां ह्री

O Kameshwar, bring such and such a woman under subjection to me.

The form of use is as follows;—Accompany the word Kámeshwar with the mystic "Om," or Pranava. Then let the woman's name precede the words, A'naya! A'naya! and follow

with the Bija (the seed, or cabalistic conclusion.) The charm is
to be repeated mentally 10,000 times, counted by a string
(rosary) 108 Kadamba blossoms (*nauclea cadamoa*), or those of
the Palasa (*butea frondosa*). The sacrifice or offering consists of
burning the same kind of flowers, counting a tenth part of the
number of repetition, that is to say, one thousand. Thus the
Mantra-devatá is brought under our power.[7] One of the flowers,
which has been charmed by this verset being recited over it, is
finally given to the woman whose name has been pronounced,
and thus her subjugation is effected.

## 2. CHAMUNDA MANTRA.[8]

### चामुंडे मोहय धष्ठतां श्रमुकीं

Repeat the Mantra mentally a lakh of times (100,000) with
the pranava. Sacrifice 10,000 flowers of the Butea frondosa,
at the same time offering the Tarpana[9] (or presenting water to
the object of worship). When the ceremonies and works of
propitiation are performed, the Mantra-devatá is subdued,
and the woman is fascinated by a gift of a flower over which
the verset has been repeated seven times.

## 3. THE MANTRA THAT SUBDUES THE PADMINI.

### कामेश्वर मोहय मोहय स्वाहा:

Repeat this Mantra, with the Pravana, till the Mantra-devatá
has been mastered.[10] Then write this Kameshvara-Mantra
upon a betel-leaf with the flower steeped in honey, choosing
Sunday for the act. Finally, after repeating the same Mantra a
hundred times, give the flower to the Padminí, who will
undoubtedly be subdued.

## 4. THE MADANASTRA-MANTRA THAT SUBDUES THE CHITRINI.

विहंगम विहंगम कामदेवात्मै

Repeat this Mantra with Pranava (10,000—100,000 times) till the deity which it contains is mastered. Then moisten nutmeg-powder in the juice squeezed from the root of the plantain tree, place it in a roll of betel-leaf which has been charmed by repeating over it the Mantra on Sunday, and let the Chitriní woman eat it.[11] She will certainly be subjected

## 5. THE MANTRA THAT SUBDUES THE SHANKHINI.

पचपच खाहा

It is said by the ancient learned men conversant with the science of fascination, that this Mantra is exceedingly efficacious. After the Mantra-devatá is subdued in the usual manner, let the root of the Tagar and cocoa-nut, or the Belfruit (*aegle marmaros,* or *crataera religiosa,* a tree sacred to Shiva) be charmed and given to the Shankhiní; if she eat any part of it, she is subject to obedience.

धिरांधिरांकामदेवाय तक्षे खाहा

After subduing the Mantra-devatá, pound the wing of a pigeon[12] in honey, make pills of it, and administer to the Hastiní, who will at once become fascinated.

## ➤ CHAPTER EIGHT ➤

# OF DIFFERENT SIGNS IN
# MEN AND WOMEN

THE CHARACTERISTICS OF A WOMAN WHOM WE SHOULD TAKE TO
wife, are as follows:—She should come from a family of equal rank
with that of her husband, a house which is known to be valiant
and chaste, wise and learned, prudent and patient, correct and
becomingly behaved, and famed for acting according to its religion, and for discharging its social duties. She should be free from
vices, and endowed with all good qualities, possess a fair face and
fine person, have brothers and kinsfolk, and be a great proficient
in the Kama-shástra; or Science of Love. Such a girl is truly fitted
for marriage; and let a sensible man hasten to take her, by performing the ceremonies which are commanded in the Holy Law.

And here may be learned the marks whereby beauty and
good shape of body are distinguished. The maiden whose face is
soft and pleasing as the moon; whose eyes are bright and liquid
as the fawn's, whose nose is delicate as the sesamum flowers;
whose teeth are clean as diamonds and clear as pearls; whose
ears are small and rounded; whose neck is like a sea-shell, with
three delicate lines or tracings behind; whose lower lip is red as
the ripe fruit of the bryony; whose hair is black as the Bhramara's
wing; whose skin is brilliant as the flower of the dark-blue lotus,
or light as the surface of polished gold; whose feet and hands
are red, being marked with the circular Chakrá or discus;[2]

whose stomach is small, whilst the umbilical region is drawn in; whose shape below the hips is large; whose thighs, being well-proportioned and pleasing as the plantain-tree, make her walk like the elephant, neither too fast nor too slow; whose voice is sweet as the Kokila-bird's—such a girl, especially if her temper be good, her nature kindly, her sleep short, and her mind and body not inclined to laziness, should at once be married by the wise man.

But the girl who comes from a bad family; whose body is either very short or very tall, very fat or very thin; whose skin is ever rough and hard; whose hair and eyes are yellowish, the latter like a cat's; whose teeth are long, or are wholly wanting; whose mouth and lips are wide and projecting,[3] with the lower lip of dark colour, and tremulous when speaking; who allows her tongue to loll out; whose eyebrows are straight; whose temples are depressed; who shows signs of beard, mustachios, and dense body-pile; whose neck is thick; who has some limbs shorter and others longer than the usual proportion; whose one breast is large or high, and the other low or small; whose ears are triangular, like a sifting or winnowing fan; whose second toe is larger and longer than the big toe;[4] whose third toe is blunt, without tip or point, and whose little toes do not touch the ground; whose voice is harsh and laugh is loud; who walks quickly and with uncertain gait; who is full grown; who is disposed to be sickly, and who bears the name of a mountain (as Govardhan),[5] of a tree (as Anbí), of a river (as Taranginí), of a bird (as Chimaní), or of a constellation (as Revatí, the 27th lunar mansion)—such a girl, especially if her disposition be irascible and temper violent; if she eat and sleep much; if she be always vexed, troubled and distressed; if her disposition be restless and fidgetty; if she has little understanding in worldly matters; if she be destitute of shame and if her natural disposition be wicked, should be carefully avoided, under all circumstances, by the wise.

So much for the characteristics of the woman. On the other hand, man should be tried, even as gold is tested, in four ways: 1, by the touchstone; 2, by cutting; 3, by heating; and, 4, by hammering. Thus should we take into consideration— 1, learning; 2, disposition; 3, qualities; and 4, action. The first characteristic of a man is courage, with endurance; if he attempt any deed, great or small, he should do it with the spirit of a lion. Second, is prudence: time and place must be determined, and opportunity devised, like the Bak-heron, that stands intently eyeing its prey in the pool below. The third is early rising, and causing others to do the same. The fourth is hardihood in war. The fifth is a generous distribution and division of food and property amongst family and friends. The sixth is duly attending to the wants of the wife. The seventh is circumspection in love matters. The eighth is secrecy and privacy in the venereal act. The ninth is patience and perseverance in all the business of life. The tenth is judgment in collecting and in storing up what may be necessary. The eleventh is not to allow wealth and worldly success to engender pride and vanity, magnificence and ostentation. The twelfth is never aspiring to the unattainable. The thirteenth is contentment with what the man has, if he can get no more. The fourteenth is plainness of diet. The fifteenth is to avoid over sleep. The sixteenth is to be diligent in the service of employers. The seventeenth is not to fly when attacked by robbers and villains. The eighteenth is working willingly; for instance, not taking into consideration the sun and shade if the labourer be obliged to carry a parcel. The nineteenth is the patient endurance of trouble. The twentieth is to keep the eye fixed upon a great business; and the twenty-first is to study the means properest for success. Now, any person who combines these twenty-one qualities is deservedly reputed an excellent man.

When choosing a son-in-law, the following characteristics should be aimed at:—He must come from a large family, which has never known sin and poverty. He must be young, handsome, wealthy, brave and influential; diligent in business, moderate in enjoying riches, sweet of speech, well versed in discharging his own duties, known to the world as a mine of virtues, steadfast in mind, and a treasury of mercy, who gives alms and makes charities as far as his means permit. Such a man is described by celebrated poets as a fit person to whom the daughter should be given in marriage.

And these are the defects and blemishes of a son-in-law;— The man who is born in a low family, who is vicious, a libertine, pitiless, and ever sickly with dangerous disease, sinful and very wicked, poor and miserly, impotent, prone to conceal the virtues and to divulge the vices of others; a constant traveller, an absentee, one ever away from his home and residing abroad; a debtor, a beggar, a man who has no friendship with the good, or who, if he have it, breaks into quarrel upon trifling things—such a person, the wise will not accept as a son-in-law.

We now proceed to the Sámudrika-lakshana or chiromantic signs, good and bad, which affect present and future happiness. The length of a man's and woman's life, and the marks which denote it, must first be treated of, because it is useless to see suspicious details if death may shortly be expected. And first of all the palmistry of the man.

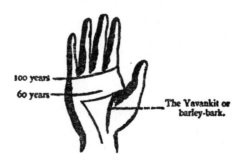

100 years

60 years

The Yavankit or barley-bark.

Every perfect hand and foot consists of five members, namely the Angushthá (thumb), the Tarjaní (forefinger), the Madhyamá (middle-finger), the Anámiká (ring-finger), and the Kanishthiká (little finger). Now, if an unbroken line in the palm[6] run from the "mount" or base of the little finger, to that of the forefinger, it is a sign that the bearer will live a hundred years. But the man in whose palm an unbroken line runs from the ball or cushion of the little finger to that of the middle-finger, should be considered as likely to live for a period of sixty years. Moreover, the man upon whose thumb or chest there is a figure shaped like a barley grain,[7] the same will eat bread earned by his own exertions, and he will ever remain happy. As a rule, if the lines in the palms be few, men are poor and penniless; if there be four they are happy; and if more than four, they are threatened with mean and wretched fortunes; moreover, the much streaked palm shows a quarrelsome nature.

The man whose eye is red, whose body is fair and of good complexion like gold; whose trunk is fleshy and whose arms reach his knees,[8] the same will always remain rich and enjoy grandeur, opulence, lordship and supremacy.

The man whose thighs are large, will win great wealth; the man whose waist is broad, will be blessed in his wife and many children; the man whose feet are long,[9] and whose hands are very delicate, will always enjoy happiness; and the man whose head is large and lengthy,[10] will rise to be a prince.

The man whose Linga is very long, will be wretchedly poor. The man whose Linga is very thick, will ever be very lucky; and the man whose Linga is short, will be a Rajah.[11] So much concerning the characteristics of men.

And now as regards the other sex. The woman of inauspicious signs, will be, or become an orphan, a widow, destitute of brothers and sisters, and without connections, as well as relations, so that her life ends, as it began, in bitterness. Her characteristics, therefore, should be carefully examined before marriage with her is contracted.

Let it be understood that the woman who bears on the sole of her left foot the signs of the Chakra (quoit, peculiar to Vishnu), the Padma (lotus), the Dhvaja (flag), the Chatra (umbrella), the mystical Svastika,[12] and the Kamala, that is circular lines,[13] and not conch-shaped on her finger-tips, that woman will be a Rani (queen). If, however, one or more of these figures be wanting, she will enjoy all the happiness of a crowned head.

The woman who bears on the sole of her left foot a line extending from the "mount" or cushion of the little toe, to the ball of the big toe, that woman will readily obtain a good husband, and will find great happiness in his love.

The woman whose two little toes do not touch the ground whilst walking, will certainly lose her husband; and during her widowhood, she will not be able to keep herself chaste.

The woman whose Tarjaní or second toe is the longest of all the toes, will be unchaste even before marriage. What doubt, then, is there of her being an adulteress as long as her youth endures?

The woman whose breasts are fleshy, firm, and handsome, whose bosom is without hair, and whose thighs are like the trunk of an elephant, will enjoy a life of happiness.

The maiden who has black moles upon her left breast, throat and ears, will marry and bear a son having auspicious marks; and by her means, all the family will be called blessed.

The maiden whose neck is very long, will be of a wicked and cruel disposition. The maiden whose neck is very short, will be wretchedly poor. The maiden whose neck has three lines or wrinkles, will be of a good disposition, and her lot will be ever fortunate.

The maiden who bears in the palm of her hand lines resembling enclosing walls, and "Toran" or garlands of flowers, and twigs of trees bent into circles,[14] will become the wife of a King, although she have been born in a servant's house.

The maiden whose palms have lines in the shape of an Ankush (spiked hook for guiding elephants), a Kuntala (or spur), and a Chakra (quoit or discus), will intermarry with a royal house, and bear a son who shows the most fortunate signs.

It is written in he book Náradokta[15] that marriage should never be contracted with a girl, unless the lines and spots, as interpreted by treatises on Chiromancy, are first examined and found good. The consequence of unauspicious signs is that her birth will cause the death of her father, mother and brother in sucession. The man who marries such a maiden, will presently die, and be followed by all his brethren, and the two families will be destroyed.

There are seven kinds of troubles which result from having intercourse with the wife of another man. Firstly, adultery shortens or lessens the period of life; secondly, the body becomes spiritless and vigourless; thirdly, the world derides and reproaches the lover; fourthly, he despises himself; fifthly, his wealth greatly decreases; in thought how to woo and win the woman in question; sixthly, he suffers much in this world; and, seventhly, he will suffer more in the world to come. Yet, despite all this ignominy, disgrace and contumely, it is absolutely necessary to have connection with the wife of another, under certain circumstances, which will be presently specified.

Great and powerful monarchs have ruined themselves and their realms by their desire to enjoy the wives of others. For instance, in former days the family of the Rávana, King of Lanká (Ceylon), was destroyed because he forcibly abducted Síta, the wife of Ráma, and this action gave rise to the Ramáyana poem, which is known to the whole world. Válí lost his life for attempting to have connection with Tárá, as is fully described in the Kishkindá-kánd, a chapter of that history. Kíchaka, the Kaurava, together with all his brethren, met with destruction, because he wished to have Draupada[16] (daughter of Drupad), the common wife of the Pandu brothers, as is described in the Virát-parví (section) of the Mahabhárat. Such are the destructions which in days past have happened to those who coveted other men's wives; let none, therefore, attempt adultery even in their thoughts.

But there are ten changes in the natural state of men, which require to be taken into consideration. Firstly, when he is in a state of Dhyása (*desiderium*), at a loss to do anything except to see a particular woman; secondly, when he finds his mind wandering, as if he were about to lose his senses; thirdly, when he is ever losing himself; fourthly, when he passes restless nights without the refreshment of sleep; fifthly, when his looks become haggard and his body emaciated; sixthly, when he feels himself growing shameless and departing from all sense of decency and decorum; seventhly, when his riches take to themselves wings and fly; eighthly, when the state of mental intoxication verges upon madness; ninthly, when fainting fits come on; and tenthly, when he finds himself at the door of death.[17]

That these states are produced by sexual passion may be illustrated by an instance borrowed from the history of bygone days. Once upon a time there was a king called Parŭravá, who was a devout man, and who entered upon such a course of mortification and austerities that Indra, Lord of the Lower Heaven, began to fear lest he himself might be dethroned. The god, therefore, in order to interrupt these penances and other religious acts, sent down from Svarga, his own heaven, Urváshí, the most lovely of the Apsaras (nymphs). The king no sooner saw her than he fell in love with her, thinking day and night of nothing but possessing her, till at last succeeding in his project, both spent a long time in the pleasures of carnal connection. Presently Indra, happening to remember the Apsara, despatched his messenger, one of the Gandharvas (heavenly minstrels), to the world of mortals, and recalled her. Immediately after her departure, the mind of Parŭravá began to wander; he could no longer concentrate his thoughts upon worship and he felt upon the point of death.

See, then, the state to which that king was reduced by thinking so much about Urváshi! When a man has allowed himself to be carried away captive of desire, he must consult a physician, and the books of medicine which treat upon the subject. And, if he come to the conclusion that unless he enjoy his neighbour's wife he will surely die, he should, for the sake of preserving his life, possess her once and once only.[18] If, however, there be no such peremptory cause, he is by no means justified in enjoying the wife of another person, merely for the sake of pleasure and wanton gratification.

Moreover, the book of Vatsayáyana, the Rishi, teaches us as follows: Suppose that a woman, having reached the lusty vigour of her age, happened to become so inflamed with love for a man, and so heated by passion that she feels herself falling into the ten states before described, and likely to end in death attended with phrenzy, if her beloved refuse her sexual commerce. Under these circumstances, the man, after allowing himself to be importuned for a time, should reflect that his refusal will cost her life; he should, therefore, enjoy her on one occasion, but not always.

The following women, however, are absolutely, and under all circumstances, to be excluded from any commerce of the kind. The wife of a Brahman; of a Shrotíya (Brahman learned in the Vedas); of an Agnihotrí (priest who keeps up the sacred fire), and of a Puránik (reader of the Puránas). To look significantly at such a woman, or to think of her with a view of sensual desire, is highly improper: what, then, must we think of the sin of carnal copulation with her? In like manner, men prepare to go to Naraka (hell) by lying with the wife of a Khatríya (king, or any man of the warrior caste, now extinct); of a friend or of a relation. The author of this book strongly warns and commands his readers to avoid all such deadly sins.

Indeed, there are certain other women who are never to be enjoyed, however much a man may be tempted. First, a virgin without marrying her; second, a widow;[19] third a woman living chastely or virtuously with her husband; fourth, the wife of our friend; fifth, the wife of our foe; sixth, any of the reverend women specified above; seventh, the wife of a pupil or a disciple; eighth, a woman born in one's own family; ninth, a woman afflicted with any serious complaint; tenth, a woman who has been defiled; eleventh, a mad woman; twelth, a woman older than oneself;[20] thirteenth, the wife of a Guru, spiritual tutor, instructor or guide; fourteenth, one's mother-in-law; fifteenth, one's maternal aunt (mother's sister); sixteenth, the wife of one's maternal uncle;[21] seventeenth, one's paternal aunt (father's sister); eighteenth, one's paternal uncle's wife; nineteenth, a sister; twentieth, a pregnant woman; twenty-first, a woman who has committed mortal sins and crimes; twenty-third, a woman whose complexion is entirely yellow; twenty-fourth, a woman whose complexion is quite black. It is laid down in the Shástras (scriptures), that the wise should never, under any circumstances, have connection with these twenty-four kinds of women, as well as with others, bearing any relationship to one.

The following is a list of the women who serve but as go-betweens:[22] First, a gardener's wife. Second, a woman, who is a personal friend. Third, a widow. Fourth, a nurse. Fifth a dancing-girl. Sixth, a woman engaged in manual or mechanical arts. Seventh, a woman hired as a servant or maid to the women of the family. Eighth, an attendant as distinguished from a slave girl. Ninth, a woman who goes from house to house speaking sweet words. Tenth, a woman with whom we can talk freely about love and enjoyment. Eleventh, a young woman under sixteen. Twelfth, a female ascetic or mendicant in the name of religion. Thirteenth, a woman who sells milk and buttermilk. Fourteenth, a tailoress. Fifteenth, a woman fit to be called "Mistress Grandmother." The amorous should prefer these kind of persons, as, when deputed upon such messages, they do their work kindly and well.

The following is a list of the women who can most easily be subdued.[23] First a woman whose deportment shows signs of immodesty. Second, a widow. Third, a woman who is highly accomplished in singing, in playing musical instruments, and in similar pleasant arts. Fourth, a woman who is fond of conversation. Fifth, a woman steeped in poverty. Sixth, the wife of an imbecile or an impotent person. Seventh, the wife of a fat and tun-bellied man. Eighth, the wife of a cruel and wicked man. Ninth, the wife of one who is shorter than herself. Tenth, the wife of an old man. Eleventh, the wife of a very ugly man. Twelfth, a woman accustomed to stand in the doorway and to stare at passers by. Thirteenth, women of variable disposition. Fourteenth, the barren woman, especially if she and her husband desire the blessing of issue. Fifteenth, the woman who brags and boasts. Sixteenth, the woman who has long been separated from her husband and deprived of her natural refreshment. Seventeenth, the woman who has never learned the real delight of carnal copulation;[24] and, eighteenth, the woman whose mind remains girlish.

And now to describe the signs and symptoms by which we are to know when women are enamoured of us. Firstly, that woman loves a man when she is not ashamed of looking at him,[25] and of boldly and without fear or deference keeping her eyes fixed upon his. Secondly, when she moves her foot to and fro whilst standing up, and draws, as it were, lines upon the ground. Thirdly, when she scratches divers limbs without a sufficient reason. Fourthly, when she leers, looks obliquely, and casts side-glances. Fifthly, when she laughs causelessly at the sight of a man.

And furthermore, the woman who, instead of answering a straightforward question, replies by joking and jesting words; who slowly and deliberately follows us wherever we go; who under some pretext or other, dwells upon our faces or forms with a wistful and yearning glance; who delights in walking before us and displaying her legs or her bosom; who behaves to us with a mean and servile submission, ever praising and flatering; who contracts friendship with our friends and who is ever asking them, "In the house of such and such a person, are there any wives? Does he love them much? And are they very beautiful?" Who, looking towards us, sings a sweet air; who passes her hands frequently over her breasts and her arms; who cracks her fingers; who yawns and sighs when not expected to do so; who will never appear before us, though we call and summon her, unless in her most becoming dress; who throws flowers and similar articles upon us; who pretexting various things, often goes into and comes forth from the house; and finally, whose face, hands and feet break into perspiration when she casually sees us; that woman showing any such signs and symptoms, is enamoured of us, and is strongly excited by passion; all we have to do, if versed in the art of love, is to send an able go-between.

On the other hand, the following women are hard to be subdued:—First, the wife who is full of love for her husband. Second, the woman whose cold desires and contempt for congress keep her chaste. Third, the woman who is envious of another's prosperity and success. Fourth, the mother of many children. Fifth, a dutiful daughter or daughter-in-law. Sixth, a courteous and respectful woman. Seventh, a woman who fears and stands in awe of her parents and those of her husband. Eighth, a wealthy woman, who ever suspects and often wrongly, that we love her money better than herself. Ninth, a woman who is shy, bashful, and retiring in the presence of strangers. Tenth, an avaricious and covetuous woman. Eleventh, a woman who has no avarice or covetuousness. Such women are not easily secured, nor is it worth our while to waste our hours in pursuing them.

The following are the places where a woman should not be enjoyed:—First, the place where fire is lighted with the religious formula Agni-mukha and other Mantras. Second, in the presence of a Brahman or any other reverend man. Third, under the eyes of an aged person, to whom respect is due, as a Guru (spiritual guide), or a father. Further, when a great man is looking on. Fifth, by the side of a river or any murmuring stream. Sixth, at a Pánwatá, a place erected for drawing water from wells, tanks and so forth. Seventh, in a temple dedicated to the gods. Eighth, in a fort or castle. Ninth, in a guardroom, police-station, or in any government place where prisoners are confined. Tenth, on a highway. Eleventh, in a house of another person. Twelfth, in the forest. Thirteenth, in an open place, such as a meadow or an upland. Fourteenth, on ground where men are buried or burned. The consequences of carnal connection at such places are always disastrous; they breed misfortunes, and, if children be begotten, these turn out bad and malicious persons.

The following are the times when women are not to be enjoyed:—First, by day, unless their class and temperament require coition during the light hours. Second, during or at the Sankránti-parvaní, that is to say, when the sun or a planet passes from one side of the zodiac to another.[26] Third, during the Sharad, or cold season[27] (October to November.) Fourth, during the Grishma, or hot season[28] (June to July). Fifth, in the Amávásyá (the last, the thirtieth, or the new moon day of the Hindu month), unless the Love-shástra specify the contrary. Sixth, during the periods when the man's body suffers from fever. Seventh, during the time of a "Vrata," any self-imposed religious observance, with obligation to carry it out. Eighth, in the evening time; and ninth, when wearied with wayfare. The consequences of congress at such epochs are as disastrous as if the act took place in a prohibited spot.

The following is the situation which the wise men of old have described as being best fitted for sexual intercourse with women. Choose the largest, and finest, and the most airy room in the house; purify it thoroughly with whitewash, and decorate its spacious and beautiful walls with pictures and other objects upon which the eye may dwell with delight.[29] Scattered about this apartment place musical instruments, especially the pipe and the lute; with refreshments, as cocoa-nut, betel-leaf and milk, which is so useful for retaining and restoring vigour; bottles of rose water and various essences, fans and chauris for cooling the air, and books containing amorous songs, and gladdening the glance with illustrations of love-postures. Splendid Diválgiri, or wall lights, should gleam around the hall, reflected by a hundred mirrors, whilst both man and woman should contend against any reserve, or false shame, giving themselves up in complete nakedness to unrestrained voluptuousness, upon a high and handsome bedstead, raised on tall legs, furnished with many pillows, and covered by a rich chatra, or canopy; the sheets being besprinkled with flowers and the coverlet scented by burning luscious incense, such as aloes and other fragrant woods.[30] In such, a place, let the man, ascending the throne of love, enjoy the woman in ease and comfort, gratifying his and her every wish and every whim.

## CHAPTER NINE

# TREATING OF
# EXTERNAL ENJOYMENTS

By "external enjoyments" are meant the processes which should always precede internal enjoyment or coition. The wise have said that before congress, we must develope the desire of the weaker sex through certain perliminaries, which are many and various; such as the various embraces and kisses; the Nakhadána, or unguiculations; the Dashanas, or morsications; the Kesha-grahanas, or manipulating the hair, and other amorous blandishments. These affect the senses and divert the mind from coyness and coldness. After which tricks and toyings, the lover will proceed to take possession of the place.

There are eight A'linganas, or modes of embracing, which will here be enumerated and carefully described.[1]—

1. Vrikshádhirūdha is the embrace which simulates the climbing of a tree,[2] and it is done as follows:—When the husband stands up the wife should place one foot upon his foot,[3] and raise the other leg to the height of his thigh, against which she presses it. Then encircling his waist with her arms, even as a man prepares to swarm up a palm-trunk, she holds and presses him forcibly, bends her body over his, and kisses him as if sucking the water of life.

2. Tila-Tandula, the embrace which represents the mixture of sesamum-seed with husked rice (Tandul). The man and woman, standing in front of each other, should fold each other

to the bosom by closely encircling the waist. Then taking care to remain still, and by no means to move, they should approach the Linga to the Yoní, both being veiled by the dress, and avoid interrupting the contact for some time.

3. Lálátika, so called because forehead (lálata) touches forehead. In this position great endearment is shown by the close pressure of arms round the waist, both still standing upright, and by the contact of brow, cheek, and eyes, of mouth, breasts, and stomach.

4. Jághan-álingana, meaning "hips, loins, and thighs." In this embrace the husband sits[4] upon the carpet and the wife upon his thighs, embracing and kissing him with fond affection. In returning her fondling, her Lungaden, or petticoats, are raised, so that her Lungi, or undergarments, may come in contact with his clothes, and her hair is thrown into the dishevelled state symbolizing passion; or the husband, for variety's sake, may sit upon the wife's lap.

5. Viddhaka, when the nipples touch the opposite body. The husband sits still, closing his eyes, and the wife, placing herself close to him, should pass her right arm over his shoulder and apply her bosom to his, pressing him forcibly whilst he returns her embrace with equal warmth.

6. Urupagudha, so called from the use of the thighs. In this embrace both stand up, passing their arms round each other, and the husband places his wife's legs between his own so that the inside of his thighs may come in contact with the outside of hers. As in all cases, kissing must be kept up from time to time. This is a process peculiar to those who are greatly enamoured of each other.

7. Dughdanír-álingana, or the "milk and water embrace," also called "Kshíraníra," with the same signification. In this mode the husband lies upon the bed, resting on one side, right or left; the wife throws herself down near him with her face to

his, and closely embraces him, the members and limbs of both touching, and entangled, as it were, with the corresponding parts of the other. And thus they should remain until desire is thoroughly aroused in both.

8. Vallarí-vreshtita, or "embracing as the creeper twines about the tree," is performed as follows:—Whilst both are standing upright, the wife clings to her husband's waist, and passes her leg around his thigh, kissing him repeatedly and softly until he draws in his breath like one suffering from the cold. In fact, she must endeavour to imitate the vine enfolding the tree which supports it.

Here end the embracements; they should be closely studied, followed up by proper intelligence of the various modes of kisses, which must accompany and conclude the A'linganas. And understand at once that there are seven places highly proper for osculation, in fact, where all the world kisses. These are—First, the lower lip. Second, both the eyes. Third, both the cheeks. Fourth, the head.[5] Fifth, the mouth. Sixth, both breasts; and seventh, the shoulders. It is true that the people of certain countries have other places, which they think proper to kiss; for instance, the voluptaries of Sáta-desha have adopted the following formula:—

But this is far from being customary with the men of our country or of the world in general.

Furthermore, there are ten different kinds of kisses, each of which has its own and proper name, and these will be described in due order.

1. Milita-kissing, which means "mishrita," mixing or reconciling. If the wife be angry, no matter however little, she will not kiss the face of her husband; the latter then should forcibly fix his lips upon hers and keep both mouths united till her ill-temper passes away.

2. Sphurita-kissing, which is connected with twitching and vellication. The wife should approach her mouth to that of her husband's, who then kisses her lower lip, whilst she draws it away, jerking, as it were, without any return of osculation.

3. Ghatika, or neck-nape kissing, a term frequently used by the poets. This is done by the wife, who, excited with passion, covers her husband's eyes with her hands, and closing her own eyes, thrusts her tongue into his mouth, moving it to and fro with a motion so pleasant and slow that it at once suggests another and a higher form of enjoyment.

4. Tiryak, or oblique kissing. In this form the husband, standing behind or at the side of his wife, places his hand beneath her chin, catches hold of it and raises it, until he has made her face look up to the sky;[6] then he takes her lower lip beneath his teeth, gently biting and chewing it.

5. Uttaroshtha, or "upper-lip-kissing." When the wife is full of desire, she should take her husband's lower lip between her teeth, chewing and biting it gently; whilst he does the same to her upper lip. In this way both excite themselves to th height of passion.

6. Pindita, or "lump-kissing." The wife takes hold of her husband's lips with her fingers, passes her tongue over them and bites them.

7. Samputa, or "casket-kissing." In this form the husband kisses the inside mouth of his wife, whilst she does the same to him.

8. Hanuvatra-kissing.[7] In this mode the kiss should not be given at once, but begin with moving the lips towards one another in an irritating way, with freaks, pranks, and frolics.

After toying together for some time, the mouths should be advanced, and the kiss exchanged.

9. Pratibodha, or "awakening kiss." When the husband, who has been absent for some time, returns home and finds his wife sleeping upon the carpet in a solitary bedroom, he fixes his lips upon hers, gradually increasing the pressure until such time as she awakes. This is by far the most agreeable form of osculation, and it leaves the most pleasant of memories.

10. Samaushtha-kissing. This is done by the wife taking her husband's mouth and lips into hers, pressing them with her tongue, and dancing about him as she does so.

Here end the sundry forms of kisses. And now must be described the various ways of Nakhadána, that is, of titillating and scratching with the nails. As it will not be understood what places are properest for this kind of dalliance, it should be explained as a preliminary that there are eleven parts upon which pressure may be exerted with more or less force. These are:—First, the neck. Second, the hands. Third, both thighs. Fourth, both breasts. Fifth, the back. Sixth, the sides. Seventh, both axillæ. Eighth, the whole chest or bosom. Ninth, both hips. Tenth, the Mons Veneris and all the parts about the Yoní; and, eleventh, both the cheeks.

Furthermore, it is necessary to learn the times and seasons when this style of manipulation is advisable. These are:—First, when there is anger in the mind of the woman. Second, at the time of first enjoying her or of taking her virginity. Third, when going to separate for a short time. Fourth, when about journeying to a foreign and distant country. Fifth, when a great pecuniary loss has been sustained. Sixth, when excited with desire of congress; and, seventh, at the season of Virati, that is to say, when there is no Rati, or furor venereus.[8] At such times the nails should be applied to the proper places.

The nails, when in good condition and properest for use, are without spots[9] and lines, clean, bright, convex,[10] hard, and unbroken. Wise men have given in the Shastras these six qualities of the nails.

There are seven different ways of applying the nails, which may be remembered by the following Mandalaka or oblong formula:—

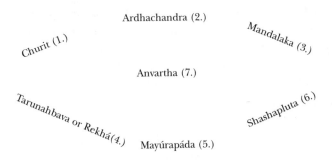

Ardhachandra (2.)

Mandalaka (3.)

Churit (1.)

Anvartha (7.)

Tarunahbava or Rekhá (4.)

Shashapluta (6.)

Mayúrapáda (5.)

1. Churit-nakhadána is setting the nails in such a way upon the cheeks, lower lip and breasts, without leaving any marks, but causing horripilation, till the woman's body-hair bristles up, and a shudder passes all over the limbs.[11]

2. Ardhachandra-nakhadána is effected by impressing with the nails upon the neck and breasts a curved mark, which resembles a half-moon (Ardha-chandra).

3. Mandalaka is applying the nails to the face for some time, and indeed until a sign is left upon it.

4. Tarunabhava or Rekhá (a line) is the name given by men conversant with the Kámashastra to nail-marks longer than two or three finger-breadths on the woman's head, thighs and breasts.

5. The Mayŭrapáda ("peacock's foot" or claw) Is made by placing the thumb upon the nipple, and the four fingers upon the breast adjacent, at the same time pressing the nails till the

mark resembles the trail of the peacock, which he leaves when walking upon mud.

6 Shasha-pluta, or the "hopping of a hare," is the mark made upon the darker part of the breast when no other portion is affected.

7. Anvartha-nakhadána is a name applied to the three deep marks or scratches made by the nails of the first three fingers on the back, the breasts and the parts about the Yoní. This Nakhadána or unguiculation is highly proper when going abroad to a distant country, as it serves for a keepsake and a token of remembrance.

The voluptuary, by applying the nails as above directed with love and affection, and driven wild by the fury of passion, affords the greatest comfort to the sexual desires of the woman; in fact, there is nothing, perhaps, which is more delightful to both husband and wife than the skilful use of unguiculation.

Furthermore, it is advisable to master the proper mode of morsication or biting. It is said by persons who are absorbed in the study of sexual intercourse, that the teeth should be used to the same places where the nails are applied with the exception, however, of the eyes, the upper lip, and the tongue. Moreover, the teeth should be pressed until such time as the woman begins to exclaim, Hu! hu![12] after which enough has been done.

The teeth to be preferred in the husband, are those whose colour is somewhat rosy,[13] and not of a dead white; which are bright and clean, strong, pointed and short, and which form close and regular rows. On the other hand, those are bad which are dingy and unclean, narrow, long, and projecting forward, as though they would leave the mouth.[14]

Like the unguiculations, there are seven different Dashanas or ways of applying the teeth, which may be remembered by the following Mandalaka or oblong formula:[15]

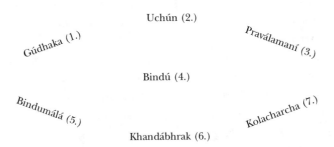

Uchún (2.)

Gúdhaka (1.)

Praválamaní (3.)

Bindú (4.)

Bindumálá (5.)

Kolacharcha (7.)

Khandábhrak (6.)

1. Gŭdhaka-dashana, or "secret-biting," is applying the teeth only to the inner or red part[16] of the woman's lip, leaving no outside mark so as to be seen by the world.

2. Uchŭn-dashana, the wise tell us, is the word applied to biting any part of a woman's lips or cheeks.

3. Praválamaní-dashana, or "coral-biting," is that wonderful union of the man's tooth and the woman's lips, which converts desire into a burning flame; it cannot be described, and is to be accomplished only by long experience, not by the short practice of a few days.

4. Bindu-dashana ("dot" or "drop-biting") is the mark left by the husband's two front teeth upon the woman's lower lip, or upon the place where the Tillá or brow-mark is worn.

5. Bindu-málá, a "rosary," or "row of dots" or "drops," Is the same as the preceding, except that all the front teeth are applied, so as to form a regular line of marks.

6. Khandábhrak is the cluster or multitude of impressions made by the prints of the husband's teeth upon the brow and cheek, the neck and breast of the wife. If disposed over the body like the Mandalaka, or Dashanágramandal, the mouth-shaped oblong traced above, it will add greatly to her beauty.

7. Kolacharcha is the name given by the wise to the deep and lasting marks of his teeth which the husband, in the heat of passion, and in the grief of departure when going to a foreign

land, leaves upon the body of his wife. After his disappearance, she will look at them, and will frequently remember him with yearning heart.

So far for the styles of morsication. And now it is advisable to study the different fashions of Keshagrahana, or manipulating the hair, which, upon a woman's head, should be soft, close, thick, black, and wavy, nor curled, nor straight.

One of the best ways of kindling hot desire in a woman is, at the time of rising, softly to hold and handle the hair, according to the manner of doing so laid down in the Kamashastra.

The Keshagrahana are of four kinds, which may be remembered by the

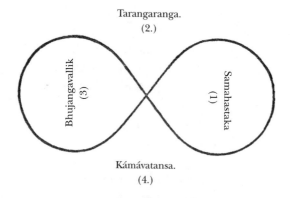

Tarangaranga.
(2.)

Bhujangavallik
(3)

Samahastaka
(1)

Kámávatansa.
(4.)

1. Samahastakakeshagrahana, or "holding the hair with both hands," is when the husband encloses it between his two palms behind his wife's head, at the same time kissing her lower lip.

2. Tarangarangakeshagrahana, or "kissing the hair in wavy (or sinuous) fashion," is when the husband draws his wife towards him by the back hair, and kisses her at the same time.

3. Bhujangavallika, or the "dragon's turn,"[17] is when the husband, excited by the approaching prospect of sexual congress amorously seizes the hind knot of his wife's hair, at the same time

closely embracing her. This is done in a standing position, and the legs should be crossed with one another. It is one of the most exciting of all toyings.

4. Kámávatansakeshagrahana, or "holding the crest-hair of love,"[18] is when, during the act of copulation, the husband holds with both hands his wife's hair above her ears, whilst she does the same thing to him, and both exchange frequent kisses upon the mouth.

Such, then, are the external enjoyments described in the due order according to which they ought to be practised. Those only are mentioned which are well known to, and are highly appreciated by the world. There are many others by no means so popular, and these are omitted, lest this treatise become an unwieldly size.[19] The following may, however, be mentioned:—

The blandishments of love are a manner of battle, in which the stronger wins the day. And in order to assist us in the struggle, there are two forms of attack, known as Karatádana and Sitkreutoddesha.

Karatádana, as the word denotes,[20] are soft tappings and pattings with the hand, by the husband or the wife, upon certain members of each other's persons. And in this process there are four divisions, which the man applies to the woman:—

1. Prasritahasta, or patting with the open, palm.

2. Uttányahasta, the same reversed; done with the back of the hand.

3. Mushti, or striking gently with the lower or fleshy part of the closed hand; softly hammering, as it were.

4. Sampátahasta, or patting with the inner part of the hand, which is slightly hollowed for the purpose, like the cobra's hood.

And here may be specified the several members that should thus be operated upon. First, the flesh below the ribs, with No. 1. Second the Mons Veneris and vicinity of the Yoní; also with

No. 1. Third, the bosom and breasts, with No. 2. Fourth, the back and hip, with No, 3. Fifth, the head with No. 4.

There are also four corresponding divisions of the practices used by the woman to the man:—

1. Santánika, a name given by learned men to the act of a wife gently patting with the closed fist her husband's breast, when the two have become one, so as to increase his pleasure.

2. Patáká is when the wife, also during congress, pats her husband gently with the open hand.

3. Bindumálá is the name given only by men when the wife, at the time of coition, fillips her husband's body with the thumbs only.

4. Kundalá is the name given by the older poets when the wife, during copulation, fillips her husband's body with thumb and fore-finger, not with the rest of the hand.

And now of the Sítkrití, or inarticulate sound produced by drawing in the breath between the closed teeth; these are the peculiar privilege and prerogative of women, and the wise divide them into five kinds:—

1. Hinkrití is the deep and grave sound, like "Hun! hun! hun!" "Hin! hin! bin!"[21] produced in the nose and mouth with the slightest use of the former member.

2. Stanita is the low rumbling, like distant thunder, expressed by "Ha! ha!" or by "Hán! hán! hán!" produced by the throat without the concurrence of the nasal muscles.

3. Sítkrití is the expiration or emission of breath, like the hissing of a serpent, expressed by "Shan! shan!" or "Shish! shish!" and produced only in the mouth.

4. Utkriti is the crackling sound, resembling the splitting of a bamboo, expressed by "T'hat! t'hat!" and formed by applying the tongue-tip to the palate,[22] and by moving it as rapidly as possible, at the same time pronouncing the interjection.

5. Bhavakriti is a rattling sound, like the fall of heavy rain-drops, expressed by "T'hap! t'hap!" produced by the lips; but it can be produced only at the time of congress.

These several Sítkritís in the woman's mouth at the moment of enjoyment, will respectively resemble the cry of the quail (Láva), of the Indian cuckoo (Kokila), of the spotted-necked pigeon (Kapota), of the Hansa-goose and of the peacock. The sounds should especially be produced when the husband kisses, bites, and chews his wife's lower lip; and the sweetness of the uterance greatly adds to enjoyment, and promotes the congress of the sexual act.

Furthermore, be it known to men the peculiar characteristics of the Ashtamahánáyika, or the eight great forms of Nayiká:[23]—

1. Khanditanáyiká, when the husband bears upon his body all the marks of sexual enjoyment, produced by sleeping with a rival wife; and when, with eyes reddened by keeping late hours, he returns to his beloved struck with fear and in an agitated state, coaxing her, and speaking sweet words, for the purpose of sueing her to congress, and she half listens to him, but yields at last. Such is the name given to her by the great poets of the olden time.

2. Vásakasajjitá is the word applied by the learned to the wife, who, having spread a soft, fine bed, in a charming apartment, sits upon it at night-time, and awaits her husband, with great expecta-tion, now half closing her eyes, then fixing her glance on the door.

3. Kalakántaritá, say the wise men, is the term for a wife, who when her husband, after grossly injuring her, falls at her feet and begs for pardon, answers loudly and in great wrath, drives him from her presence, and determines not to see him again; but presently, waxing repentant, laments in various ways the pains and sorrows of separation, and at last recovers quietude by the hope of reunion.

4. Abhisáriká is the woman whose sexual passions being in a state of overflowing, dresses herself, and goes forth shamelessly, and wantonly at night-time to the house of some strange man, in the hope of carnal copulation with him.

5. Vipralabdhá is the disappointed woman, who, having sent a go-between to some strange man, appointing him to meet her at a certain place, repairs there, confused and agitated with the prospect of congress, but sees the go-between returning alone, and without the lover, which throws her into a state of fever.

6 Viyogini is the melancholy woman, who, during the absence of her husband in a far country, smells the fragrant and exciting perfumes[24] of sandal-wood, and other odorous substances, and looking upon the lotus-flower and the moon-light, falls into a passion of grief.

7. Svádhinapúrvapatiká is the name given to the wife whose husband instead of gratifying her amorous desires, and studying her carnal wants, engages in the pursuit of philosophic knowledge derived from meditation.

8. Utkanthitá, according to the best poets, is the woman who loves her husband very dearly, whose eyes are light and lively, who has decorated herself with jewels and garlands, well knowing the wishes of her man, and who, burning with desire, awaits his coming, propped up with pillows in a sleeping-apartment appropriated to pleasure, and sumptuously adorned with mirrors and pictures.[25]

## CHAPTER TEN

# TREATING OF INTERNAL ENJOYMENTS
# IN ITS VARIOUS FORMS

By "internal enjoyment" is meant the art of congress which follows the various external preliminaries described in the last chapter. These embraces, kisses and sundry manipulations, must always be practised according to the taste of husband and wife, and if persisted in as the Shastra directs, they will excessively excite the passions of the woman, and will soften and loosen her Yoní so as to be ready for carnal connection.

The following verses show how much art and science there is in a matter which appears so simple to the uneducated and vulgar.

"What is the remedy when a woman is mightier than a man? Although she be very strong, yet no sooner are her legs placed wide apart, than she loses her force of passion, and is satisfied."

"Thus the Yoní from being tight and compact, becomes slack and loose; let the husband, therefore, press her thighs together, and she will be equally able to struggle with him at the time of congress."

"Well, if a woman be only twelve or thirteen years old, and the man is quite grown up, and has lost the first vigour of his youth, what must be done to make them equal?"

"In such a case, the legs of the woman must be stretched out to the fullest extent, so as to weaken the powers, and by these means the man will prove himself her equal."

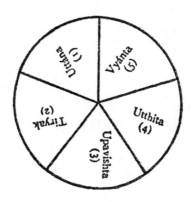

There are five main Bandha or A'sana—forms or postures of congress—which appear in the following shape, and each

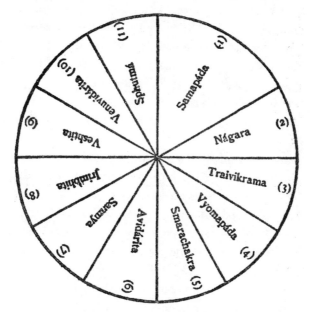

of these will require its own description successively, and in due order.[1]

(A) Uttána-bandha (*i. e.*, supine posture) is the great division so-called by men well versed in the art of Love, when a woman lies upon her back, and her husband sits close to her upon his hams. But is this all that can be said of it? No! no! there are eleven subdivisions, as shown in fee following table:—

And now of the several sub-divisions:—

1. Samapáda-ŭttána-bandha, is when the husband places his wife upon her back, raises both her legs, and placing them upon his shoulders, sits close to her and enjoys her.

2. Nágara-ŭttána-bandha, is when the husband places his wife upon her back, sits between her legs, raises them both, keeping them on the other side of his waist, and thus enjoys her.

3. Traivikrama-ŭttána-bandha, is when one of the wife's legs is left lying upon the bed or carpet, the other being placed upon the head of the husband, who supports himself upon both hands. This position is very admirable.

4. Vyomapáda-ŭttána-bandha, is when the wife, lying upon her back, raises with her hands both legs, drawing them as far back as her hair; the husband, then sitting close to her, places both hands upon her breasts and enjoys her.

5. Smarachakrásana, or the position of the Kama's wheel, a mode very much enjoyed by the voluptuary. In this form, the husband sits between the legs of his wife, extends his arms on both sides of her as far as he can, and thus enjoys her.

6. Avidárita is that position when the wife raises both her legs, so that they may touch the bosom of her husband, who, sitting between her thighs, embraces and enjoys her.

7. Saumya-bandha is the name given by the old poets to a form of congress much in vogue amongst the artful students of the Kámashastra. The wife lies supine, and the husband, as usual, sits;[2] he places both hands under her back, closely embracing her, which she returns by tightly grasping his neck.

8. Jrimbhita-ásana. In order to bend the wife's body in the form of a bow, the husband places little pillows or pads beneath her hips and head, he then raises the seat of pleasure and rises to it by kneeling upon a cushion. This is an admirable form of congress, and is greatly enjoyed by both.

9. Veshtita-ásana, is when the wife lies upon her back cross legged,[3] and raises her feet a little; this position is very well fitted for those burning with desire.

10. Venuvidárita is that in which the wife, lying upon her back, places one leg upon her husband's shoulder, and the other on the bed or carpet.

11. Sphutmá-úttána-bandha is when the husband, after insertion and penetration, raises the legs of his wife, who still lies upon her back, and joins her thighs closely together.

Here end the eleven forms of Uttána-bandha; we now proceed to the:—

(B) Tiryak (*i. e.,* aslant, awry posture) whose essence consists of the woman lying upon her side. Of this division, there are three sub-divisions:—

1. Vínaka-tiryak-bandha is when the husband, placing himself alongside of his wife, raises one of his legs over his hip and leaves the other lying upon the bed or carpet. This A'sana (position) is fitted only for practice upon a grown-up woman; in the case of a younger person, the result is by no means satisfactory.

2. Samputa-tiryak-bandha is when both man and woman lie straight upon their sides, without any movement or change in the position of their limbs.

3. Karkata-tiryak-bandha is when both being upon their sides, the husband lies between his wife's thighs, one under him, and the other being thrown over his flank, a little below the breast.

Here end the three forms of the Tiryak-bandha; and, we now proceed to the:—

(C) Upavishta (*i. e.,* sitting) posture. Of this division there are ten sub-divisions shown in the following figure:

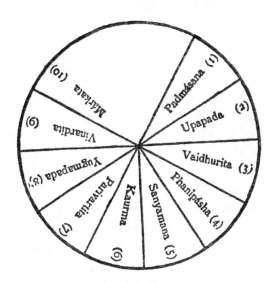

1. Padm-ásana. The husband in this favourite position sits crossed-legged upon the bed or carpet, and takes his wife upon his lap, placing his hands upon her shoulders.

2. Upapad-ásana. In this posture, whilst both are sitting, the woman slightly raises one leg by placing the hand under it, and the husband enjoys her.

3. Vaidhurit-ásana. The husband embraces his wife's neck very closely, and she does the same to him.

4. Phanipásh-ásana. The husband holds his wife's feet, and the wife those of her husband.

5. Sanyaman-ásana. The husband passes both legs of his wife under his arms at the elbow, and holds her neck with his hands.

6. Kaurmak-ásana (or the tortoise posture). The husband must so sit that his mouth, arms, and legs, touch the corresponding members of his wife.

7. Parivartit-ásana. In addition to the mutual contact of mouth, arms, and legs, the husband must frequently pass both the legs of his wife under his arms at the elbow.

8. Yugmapad-ásana is a name given by the best poets to that position in which the husband sits with his legs wide apart, and, after insertion and penetration, presses the thighs of his wife together.

9. Vinarditásana, a form possible only to a very strong man with a very light woman, he raises her by passing both her legs over his arms at the elbow, and moves her about from left to right, but not backwards or forwards, till the supreme moment arrives.

10. Márkatásana, is the same position as No. 9; in this, however, the husband moves the wife in a straight line away from his face, that is, backwards and forwards, but not from side to side.

Here end the forms of Upavishta, or sitting-posture. The next is:—

(D) Utthita, or the standing posture, which admits of three sub-divisions:—

1. Jánu-kŭru-utthitha-bandha (that is, "knee and elbow standing-form,") a posture which also requires great bodily strength in the man. Both stand opposite to each other, and the husband passes' his two arms under his wife's knees, supporting her upon the *saignée*, or inner elbow; he then raises her as high as his waist, and enjoys her, whilst she must clasp his neck with both her hands.

2. Hari-vikrama-utthita-bandha: in this form the husband raises only one leg of his wife, who with the other stands upon the ground. It is a position delightful to young women, who thereby soon find themselves *in gloriâ*.

3. Kírti-utthita-bandha: this requires strength in the man, but not so much as is wanted for the first subdivision. The wife, clasping her hands and placing her legs round her husband's

waist, hangs, as it were, to him, whilst he supports her by placing his fore-arms under her hips.

Here end the forms of Utthita, or standing-posture; and we now come to the:—

(E) Vyánta-bandha, which means congress with a woman when she is prone, that is, with the breast and stomach to the bed or carpet. Of this A'sana, there are only two well-known sub-divisions:—

1. Dhenuka-vyánta-bandha (the cow-posture[4]): in this position the wife places herself upon all fours, supported on her hands and feet (not her knees), and the husband, approaching from behind, falls upon her waist, and enjoys her as if he were a bull. There is much religious merit in this form.

2. Aybha-vyánta-bandha (or Gajásawa, the elephant posture[5]). The wife lies down in such a position that her face, breast; stomach, and thighs all touch the bed or carpet, and the husband, extending himself upon her, and bending himself like an elephant, with the small of the back much drawn in, works underneath her, and effects insertion.

"O Rajah," said the arch-poet Kalyâna-Malla, "there are many other forms of congress, such as Harinásana, Sukrásana, Gardhabásana, and so forth; but they are not known to the people, and being useless as well as very difficult of performance, nay, sometimes so full of faults as to be excluded or prohibited, I have, therefore, not related them to you. But if you desire to hear anything more about postures, be pleased to ask, and your servant will attempt to satisfy your curiosity."

"Right well!" exclaimed the king. "I much wish to hear you describe the Purŭsháyitabandha."

"Hear, O Rajah," resumed the poet, "whilst I relate all that requires to be known concerning that form of congress."

Purŭsháyitabandha[6] is the reverse of what men usually practise. In this case the man lies upon his back, draws his wife upon him and enjoys her. It is especially useful when he, being exhausted, is no longer capable of muscular exertion, and when she is ungratified, being still full of the water of love. The wife must, therefore, place her husband supine upon the bed or carpet, mount upon his person, and satisfy her desires. Of this form of congress there are three sub-divisions:—

1. Viparíta-bandha, or "contrary postition," is when the wife lies straight upon the outstretched person of her husband, her breast being applied to his bosom, presses his waist with her hands, and moving her hips sharply in various directions, enjoys him.

2. Purŭsháyita-bhramara-bandha ("like the large bee"): in this, the wife, having placed her husband at full length upon the bed or carpet, sits at squat upon his thighs, closes her legs firmly after she has effected insertion; and, moving her waist in a circular form, churning, as it were, enjoys her husband, and thoroughly satisfies herself.

3. Utthita-uttána-bandha. The wife, whose passion has not been gratified by previous copulation, should make her husband lie upon his back, and sitting cross-legged upon his thighs, should seize his Linga, effect insertion, and move her waist up and down, advancing and retiring; she will derive great comfort from this process.

Whilst thus reversing the natural order in all these forms of Purŭsháyita, the wife will draw in her breath after the fashion called Sitkâra; she will smile gently, and she will show a kind of half shame, making her face so attractive that it cannot well be described. After which she will say to her husband, "O my dear! O thou rogue; this day thou hast come under my control, and hast become subjected to me, being totally defeated in the battle of love!" Her husband manipulates her hair according to art, embraces her and kisses her lower lip; whereupon all her members will relax, she will close her eyes and fall into a swoon of joy.

Moreover, at all times of enjoying Purŭsháyita the wife will remember that without an especial exertion of will on her part, the husband's pleasure will not be perfect. To this end she must ever strive to close and constrict the Yoní until it holds the Linga, as, with a finger,[7] opening and shutting at her pleasure, and finally, acting as the hand of the Gopâla-girl, who milks the cow. This can be learned only by long practice, and especially by throwing the will into the part to be affected, even as men endeavour to sharpen their hearing,[8] and their sense of touch. While so doing, she will mentally repeat" Kámadeva! Kámadeva," in order that a blessing may rest upon the undertaking. And she will be pleased to hear that the act once learned, is never lost. Her husband will then value her above all women, nor would he exchange her for the most beautiful Pâní (queen) in the three worlds. So lovely and pleasant to man is she who constricts.

Let it now be observed that there are sundry kinds and conditions of women whom the wise peremptorily exclude from Purŭsháyita, and the principal exceptions will here be mentioned. First, the Karíní-woman. Second, the Haríní. Third, she who is pregnant. Fourth, she who has not long left the lying-in chamber. Fifth, a woman of thin and lean body, because the exertion will be too great for her strength. Sixth, a woman suffering from fever or other weakening complaint. Seventh, a virgin; and, eighth, a girl not yet arrived at puberty.

And now having duly concluded the chapter of internal enjoyments, it is good to know that if husband and wife live together in close agreement, as one soul in a single body, they shall be happy in this world, and in that to come. Their good and charitable actions will be an example to mankind, and their peace and harmony will effect their salvation. No one yet has written a book to prevent the separation of the married pair and to show them how they may pass through life in union. Seeing this, I felt compassion, and composed the treatise, offering it to the god Pandurang.

The chief reason for the separation between the married couple and the cause, which drives the husband to the embraces of strange women, and the wife to the arms of strange men, is the want of varied pleasures and the monotony which follows possession. There is no doubt about it. Monotony begets satiety, and satiety distaste for congress, especially in one or the other; malicious feelings are engendered, the husband or the wife yield to temptation, and the other follows, being driven by jealousy. For it seldom happens that the two love each other equally, and in exact proportion, therefore is the one more easily seduced by passion than the other. From such separations result polygamy, adulteries, abortions, and every manner of vice, and not only do the erring husband and wife fall into the pit, but they also drag down the names of their deceased ancestors from the place of beautified mortals, either to hell or back again upon this world. Fully understanding the way in which such quarrels arise, I have in this book shown how the husband, by varying the enjoyment of his wife, may live with her as with thirty-two different women, ever varying the enjoyment of her, and rendering satiety impossible. I have also taught all manner of useful arts and mysteries, by which she may render herself pure, beautiful and pleasing in his eyes. Let me, therefore, conclude with the verse of blessing:—

"May this treatise, "Ananga-ranga," be beloved of man and woman, as long as the Holy River Ganges springeth from Shiva, with his wife Gauri on his left side; as long as Lakshmí loveth Vishnŭ; as long as Bramhá is engaged in the study of the Vedas; and as long as the earth, the moon and the sun endure."

FINIS.

# APPENDIX I[1]

## ASTROLOGY IN CONNECTION WITH MARRIAGE.

NOW IS RELATED THE EFFECT RESULTING FROM THE CONSONANCE and dissonance, amity and hospitality, between the stars (and destinies) of a couple proposed to be bride and bridegroom.[2] Having ascertained that the houses (*kula*), the family names (*gotra*), and the individual dispositions (*svabháva*), of the postulants are free from inherent blemish,[3] their Gunas (qualities or requisites) must be determined from the zodiacal signs and the asterisms presiding over their birth.[4]

The Gunas, number in total thirty-six, of which at least nineteen are requisite for a prosperous match; and thence upwards, the fruit resulting from their influence is proportioned to their number.

Observations upon these subjects will be facilitated by the three following tables:—

Table I. shows the presiding planet, the genus (or nature) and the caste (in theory not in practice) of the questioner, when the zodiacal sign of his birth-time is known, for instance, if Sol be in Aries at the birth of the patient, his planet is Mars; he belongs to the genus quadruped, and he is by caste a Kshatriya or fighting-man.

## TABLE I.

| Zodiacal Sign. | Presiding Planet | Genus | Caste |
|---|---|---|---|
| Aries | Mars | Quadruped | Kshatriya |
| Taurus | Venus | Quadruped | Vaishya |
| Gemini | Mercury | Human | Shudra |
| Cancer | Moon | Insect | Brahman |
| Leo | Sun | Quadruped | Kshatriya |
| Virgo | Mercury | Human | Vaishya |
| Libra | Venus | Human | Shudra |
| Scorpio | Mars | Insect | Brahman |
| Sagittarius | Jupiter | Man-horse | Kshatriya |
| Capricornus | Saturn | Water-man | Vaishya |
| Aquarius | Saturn | Human | Shudra |
| Pisces | Jupiter | Aquatic animal | Brahman |

Table II. shows the number of Guna, or qualities, requisite for a prosperous match, distributed under eight heads:—

TABLE II.

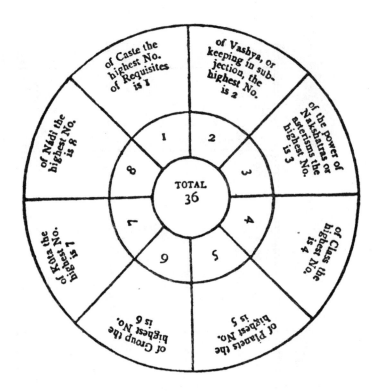

Table III. shows the group and class to which a person belongs when the asterism (Nakshatra, or lunar mansion) of his birth-time is known, together with his Nádi, or hour of twenty-four minutes. The twenty-seven asterisms are classed under three heads; of gods, of men and of demons (Rakshasas), and the asterism determines to which the querent belongs. Moreover, each asterism is divided in four quarters, and of these nine make one zodiacal sign. The name-letter used in that quarter stands for that quarter.

## TABLE III.

| Asterism (Nakshatra). | Group. | Class. | Nadi. Hour of 24 m. | Quarters of Asterisms, showing changes of the Zodiacal signs. 1 | 2 | 3 | 4 |
|---|---|---|---|---|---|---|---|
| Ashviní | God | Horse | First | Cha, 1, i. e. Aries | Che, 1, i. e. do. | Cho, 1, i. e. do. | Lá, 1, i. e. do. |
| Bharaní | Man | Elephant | Middle | Li, 1, i. e. do. | Lu, 1, i. e. do. | Le, 1, i. e. do. | Lo, 1, i. e. do. |
| Krittiká | Demon | Ram | Last | A, 1. i. e. do. | I, 2, i. e. Taurus | U', 2, i. e. do. | Ve, 2, i. e. do. |
| Rohiní | Man | Serpent | Last | O, 2, i. e. do. | Vá, 2, i. e. do. | Vi, 2, i. e. do. | Vu, 2, i. e. do. |
| Mriga | God | Serpent | Middle | Ve, 2, i. e. do. | Vo, 2, i. e. do. | Ká, 3, i. e. Gemini | Ki, 3, i. e. do. |
| Ardrá | Man | Dog | First | Ku, 3, i. e. do. | Gha, 3, i. e. do. | Na, 3, i. e. do. | Chha, 3, i. e. do. |
| Punarvasu | God | Cat | First | Ke, 3, i. e. do. | Ko, 3, i. e. do. | Ha, 3, i. e. do. | Hi, 4, i. e. Cancer |
| Pushya | God | Ram | Middle | Hu, 4, i. e. do. | He, 4, i. e. do. | Ho, 4, i. e. do. | Da, 4, i. e. do. |
| A'shleshá | Demon | Cat | Last | Di, 4, i. e. do. | Du, 4, i. e. do. | De, 4, i. e. do. | Do, 4, i. e. do. |
| Maghá | Demon | Mouse | Last | Ma, 5, i. e. Leo | Mi, 5, i. e. do. | Mu, 5, i. e. do. | Me, 5, i. e. do. |
| Purvá | Man | Mouse | Middle | Mo, 5, i. e. do. | Tá, 5, i. e. do. | Ti, 5, i. e. do. | Tu, 5, i. e. do. |
| Uttará | Man | Cow | First | Te, 5, i. e. do. | To, 6, i. e. Virgo | Pa, 6, i. e. do. | Pi, 6, i. e. do. |
| Hasta | God | Buffalo | First | Pu, 6, i. e. do. | Shá, 6, i. e. do. | Ná, 6, i. e. do. | Dhá, i. e. do. |

TABLE III.—*continued*

| Asterism (Nakshatra). | Group. | Class. | Nadi. Hour of 24 m. | Quarters of Asterisms, showing changes of the Zodiacal signs. | | | |
|---|---|---|---|---|---|---|---|
| | | | | 1 | 2 | 3 | 4 |
| Chitrá | Demon | Tiger | Middle | Pe, 6, i. e. do. | Po, 6, i. e. do. | Rá, 7, i. e. Libra | Ri, 7, i. e. do. |
| Svátí | God | Buffalo | Last | Ru, 7, i. e. do. | Re, 7, i. e. do. | Ro, 7, i. e. do. | La, 7, i. e. do. |
| Vishákhá | Demon | Tiger | Last | Zi, 7, i. e. do. | Zu, 7, i. e. do. | Ze, 7, i. e. do. | Zo, 8, i. e. Scorpio |
| Anurádhá | God | Deer | Middle | Ná, 8, i. e. do. | Ni, 8, i. e. do. | Nu, 8, i. e. do. | Ne, 8, i. e. do. |
| Jyeshthá | Demon | Deer | First | No, 8, i. e. do. | Yá, 8, i. e. do. | Yi, 8, i. e. do. | Tu, 8, i. e. do. |
| Múla | Demon | Dog | First | Ye, 9, i. e. Sagittarius | Yo, 9, i. e. do. | Bhá, 9, i. e. do. | Bhi, 9, i. e. do. |
| Purváshádhá | Man | Monkey | Middle | Bhu, 9, i. e. do. | Dha, 9, i. e. do. | Phá, 9, i. e. do. | Dhá, 9, i. e. do. |
| Uttaráshádhá | Man | Ichneumon | Last | Bhe, 9, i. e. do. | Bho, 10, i. e. Capricornus | Ga, 10, i. e. do. | Gí, 10, i. e. do. |
| Shravana | God | Monkey | Last | Khi, 10, i. e. do. | Khu, 10, i. e. do. | Khe, 10, i. e. do. | Kho, 10, i. e. do. |
| Dhanishthá | Demon | Lion | Middle | Gá, 10, i. e. do. | Gi, 10, i. e. do. | Gu, 11, i. e. Aquarius | Ge, 11, i. e. do. |
| Shatatáraká | Demon | Horse | First | Go, 11, i. e. do. | Sá, 11, i. e. do. | Si, 11, i. e. do. | Su, 11, i. e. do. |
| Purvábhádrapada | Man | Lion | First | Se, 11, i. e. do. | So, 11, i. e. do. | Dá, 11, i. e. do. | Di, 12, i. e. Pisces |
| Uttarábhádrapadá | Man | Cow | Middle | Du, 12, i. e. do. | Zam, 12, i. e. do. | N, 12, i. e. do. | Yo, 12, i. e. do. |
| Retatí | God | Elephant | Last | Do, 12, i. e. do. | Do, 12, i. e. do. | Chá, 12, i. e. do. | Chi, 12, i. e. do. |

And now to consider the tables more carefully. As is shown by No. II. the Gunas are of various values, and are distributed under eight heads.

1. Caste. If both be of the same, or the caste of the bridegroom be higher, there is one Guna (of the thirty-six) otherwise there is none.

2. Vashya, or keeping in subjection, one of the prime considerations of marriage. If the zodiacal signs of the bride and bridegroom be of the same genus (Table I.) this represents two Gunas. If the person kept in subjection be also the "food" of the other, this counts for only one-half (Guna). If there be natural friendship between the genera of the bride and bridegroom this stands for two Gunas; and if one be an enemy to the other, and also keep the other in subjection, it represents only one Guna. The consideration is as follows:—To the human genus every quadruped, saving only the lion, remains in supbjection; for instance, the quadruped ram is subject to, and is the "food" of the human genus, with no exception except the Brahman. The same is the case with the fish and the crab amongst lower animals. The scorpion is the general enemy to the human race, and other animals are enemies as well as food. Thus we discover which of the two persons will hold the other in subjection.

3. The Nakshatras (Table III.) must be considered as follows:— The bride's asterism should be counted from that of the bridegroom, and the number be divided by nine. If the remainder be three, five or seven, it is a sign of bad fortune; and *vice versâ* with all others. Similarly the bridegroom's lunation should be counted from the bride's; and if, after dividing as before by nine, the remainders of both parties indicate good fortune, this counts as three Gunas, the maximum. Only if one portend well, it counts as one Guna and a-half: otherwise there is no Guna.

4. Class. Perfect friendship counts for four Gunas; common friendship as three, indifference as two; enmity as one, an exceeding enmity as half a Guna. Perfect friendship can subsist only between two human beings of the same caste. Cows and buffalos, elephants and rams, live in common friendship. Cows and tigers, horses and buffalos, lions and elephants, rams and monkeys, dogs and deer, cats and mice, snakes and ichneumons are exceedingly inimical. Common enmity and indifference are easily exemplified by the lives or ordinary men and beasts.

5. Planets. If the presiding planets of both persons be the same, and there be perfect friendship, this counts for five Gusas; or four if only common friendship. If there be friendship with an enemy of the other person it reduces the value to one Guna, and if both have such friendship to one half. In cases of mutual indifference the Gunas amount to three, and if there be mutual enmity there is no Guna.

6. Groups as in Table III. If both belong to the same group, six Gunas are present; also if the bridegroom belong to the god-group and the bride to the man-group. The reverse reduces it five: if the bridegroom be of demon-group, and the bride of god-group, there is only one Guna, and in all other cases none.

7. Kùta, that is the agreement of the zodiacal signs and asterisms of bride and bridegroom. It is of two kinds, auspicious and ill-omened. The Kŭta is fortunate if the bride and bridegroom be born in the same sign, but in different asterisms, or in the same asterisms, but in different signs, or, lastly, in the same asterisms but in different quarters. A difference of seven asterisms is also auspicious; for instance, if the bridegroom's asterism be Ashvini (Table III.), and that of the bride Pushya. The same is the case with three, four, ten, and eleven asterisms, and with a second sign from an even sign; for instance, Cancer being the fourth is an even sign, and if the sign of one party be Cancer and

the other Virgo, the Kŭta is auspicious. This is also the case with a sixth sign from an even sign; and an eighth and a twelfth from an odd sign. But a second sign, a fifth, a sixth, a ninth, and a twelfth from an odd sign, and an eighth from an even sign, are unfortunate Kŭtas. The Gunas of Leo and Virgo are both auspicious. If there be a fortunate Kŭta, and the sign of the bridegroom be remote from that of the bride, and if there be enmity between the classes of the two, this conjunction will represent six Gunas. If there be the same sign and different asterisms, or the same asterism and different signs, the Gunas number five. In an unfortunate Kŭta if there be friendship between the classes of the postulants, and the bride's asterism be remote from that of the bridegroom this counts for four Gunas; but if there be only a single condition, it reduces the requisites to one. In all other cases there is no Kŭta.

1. The Nádi or point of time. If the nádis of the bride and bridegroom be different, as *e. g.,* first and last, first and middle, last and middle, this conjunction represents eight Gunas. The requisites are nil when the Nádi is alike.

# APPENDIX II

NOW IS RELATED THE RASÁYANA, OR PREPARATION OF METALS for medicinal purposes.

### FIRST RECIPE.

For the curing of diseases caused by quicksilver.[1] Take sixty-four Tolas (each three drachms) of the juice of betel-plant (*piper betel*); mix with equal quantities of the juice of Bhringárajá (*eclipta prostrata*), juice of the Tulsi (*ocymum basilicum*=herb basil) and goat's milk; and rub the mixture into all parts of the body for two days, each day two pahárs (= six hours) followed by a cold bath.

### SECOND RECIPE.

For reducing mercury to Bhasma (ashes=metallic oxide). Take of purified quicksilver and sulphur equal parts, and levigate with the sap of the Banyan-tree (*ficus indica*); place the preparation in an earthern pot over a slow fire and stir with a stick of the Banyan-tree for a whole day. If two Gunjas (= 1 $^5/_{10}$ grs. troy) of this medicine be eaten at early morning in betel leaf; digestion is improved and the powers of copulation are increased.

### THIRD RECIPE.

For preparing Hemagarbha, the Elixir vitæ which contains gold. Take three parts of purified quicksilver; one part and a half of sulphur; one part of gold; two parts of the ashes (metallic oxide) of copper and calx of pearls and coral, each one-tenth of a part. Levigate in a mortar for seven days with the juice of the Kumári (*aloe perfoliata,*) make into a ball, cover well with a piece of cotton cloth and place in an earthen vessel, containing a little sulphur: the mouth must be well closed, leaving for the escape of smoke a small hole which must be kept open with a needle if necessary. Set the vessel over a Válukayantra (bain marie, or sand-bath) under which a slow fire is kindled. After about half a Ghataká (= 12 minutes) the fire must be diminished and allowed to extinguish. Remove the ball and use as the doctor directs.

### FOURTH RECIPE.

For reducing Haritál (Sansk, hartálaka, = sulphuret of arsenic, yellow orpiment) to ashes, or metallic oxide. Levigate yellow orpiment and knead it with the juice of the plant Nágar-jŭni (a Cyperus-grass.) Levigate again with the juice of the Pinpalli (*piper longum*) and the Piper betel for two days. Make balls of the preparation; dry in shade; then set in earthen vessel in a bain marie. A hot fire must be kept up till the orpiment is thoroughly "cooked," and allow the fire to diminish and extinguish. Remove the balls from the vessel and use in every disease.

### FIFTH RECIPE.

For absorbing all other metals by purified mercury. Thoroughly levigate quicksilver with the juice of the "seven minor poisons," *viz.,* Arka (*Callotropis gigantea*) Sehunda

(*Euphorbia*), Dhatura (Stramonium, white thorn-apple), Lángali (*Jussiæa repens*), Karavira (oleander or Soma[2]) and opium. By this means mercury loses its wings and cannot fly, while it gets a mouth and eats up every metal with speed.

### SIXTH RECIPE.

A sovereign remedy against all diseases and death. Take Abhraka (tale) and levigate with the milky sap of the Arka for the space of a day. Then wrap up the preparation in Arka-leaves and boil in a heap of Gobar (cow dung) cakes about two feet thick. Repeat this boiling with fresh leaves for seven times, then infuse the preparation three times in a decoction of Parámbi Maráthi, the fibrous roots of the Banyan-tree. In this way the mineral is "killed;" its impurities are removed and it becomes nishchandra talc. Boil equal parts of this and Ghi (clarified butter) in an iron vessel till the butter is absorbed, and it is ready for use; it cures every complaint, including old age and death.

# ENDNOTES

## THE KAMA SUTRA

### INTRODUCTION

1 "Introduction" to the *Kamasutra*. A New Translation by Wendy Doniger and Sudhir Kakar. New York: Oxford University Press, 2002. liii.
2 Ibid. lvii.
3 Andrea Pinkney and Lance Dane. *The Kama Sutra Illuminated: Erotic Art of India*. New York: Harry N. Abrams, 2002. 45.

### INTRODUCTORY PREFACE

1 Dharma is acquisition of religious merit, and is fully described in Chapter 5, Volume III, of James Talboys Wheeler's *History of India*, and in the edicts of Asoka.
2 Artha is acquisition of wealth and property, etc.
3 Kama is love, pleasure, and sensual gratification.

### CHAPTER II

1 These were certainly materialists who seemed to think that a bird in the hand was worth two in the bush.
2 Among the Hindus the four classes of men are the Brahmans, or priestly class; the Kshatriyas, or warrior class; the Vaishya, or agricultural and mercantile class; and the Shudra, or menial class. The four stages of life are: the life of a religious student (Brahmacarin), the life of the householder (Grihastha), the life of a Vana prastha, or forest dweller, and the life of a Sannyas, or wandering ascetic.
3 Bali was a demon who had conquered Indra and gained his throne, but was afterward overcome by Vishnu at the time of his fifth incarnation.

⁴ Dandakya is said to have abducted from the forest the daughter of a Brahman, named Bhargava, and being cursed by the Brahman, was buried with his kingdom under a shower of dust The place was called after his name the Dandaka Forest, celebrated in the Ramayana, but now unknown.

⁵ Ahalya was the wife of the sage Gautama. Indra caused her to believe that he was Gautama, and thus enjoyed her. He was cursed by Gautama and subsequently afflicted with a thousand ulcers on his body.

⁶ Kichaka was the brother-in-law of King Virata, with whom the Pandavas had taken refuge for one year. Kichaka was killed by Bhima, who assumed the disguise of Draupadi. For this story the Mahabharata should be referred to.

⁷ The story of Ravana is told in the Ramayana; the Ramayana and the Mahabharata are the two great epic poems of the Hindus; the latter was written by Vyasa, and the former by Vlamiki.

### CHAPTER III

¹ The author wishes to prove that a great many things are done by people from practice and custom, without their being acquainted with the reason of things, or the laws on which they are based, and this is perfectly true.

² The proviso of being married applies to all the teachers.

### CHAPTER IV

¹ This term would appear to apply generally to an inhabitant of Hindustan. It is not meant only for a dweller in a city, like the Latin Urbanus as opposed to Rusticus.

² Gift is peculiar to a Brahman, conquest to a Kshatriya, while purchase, deposit, and other means of acquiring wealth belong to the Vaishya.

³ Natural garden flowers.

⁴ Such as quails, partridges, parrots, starlings, etc.

⁵ The calls of nature are always performed by the Hindus the first thing in the morning.

⁶ A color made from lac.

⁷ This would act instead of soap, which was not introduced until the rule of the Muslims.

⁸ Ten days are allowed when the hair is taken out with a pair of pincers.

⁹ These are characters generally introduced in the Hindu drama; their characteristics will be explained further on.

¹⁰ Noonday sleep is allowed only in summer, when the nights are short.

¹¹ These are very common in all parts of India.

¹² In the *Asiatic Miscellany,* and in Sir William Jones's works, will be found a spirited hymn addressed to this goddess, who is adored as the patroness of the fine arts, especially of music and rhetoric, as the inventress of the

Sanskrit language, etc. She is the goddess of harmony, eloquence, and language, and is somewhat analogous to Minerva. For further information about her see Edward Moor's *The Hindoo Pantheon.*

13 The public women, or courtesans (Vesya), of the early Hindus have often been compared with the Hetera of the Greeks. The subject is dealt with at some length in H. H. Wilson's *Select Specimens of the Theatre of the Hindoos*, in two volumes (Trübner and Co., 1871). It may be fairly considered that the courtesan was one of the elements, and an important element too, of early Hindu society, and that her education and intellect were both superior to that of the women of the household. Wilson says: "By the Vesya or courtesan, however, we are not to understand a female who has disregarded the obligation of law or the precepts of virtue, but a character reared by a state of manners unfriendly to the admission of wedded females into society, and opening it only at the expense of reputation to women who were trained for association with men by personal and mental acquirements to which the matron was a stranger."

14 According to this description a Pithamarda would be a sort of professor of all the arts, and as such received as the friend and confidant of the citizens.

15 A seat in the form of the letter *T*.

16 The Vita is supposed to represent somewhat the character of the Parasite of the Greek comedy. It is possible that he was retained about the person of the wealthy, and employed as a kind of private instructor, as well as an entertaining companion.

17 Vidushaka is evidently the buffoon and jester. Wilson says of him that he is the humble companion, not the servant, of a prince or man of rank, and it is a curious peculiarity that he is always a Brahman. He bears more affinity to Sancho Panza, perhaps, than any other character in Western fiction, imitating him in his combination of shrewdness and simplicity, his fondness of good living and his love of ease. In the dramas of intrigue he exhibits some of the talents of Mercury, but with less activity and ingenuity, and occasionally suffers by his interference. According to the technical definition of his attributes he is to excite mirth by being ridiculous in person, age, and attire.

18 This means, it is presumed, that the citizen should be acquainted with several languages. The middle part was perhaps a reference to the Thugs.

## CHAPTER V

1 This term does not apply to a widow, but to a woman who has probably left her husband, and is living with some other person as a married woman, *maritalement,* as they say in France.

[2] Any woman fit to be enjoyed without sin. The object of the enjoyment of women is twofold: pleasure and progeny. Any woman who can be enjoyed without sin for the purpose of accomplishing either the one or the other of these two objects is a Nayika. The fourth kind of Nayika which Vatsyayana admits further on is neither enjoyed for pleasure nor for progeny, but merely for accomplishing some special purpose in hand. The word Nayika is retained as a technical term throughout.

## PART TWO

### CHAPTER I

[1] High unions are said to be better than low ones, for in the former it is possible for the male to satisfy his own passion without injuring the female, while in the latter it is difficult for the female to be satisfied by any means.

[2] This is a long dissertation very common among Sanskrit authors, both when writing and talking socially. They start certain propositions, and then argue for and against them. What it is presumed the author means is that, though both men and women derive pleasure from the act of coition, the way it is produced is brought about by different means, each individual performing his own work in the matter irrespective of the other, and each deriving individually his own consciousness of pleasure from the act performed. There is a difference in the work that each does, and a difference in the consciousness of pleasure that each has, but no difference in the pleasure they feel, for each feels that pleasure to a greater or lesser degree.

### CHAPTER IV

[1] From this it would appear that in ancient times the breasts of women were not covered, and this is seen in the painting of the Ajanta and other caves, where we find that the breasts of even royal ladies and others are exposed.

### CHAPTER IX

[1] This practice appears to have been prevalent in some parts of India from a very ancient time. The *Shushruta'*, a work on medicine some two thousand years old, describes the wounding of the lingam with the teeth as one of the causes of a disease treated upon in that work. Traces of the practice are found as far back as the eighth century, for various kind of the Auparishtaka are represented in the sculptures of many Shaivite

temples at Bhubaneshwar, near Cuttack, in Orissa, which were built about that period. From these sculptures being found in such places, it would seem that this practice was popular in that part of the country at that time. It does not seem to be so prevalent now in Hindustan, its place perhaps being supplanted by the practice of sodomy introduced since the Muslim period.

### CHAPTER X

1   The fresh juice of the coconut tree, the date tree, and other kinds of palm trees are drunk in India. It will not keep fresh very long, but ferments rapidly, and is then distilled into liquor.

## PART THREE

### CHAPTER I

1   The flight of a bluejay on a person's left is considered a lucky omen when one starts on any business; the appearance of a cat before anyone at such a time is looked on as a bad omen. There are many omens of the same kind.
2   Such as the throbbing of the right eye of men and the left eye of women, etc.
3   Before anything is begun it is a custom to go early in the morning to a neighbor's house, and overhear the first words that may be spoken in his family, and according as the words heard are of good or bad import, so draw an inference as to the success or failure of the undertaking.
4   A disease consisting of any glandular enlargement in any part of the body.
5   A woman the palms of whose hands and the soles of whose feet are always perspiring.

### CHAPTER V

1   These forms of marriage differ from the four kinds of marriage mentioned in Part Three, Chapter I, and are only to be made use of when the girl is gained over in the way mentioned in Chapters III and IV.
2   About the Gandharvavivaha form of marriage, see note to page 28 of Sir R. F. Burton's *Vickram and the Vampire: or, Tales of Hindu Devilry* (Longmans, Green & Co., London, 1870): "This form of matrimony was recognised by the ancient Hindus, and is frequent in books. It is a kind of Scotch wedding—ultra-Caledonian—taking place by mutual consent without any form or ceremony. The Gandharvas are heavenly minstrels of Indra's court, who are supposed to be witnesses."

## PART IV

### CHAPTER I

[1] This probably refers to a girl married in her infancy, or when very young, whose husband had died before she arrived at the age of puberty.

### CHAPTER II

[1] A name given to the maidservants of the zenana of the king in ancient times, because they always kept their breasts covered with a cloth called Kanchuki. It was customary in the old time for the maidservants to cover their breasts with a cloth, while the queens kept their breasts uncovered. This custom is distinctly to be seen in the Ajanta cave paintings.

[2] The meaning of this word is "superior woman," so it would seem that a Mahallarika must be a person in authority over the maidservants of the harem.

[3] This was also appertaining to the rank of women employed in the harem. In later times this place was given to eunuchs.

[4] As kings generally had many wives, it was usual for them to enjoy their wives by turns. But as it happened sometimes that some of them lost their turns owing to the king's absence, or to their being unwell, then in such cases the women whose turn had been passed over, and those whose turns had come, used to have a sort of lottery, and the ointment of all the claimants were sent to the king, who accepted the ointment of one of them, and thus settled the question.

## PART V

### CHAPTER IV

[1] The wife of the sage Gautama; she was seduced by Indra the king of the gods.

[2] The heroine of one of the best, if not the best, of Hindu plays, and the best known in Sanskrit dramatic literature. It was first brought to notice by Sir William Jones, and has been well and poetically translated by Arthur W. Ryder in a volume entitled *Shakuntala and Other Writings* by Kalidasa (Dutton Paperbacks, D40).

[3] It is supposed that storms, earthquakes, famines, and pestilent diseases are here alluded to.

### CHAPTER V

[1] This is a phrase used for the man who does the work of everybody, and who is fed by the whole village.

2  The exact date of the reign of these kings is not known. It is supposed to have been about the beginning of the Christian Era.

3  These are Lust, Anger, Avarice, Spiritual Ignorance, Pride, and Envy.

## CHAPTER VI

1  The way to make oneself invisible; the knowledge of the art of transmigration, or changing ourselves or others into any shape or form by the use of charms and spells; the power of being in two places at once; and other occult sciences are frequently referred to in Oriental literatures.

2  This may be considered as meaning religious influence, and alludes to persons who might be gained over by that means.

## PART VI

## CHAPTER VI

1  The souls of men who die with their desires unfulfilled are said to go to the world of the manes, and not direct to the Supreme Spirit.

## PART VII

## CHAPTER I

1  It is a custom of the courtesans of Oriental countries to give their daughters temporarily in marriage when they come of age, and after they have received an education in the *Kama Sutra* and other arts.

2  From the earliest times Oriental authors have concerned themselves with aphrodisiacs. The following note on the subject is taken from page 29 of a translation of the Hindu *Art of Love*, otherwise the *Ananga Ranga:* "Most Eastern treatises divide aphrodisiacs into two different kinds: (1) the mechanical or natural, such as scarification, flagellation, etc.; and (2) the medicinal or artificial. To the former belong the application of insects, as is practiced by some savage races; and all Orientalists will remember the tale of the old Brahman whose young wife insisted upon his being again stung by a wasp."

## THE ANANGA RANGA

## INTRODUCTION

1  The mountain-goddess of many names, wife of Shiva, the third person of the Hindu Trinity, who is here termed Shambhu for Swayambhu, the Self-Existent. The invocation is abrupt and does not begin with the beginning, Ganesha (Janus), Lord of Incepts, who is invariably invoked by the Hindu,

that he may further the new undertaking. This god is worshipped under the form of a short stout man, with an elephant's trunk and protuberant belly. (See Vol. III. p. 38, "A View of the History, Literature, and Mythology of the Hindus," by William Ward, of Serampore, London, 1832.) The loves of Krishna and the sixteen thousand milkmaids are recorded in the Bahgavat: this eleventh incarnation of Vishnú is a dark-blue man, playing with both hands upon the pipe, whilst Rada, his wife, stands on his left side. Kámadeva, or the Hindu Cupid, the son of Bramhá, is represented as a beautiful youth, the most lovely of all the gods, holding a bow and flower-tipped arrow, with which, while wandering through perfumed glades, accompanied by Rati, his spouse, he wounds the hearts of the inhabitants of the Triloka or Three Worlds. Sir William Jones says that he appears to correspond with the Greek Eros and the Roman Cupido, but that the Indian description of his person and arms, his family, attendants and attributes has new and peculiar beauties. Sambar' Asura was one of the Rakshasas, gigantic and diabolical beings, whom Kama slew.

2  The Sakti, or female principle, representing the aptitude of conception and continuation, becomes the wives of the gods in Hindu mythology. Thus in the Shavya-Purana, Shiva says, "from the supreme spirit proceed Parusha" (the generative or male principle) "and Parkriti" (the productive, or female principle), and by them was produced the universe, the manifestation of the one god." For its origin we must go back to the Chaldaeo-Babylonian System.

3  This title has been explained: see also Ward iii. 179. Káma was the son of Maya (= Illusion, the attracting powers of Matter, Maia the mother of Mercury), he married Rati (Affection, vulgarized in our "rut") and is bosom-friend to Vasanta, Basant or Spring.

## CHAPTER I

1  Evidently the nervous temperament, with due admixture of the bilious and sanguine.

2  A lofty tree with soft and fragrant pollen.

3  The Yoni is the feminine opposed to the Linga (Priapus) or male apparatus.

4  See note, chap. iv., on the Hindu ideas of human sperm, and for the vermicules of the Yoni, chap. iii, sec. 3.

5  Usually known as the Indian cuckoo, though its voice is harsh and disagreeable; in poetry and romance it takes the place of the bulbul of Persia, and the nightingale of Europe.

6  The sanguine temperament.

7 Meaning excellent as that of the Peacock, which is not disliked by the Hindus as by Europeans. They associate it with the breaking of rainy monsoon, which brings joy to the thirsty earth and sun-parched men.

8 The bilious temperament.

9 So Apollonius of Rhodes, describing the passions of Medeia says:— "The fire which devours her, attacks all her nerves, and makes Itself felt even behind the head in that spot where pain is most poignant when an extreme fervour seizes on all the senses."

10 "Elephant"-woman, because the animal being called the "handed one," from the use of the trunk, and Hastiní corresponds with Karami, from kara, a hand. She is "mulier nigris dignissima barris," and of the lymphatic or lowest temperament. These divisions represent, we have noted, roughly and unscientifically, the four European temperaments, nervous, sanguine, bilious and lymphatic. In a future chapter, the three Hindu temperaments will be discussed.

11 The days (Tithi) are those of the lunar fortnight: the Pratipadá, for instance, being the first, when the moon's increase and wane begin.

12 As amongst the classics, day and night are divided by the Hindus with eight watches each of seven ghari, or hours (1 ghari=241.)

## CHAPTER II

1 Chandrakala is properly a digit, or one-sixteenth of the lunar orb.

2 Called Sitkára from the sound "S't! s't! s't! s't!" as a person breathing hard or drawing in cold air between the teeth, thus making an inarticulate sound. Full particulars concerning it will be found in Chapter IX.

3 In the original Sanskrit and in all translations there is an allusion to the practice described by Juvenal (IX. 4.).

4 Alluding to what Shakespeare calls "kissing with th' inner lip."

## CHAPTER III

1 These divisions again appear to represent the nervous, bilious and sanguine temperament. Some MSS. divide men only by the three Linga-lengths of 6, 9 and 12 finger breadths: the latter (6 widths) would be of African or Negro dimensions.

2 A fair anticipation of the spermatozoa: see terminal note of Chapt. iv.

## CHAPTER IV

1 In old European physiology it ranked lowest.

[2] The Hindu Plutus, god of wealth.

[3] The Semitic races domesticated the ass, and recognized its admirable qualities; they treated it with due respect, and they were not ashamed of being compared with it—e.g., "Issachar is a strong ass." The early Egyptian Kings (B. C. 4000–1000) had no horses in their invading hosts, and the law of Moses seems to condemn the use. The "Equus Caballus" was conquered and utilized by the Caucasians in Central Asia, and they overwhelmed its rival with abuse and contempt, attributing its creation to Vishvakarma, who caricatured the work of the gods.

[4] Rítu-snátá is the woman, who, on the fourth day, has bathed and become pure.

[5] This is the Hindu view: The Moslems hold that the desires of a woman are ten times stronger than those of a man. Both are right in certain exceptions; for instance the male is the stronger in dry climates, the female in the hot, damp and depressing.

[6] The "Fons et scaturigo Veneris" of the classics. It need hardly be remarked that the Hindus, like the ancients in Europe, believed the Káma-salila of women to be in every way like that of men; the microscope was required for the detection of the spermatozoa in one sex only. "Clitoris" means "shutter;" hence the French "clitoriser," to tickle it.

## CHAPTER VI

[1] In the following prescriptions no proportions are given. It is understood that for external applications the correct quantity is the quarter of a Tola, unless otherwise specified; while those taken internally are always of a whole Tola:—

> 1 Masha = 15 grains = 1-12 of Tola.
> 2 Tola  = 45 grains = 2 scruples 5 grains.
> 3 Tola  = 2 drachms = 120 grains.
> 4 Tola  = 3 drachms = 180 grains.

[2] Others translate Rúí, hogweed (Boerhavia alata diffusa).

[3] The reader is strongly cautioned against this prescription, and others which contain mercury.

[4] This process is called in Arabian medicine "Imsák," which means "holding" or "retaining". It may safely be asserted that almost every volume of the Eastern pharmacopeia is half-full of aphrodisiacs; whilst at least half the latter have for their object "Imsák". Hence, Europeans, who ignore the art and practice, are contemptuously compared by Hindu women with village cocks; and the result is that no stranger has ever been truly loved by a native girl.

5  The following is a useful list of the twenty-seven Nakshatras. Mansions of the Moon, or Asterisms in the moon's path:—

1. Ashviní a mare.
2. Bharaná, filling or satisfying.
3. Krittika; also the Pleiades.
4. Rohini, lightning; girl nine years old.
5. Mriga, a deer, any beast; the rain which falls during this asterism.
6. Ardra; wet.
7. Punarwasu; also called Thorlakunwar, "great son"—i.e., an old boy.
8. Pushya (also the month Posh), which some call Tarná.
9. Ashleshá, an embrace.
10. Maghá.
11. Púrvaphalguna.
12. Uttarphalguna, the north.
13. Hasta, the hand.
14. Chittrá.
15. Sváti, solitary; also the star Arcturus.
16. Vishákhá.
17. Anurádhá.
18. Jyeshthá.
19. Múla, root, basis, origin, first ancestor, a child.
20. Púrvásháhá.
21. Uttarásháhá.
22. Shrivan, "hearing or organ of hearing."
23. Dhanistá.
24. Shata-toraká, because it contains a hundred stars.
25. Púrvábhádrapada.
26. Uttarabhádrapada.
27. Revatí, the wife of Balarám; also a kind of Chumbelí or jasmine flower.

For more concerning the Nakshatras, see Appendix I.

6  Vájí is a horse, karan, making; applied to exciting lust by charms, etc.
7  Most eastern treatises divide aphrodisiacs into two different kinds; 1, the mechanical or external, such as scarification, flagellation, etc.; and, 2, the medicinal, or artificial. To the former belong the application of insects, as is practised by some savage races; and all Orientalists will remember the tale of old Brahman, whose young wife insisted upon his pudendum being stung by a wasp.
8  The Chinese certainly have a secret of the kind; it appears as a small pill of rhubarb colour enclosed in a waxen capsule, and as frequent analysis has shown, of vegetable matter. Dissolved in warm water and applied to the part, it produces a formication which ends in intense irritation, and greatly increases the size by inducing abnormal injection of blood.
9  Myrrh, an invaluable gum neglected by us, appears in Hindu and Arab Pharmacopeias as a kind of universal remedy, like our books about A. D. 1500, which made one drug cure every disease.

[10] Others say Karví-Dorkí, the fruit of the cucumis acutangulus or sulcatus.

[11] The "black salt" is made by fusing the fossil article in water with emblic myrobalans; it is a well-known tonic, and also used in different proportions as an aperient.

[12] This process of contraction is universally adopted in India. Europeans who, as a rule, know only prostitutes, believe that it is effected by Chunam, or slacked lime. Of course this is a vulgar error. The popular constrictor is an infusion of astringent bark, sometimes strengthened with alum.

[13] Amongst African savages the same process is effected by fumigation with odoriferous gums, which are thrown upon the fire, and the patient stands over it.

[14] Nothing in the East is considered more impure than to wear this body-hair; it is removed by men with the razor, and by woman with various depilatories, especially quicklime and orpiment in certain proportions. Even savages in the Tropics have adopted a custom, without which cleanliness cannot be. A hair of the pecten, or the axillæ, submitted to the microscope, shows excellent reason for the general practice of equatorial regions.

[15] In the original, Smarálaya, from Smara, recollection, a title of Kámadeva, and Alaya, a house, as in Himalaya, which we hideously pronounce Himaláya.

[16] According to others, "Shankha-Bhasma" is metallic oxide. Literally understood, it would supply lime for mixture with orpiment.

[17] The great perfumers of civilized cities invariably refuse to recommend a depilatory, and it will be easily understood that the hair cannot permanently be destroyed without removing the bulb, that is to say, without excoriating the part, a painful operation, systematically performed by several savage and barbarous races. Great care must be taken in applying depilatories which contain orpiment, an active poison, that will be diffused by a scratch or a sore, and the proper proportions of lime must be added (not vaguely, as in the text), otherwise the skin will be permanently marked, or even burnt off.

[18] Others read Tandulja, an esculent vegetable.

[19] Others read Rasawati. This collyrium is prepared by boiling together calx of brass and one-eighth of Daru-haldi (curcuma xanthor-rhizon), adding to the decoction an equal part of goat's milk, and reducing (or evaporating) to one-fourth.

[20] Among the people of Hindustan, Muslims as well as Hindus, there are thousands of nostrums and specifics for causing pregnancy. This is the inevitable supply caused by the demand in the harems of the wealthy, where venereal excesses and other evils which accompany riches, render want of offspring the great misery of human life. A son and heir is an absolute necessity to the Rajah and the Amir, who willingly pay enormous sums to an army of quacks and charlatans.

²¹ "Nothing new under the sun"—we again remark. During the last few years the use of clay externally as well as internally, in medicines as well as in surgery, has been revived, and many hospitals in the United States have preferred it as a wound-dressing to all poultices.

²² Others read Prasidvá——?

²³ In a MS. I find It thus:—

**ॐ यत्रिभार्या जय्रसव्रयमयमयमयबहिः** etc., etc.

The Adi-pranava (secret word) and the Bij (literally seed, here cabalistic letter or syllable, forming the essence of the charm) are properly the ineffable "Aum" or "Om" concerning which see any treatise on Hindu Theology.

²⁴ The only licit way of limiting the family in India is the practice of polyandry, which is now confined to Malabar, Ceylon, and other parts of Himalayas. Abortives, however, are common throughout the Peninsula, and many women make this form of murder their trade; instruments and violence are seldom, if ever, used; dependance is placed chiefly on poisons and nostrums, consequently the mother often shares the fate of the child.

²⁵ Others read "decoction of husks, chaff or bran of rice."

²⁶ Others read Lodhra.

²⁷ What a fortune would be such a remedy in civilized lands. Yet the Hindus have something of the kind; witness the "Jatá-wálá" mendicant, who makes his hair grow upwards of six feet long and twists it round his head like a turban.

²⁸ Besides black, the only dyes used in India are light sky-blue, the effect of indigo-leaves applied to the white beard by men of the Western coast, and Henna powder, which gives an orange tint.

²⁹ In the East there are many prescriptions to be taken internally for changing the colour of the hair; prudent men avoid them.

³⁰ Others translate Goro-chan, a "substance found in the cow's head" used in dying, painting and physic.

³¹ Others translate Vekhand by calamus aromaticus.

³² Others have Lodhra tree.

³³ The women of India proper are remarkable for round and high bosoms; and the more southerly its habitat; the firmer become the breasts of the race, although we should expect the reverse, where the climate is so distinctly hot, damp, and tropical. On the other hand, the women of Cashmere, Sind and the Panjab; of Afganistan and Persia, though otherwise beautifully shaped, and fine in face as in figure, are all more or less subject, after the birth of the first child, to the blemish of pendulous breasts. And the geographical line of sodomy corresponds with that of the flaccid bosom.

[34] The following prescriptions in the original conclude the seventh, or mystical chapter. They are transferred to this place, as they evidently belong to it.

[35] Akrota-Vriksha; others read careya arborea, salvadora persica, and even a kind of palm.

[36] Others translate Kunku-mágar, "saffron".

[37] Pán-supári, the favourite "quid" of Hindostan, is composed of Pán (the leaf of the betel pepper, P. betel), containing shredded Supárí nut (the fruit of the Areca palm), with a little catechu, cardamom, nutmeg and mace, adding a small quantity of Chunám (slaked shell-lime) to bring out the flavour.

## CHAPTER VII

[1] This is a round sectarian mark, about the size of a wafer, which the Hindu applies to his forehead, after certain rites and prayers. The reader will find this chapter interesting on account of the various abominations which it contains. The underlying idea appears to be that if any secretion of the body, the fouler the better, can be secretly administered to a person of either sex, the result is the subjection of the patient to the adhibitor. The European reader will hardly believe how extensively this practice is carried out all over the East. No Persian will drink sherbet in the house of his future, mother-in-law; and Jewish women, who are especially addicted to these practices, will mix their monthly blood in the philters which they give to men.

[2] The reader can now consult the Kama Sutra of the Sage Vatsyáyana, translated from the Sanskrit in seven Parts, gr. in 8vo, with Preface, Introduction and concluding remarks. (Benares, printed for the Hindoo Kama Shastra Society, 1883.)

[3] Nothing in Hindu eyes can be more impure or sacrilegious than such an act as this; the people having, as a rule, the highest reverence for the body from which life has departed. And the horror of the thing is, of course, the secret of its power.

[4] Others translate "Cassia buds."

[5] These, of course, would be putrid in an Indian climate.

[6] The reader need hardly be told that even in England the old-fashioned superstition of summoning an absent person is not extinct. The formulas, as a rule, are silly verses, whose sole object is apparently to control the will of the reciter. They lead to a complicated subject, the animal magnetism, or mesmerism, both names equally absurd, which has been practised in India from time immemorial.

[7] The efficacy of the Mantra is in the Devatá, or deity that resides in it, and he is conquered or conciliated by the mere act of repetition and of making offerings. This conclusion results directly from the Hindu theory of prayer.

8 Chámunda is one of the many names of Deví, the wife or Sakti of the god Shiva.

9 Literally, "satisfaction"; generally applied to the rite of offering water to the Pitris or ancestral Manes.

10 Here nothing is said concerning? the number of times, which may be 10,000 or 100,000. Of course, the more repetitions the better, as thus the Mantra-devatá, without whom the formula has no efficacy, will be the more surely bound. The Muslims of India have borrowed all these superstitions from the heathen.

11 Here the difficulty will be to persuade the women to eat the charmed betel; in the East the people are prudent in such matters, and we have seen reasons why they should be.

12 Others read Kevdá, a Francolin partridge.

13 This chapter has been left in all its original confusion of subjects; it would be easy to revise it, but then it would lose "cachet".

## CHAPTER VIII

1 The large black bee of Southern Europe, India, etc. Corresponding with the "bumble bee" of England, but without the yellow markings.

2 Alluded to in a future part of the chapter.

3 All Easterns uphold the doctrine of the Salernitan School. Noscitur a labiis quantum sit virginis antrum: nositur a naso quanta sit hasta viro.

4 In Europe there is much dispute concerning this canon. But the big toe represents the thumb which distinguishes the human from the simian hand, and the longer the better formed the two are, the higher is the organisation. In this matter races greatly differ: compare, for instance, the short thumb of the Anglo-Saxon with the long thumb of the Celt, or the common Englishman with the common Irishman.

5 The Hill in Mathura, which Krishna held up in hand.

6 As a rule the plamistry of the Gypsies is directly derived, like their language, from India, and so artificial a system speaks strongly in favour of a single origin and propagation by tradition. Here, however, the "line of life" (linea vitæ) is transferred from the base of the thumb to an unusual place, technically called the Cingulum Veneris.

7 This figure Europeans turn into an M, and hold to mean marriage. The "barley-mark" in the text seems to correspond with the triangle formed by the "supreme natural Line," the "Line of Life," and the "Line of the Lunar Mount." (Richard Saunders' "Physiognomie and Chiromancie," London, 1671; and Les Mysterés de la Main," Ad. Desbarrolles, Paris, Dentu, 1862).

8 Such was the case with the celebrated Highland cateran. Rob Roy Macgregor.

[9] An unusual conformation in the Indian, whose short thin feet are despised by the Afghans, and the adjacent mountaineers. When Ranjit Singh ordered a hundred matchlocks from a celebrated gunsmith across the Indus, he received in return a slipper with a message that the order would be executed as soon as a Sikh's foot could be found to fit that shoe.

[10] An idea long familiar to the world before the days of Dr. Gall.

[11] Here we find a Hindu origin for the naughty schoolboy lines about short and thick—long and thin.

[12] The Svastika is the crutched cross, known to the Scandinavians as the "hammer of Thor," and supposed to denote the thunderbolt. It is painted on doors in India as an auspicious mark or seal, and is affixed to documents in lieu of signatures by Hindu wives (not widows), who cannot write their names. "Svastika," amongst the Jains, is the emblem of the seventh Gurú or spiritual teacher, and the word is also applied to a temple built in the shape of a symbol.

[13] These circular lines being held particularly auspicious.

[14] These ornaments are hung from doorways or about awnings on festive occasions.

[15] That is, the book written by Nàrada, one of the twenty Rishis or Sages, and a son of Brahma. His name is properly applied to a quarrelsome and embroiling fellow.

[16] These three represent "Helen of Troy" in the classical history of Hindustan.

[17] These tea are the progressive stages of love longing.

[18] This was the heathen idea generally, and a friend would hardly have felt justified in refusing, under such circumstances, the loan of his wife. So Seleucus, King of Syria, gave the fair Stratonike to his son, Antiochus, in order to save a life which was endangered by the violence of passion. Equally generous was Socrates, the "Christian before Christianity;" which generosity may, perhaps, account in part for the temper of Xantippe.

[19] Because by Hindu custom, if not by the old law, the lover cannot marry a widow.

[20] Easterns are all agreed upon this point, and the idea is that the embraces of a woman older than the husband, "burn" and destroy his strength. It is certain that when there is considerable difference of age, the younger of the two suffers in appearance, if not in health. How many women we see in civilized countries with, that young-old look, which at once assures the observer that they are married to men much their seniors? We seldom meet in society with the reverse case, for ridicule always attaches to a

man's marrying a woman whose age greatly exceeds his own. Yet the few instances which appear, justify our belief that there is something the reverse of hygienic in the practice.

21 In Sanskrit, and in the Prakrit or modern language of Hindostan, there are different names for our "aunt": Mávashi, for instance, is the maternal aunt, and Mámí, the maternal uncle's wife.

22 This need not necessarily be taken in a bad sense, as "procuress." In Hindu, as well as in Muslim families, women are sufficiently secluded to require the assistance of feminine Mercuries in matters of marriage.

23 This can hardly be used in an honest sense: it might be translated "seduced," were not that word so liable to misuse and misconstruction. What man in his senses can believe in the "seduction" of a married woman? As a rule, indeed, the seduction is all on the other side.

24 Which, allow us to state, is the case with most Englishwomen and a case to be remedied only by constant and intelligent study of the Ananga-Ranga Scripture.

25 In the East, women take the first step in such matters. Nothing can be more ridiculous than to see the bearded and turbaned Turk blushing, "boggling," and looking silly as he is being inspected for a pair of bold feminine eyes.

26 Parvani (Sanskrit Parva), is applied to certain times, such as the solstices and the equinoxes, when good actions are most acceptable.

27 It must be remembered that during the whole period of the sun's southing (Dakshanáyana, opposed to Uttaráyana, or his northerly direction), the high-caste Hindu will not marry.

28 The other four are Vasanta, or spring (April to May); Varshá, the rains (August to September); Hermanta, or the cold season (December to January); and Shishirá, early spring (February to March). Thus the Hindu year contains six Ritú or seasons.

29 This precaution might be adopted in modern civilization. It was practised by the Greeks and Romans, for the purpose of begetting graceful and beautiful children; and, considering the history of mother-marks and other puerperal curiosities, we should be careful how we determine that the conception cannot be favourably, as well as unfavourably influenced by the aspect of objects around the parents.

30 Concerning the effect of perfumes upon the organs, see Chap, IX.

## CHAPTER IX

1 The Alinganas are illustrated in almost every edition of "Koka Pandit," and so are the broader subjects treated of in the following chapter. At Puna (Poonah) and other parts of Western India, there are artists who make this

the business of their lives, and who sell a series of about eighty body colours, at the rate of two to five Rupees each. The treatment is purely conventional, and the faces, as well as the dresses, probably date from several centuries ago. A change took place when an unhappy Anglo-Indian Officer, wishing to send home a portrait of his wife, applied to one of our artists with that admirably naive ignorance of everything "native," which is the growing custom of his race. The result was that the Englishwoman's golden hair and beautiful features appear in some fifty or sixty highly compromising attitudes, and will continue to do so for many a generation to come.

2  Compare the slang word in French, "grimper."

3  Both feet being, of course, naked.

4  Sitting invariably means cross-legged, like a tailor upon his board, or at squat, like a bird, and the seat is a mat, or carpet, in India, and a divan in the nearer East.

5  In Europe, osculation upon the head and forehead is a paternal salutation, and, as a rule, men kiss one another upon both cheeks, and only their wives and concubines on the mouth. These distinctions are ignored by Orientals.

6  A fair specimen of the verbosity of Hindu style, which is so seldom realized or copied by Europeans speaking "native" languages. We should say "hold her chin and raise her face," or, to quote Ovid's Metamorphoses, "ad lumina lumen"—Attollens, which the Hindu would only half understand. This remark might be illustrated at considerable length.

7  In Sanskrit, "Hanu" means jaw.

8  "Virati" usually signifies being freed or refraining from carnal and worldly desires and passions; the extinction of earthly affections, and so forth.

9  The Hindus do not appear to have say special superstition about the white spots on the nails, which the vulgar of Europe call "gifts," because they portend presents.

10 Some wrongly translate this word "growing," or increasing. It means convex; in fact, what we call "filbert nails," opposed to the fiat, the concave, and the spatulated.

11 The European superstition is, that when horripilation takes place without apparent cause, a person is passing over the spot where the shudderer will be buried. This idea can hardly exist amongst a people who sensibly burn their dead in fixed places, far removed from the haunts of the living; and amongst Muslims, as well as Hindus, the "goose flesh," as we call it in our homely way, is a sign of all the passions.

12 This interjection usually denotes grief or pain, and here perhaps it is used in the latter sense.

13 "Rosy teeth" suggest a resemblance to our "curly teeth," popularly associated with straight hair. The author, however, is right according to the most

modern and the best authorities, in asserting that dead white is a bad colour, liable to caries, and easily tarnishing.

[14] Prognathism and Macrodontism are unknown to the higher castes of Hindus.

[15] Also called Dashanágramandal or circle of the principle bitings.

[16] The darker Hindus, like Africans, do not show redness in the lips, and the Arabs, curious to say, exceedingly admire brown lips.

[17] Bhujanga is a dragon, a cobra, a snake generically, or a man who keeps a mistress.

[18] Avatansa means a crest, a tuft, or an earring

[19] The reader will remember that the Hindus, as a rule, are a race of vegetarians, who rarely drink any stimulant such as wine, ale and spirits, or even tea, coffee and chocolate. They look with horror upon the meat-eater, that makes his body a grave for the corpses of animals; and they attach a bad name to all narcotics except tobacco, leaving opium and Bhang or Hashísh to low fellows and ribald debauchees. It is evident that, under such circumstances, their desires, after the first heat of youth, will be comparatively cold, and that both sexes, especially the weaker, require to be excited by a multitude and a variety of preliminaries to possession, which would defeat their own object in case of Europeans. Thus also we may account for their faith in pepper, ginger, cloves, cinnamon, and other spices which go by the name of "Garm Masálà," or hot condiments; these would have scanty effect upon the beef-eating and beer-bibbling Briton, but they exert a sufficiently powerful action upon a people of water-drinkers and rice or pulse-feeders.

[20] "Kara," a hand, and Tádana, "striking."

[21] In all these interjections, the terminal liquid is a highly nasalized nunnation.

[22] Somewhat in the same way as an Englishman urges on a horse.

[23] A mistress, or one beloved, the feminine of Náyak, meaning the head, a chief, the lover, the hero of a play, or the best gem in a necklace; hence the corrupted word "Naik," a corporal in the "native" army.

[24] There are many theories upon this subject in the East. For instance, the Narcissus-flower is everywhere supposed to excite the woman and depress the man, whilst the Mimosa blossom gives an essence which the Arabs call "Fitnah," trouble or revolt, because its action is direct and powerful upon the passions of their wives as the Spanish "Viento de las mujeres."

[25] These eight Náyikás are borrowed from the language of the Hindu drama.

## CHAPTER X

[1] The reader will bear to mind that the exceeding pliability of the Hindu's limbs enables him to assume attitudes absolutely impossible to the Europeans, and his chief object in congress is to avoid tension of the

muscles, which would shorten the period of enjoyment. For which reason, even in the act of love, he will delay to talk, to caress his wife, to eat, drink, chew Pán-supári, and perhaps smoke a water-pipe.

Stripped of its excessive verbiage, the Hindu "facons de faire." are simple enough. The five great divisions represent; 1. The woman lying supine (upon her back); 2. Lying on her side (right or left); 3. Sitting in various ways; 4. Standing, or as the vulgar call, an upright; and, lastly, 5. Lying prone (upon breast and stomach). Of the first division, there are eleven subdivisions; of the second, three; of the third, ten; of the fourth, three; and two of the fifth class, making a total of twenty-nine, and with three forms of Purúháyit, a grand total of thirty-two.

As in similar European treatises, the Kámashartra is very brief and unsatisfactory, except in the principal positions, and it can hardly be understood without illustrations. Some appear to be identical with others, at least no distinction can be learnt from the text. Moreover, it is evident that the Yoní of the Hindu woman must be placed exceptionally high, otherwise many of the postures would be quite impossible—these varieties of conformation are exceedingly interesting to the ethnologist, but the matter is far too extensive for discussing here. The subject of constricting the Yoní is also ethnologically of great importance, as will be seen when the reader arrives at the paragraph. An allusion has already been made to the Hindu practice of affecting conception by both parents looking at pictures of noble and beautiful forms; a custom well-known to the ancients, but now unaccountably neglected. (See Chap. VIII).

[2] Not as a tailor, but "sitting at squat," upon both feet, somewhat like a bird, a position impossible to Europeans.

[3] Unintelligible without an illustration.

[4] There is nothing of insult in comparison with a cow, which is worshipped by the Hindus.

[5] The classical idea of elephants, like other retromingents, copulating "à tergo," was never known to the Hindus, who were too well acquainted with the habits of the animals. It is needless to say that their coition is that of other quadrupeds.

[6] This position is held in great horror by Muslims, who commonly say, "Cursed be he who makes himself earth and woman heaven!"

[7] Amongst some races the constrictor vaginæ muscles are abnormally developed. In Abyssinia, for instance, a woman can so exert them as to cause pain to a man, and, when sitting upon his thighs, she can induce the orgasm without moving any other part of her person. Such an artist is called by the Arabs, "Kabbázah," literally meaning "a holder," and it is not surprising that the slave dealers pay large sums for her. All women have more or less the power, but they wholly neglect it;

indeed, there are many races in Europe which have never even heard of it. To these the words of wisdom spoken by Kalyána-Malla, the poet, should be peculiarly acceptable.

[8] So, it is said, that Orsini, the conspirator, employed the long hours of his captivity in cultivating this sense, until he was able readily to distinguish sounds which other men could not even hear.

## APPENDIX I

[1] We have relegated the astrological and chemical chapters to an appendix. They appear (pp. 120 et seq.) in the Maratha Edit. of the Ananga-Ranga. (Bombay, 1842); but it is more than doubtful if they belong to the original work.

[2] As mere children are married in India these precautions ana considerations must be taken by the relatives. See the beginning of chapter VIII.

[3] The fault of families is hereditary ill-repute: the greatest blemish of names is when those of bride and bridegroom exactly correspond, and those of disposition are too well known to require notice.

[4] The signs and asterisms are set down in the horoscopes, which are drawn up at the child's birth by competent inquirers.

## APPENDIX II

[1] The Hindus are supposed to have introduced the internal use of mercury which, in the shape of corrosive sublimate, found its way to Europe. They must have soon discovered the hideous effects of its abuse: in countries like Central Africa, where mercury is unknown, Syphilis never attacks the bones of the nose or face. The remedy in the text can do neither good nor harm.

[2] So the Dictionaries, naming very different plants, Nerium odorum (with poisonous root) and the harmless holy Soma (Sercostamma). But Kara-vira is a word of many meanings.

# SUGGESTED READING

BRODIE, FAWN. *The Devil Drives: A Life of Sir Richard Burton.* New York: W. W. Norton & Co, 1984.

DANIELOU, ALAIN. *The Complete Kama Sutra: The First Unabridged Translation of the Classic Indian Text.* Rochester, VT: Park Street Press, 1994.

DONIGER, WENDY, AND SUDHIR KAKAR, TRANS. *Kamasutra.* New York: Oxford University Press, 2002.

KAKAR, SUDHIR. *The Ascetic of Desire: A Novel of the Kamasutra.* Woodstock, NY: The Overlook Press, Peter Mayer Publishers Inc., 2000.

KENNEDY, DANE. *The Highly Civilized Man: Richard Burton and the Victorian World.* Cambridge: Harvard University Press, 2005.

LOVELL, MARY S. *A Rage to Live: A Biography of Richard and Isabel Burton.* New York: W. W. Norton, 2000.

PINKNEY, ANDREA, AND LANCE DANE. *The Kama Sutra Illuminated: Erotic Art of India.* New York: Harry N. Abrams, 2002.

SIEGEL, LEE. *Love in a Dead Language.* Chicago: University of Chicago Press, 2000.

VANITA, RUTH, AND SALEEM KIDWAI, EDS. *Same-Sex Love in India*: *Readings from Literature and History.* New York: Palgrave, 2001.

URBAN, HUGH. *Tantra: Sex, Secrecy, Politics, and Power in the Study of Religion.* Berkeley: University of California, 2003.

WIKOFF, JOHANINA, AND DEBORAH S. ROMAINE. *The Complete Idiot's Guide to the Kama Sutra.* Indianapolis: Alpha Books, 2000.

Look for the following titles, available now from
The Barnes & Noble Library of Essential Reading.

Visit your Barnes & Noble bookstore,
or shop online at www.bn.com/loer

## FICTION AND LITERATURE

| | | | |
|---|---|---|---|
| Abbott, Edwin A. | Flatland | 0-7607-5587-6 | $5.95 |
| Apuleius | Golden Ass | 0-7607-5598-1 | $7.95 |
| Austen, Jane | Love and Freindship and Other Early Works | 0-7607-6856-0 | $6.95 |
| Braddon, Mary Elizabeth | Lady Audley's Secret | 0-7607-6304-6 | $7.95 |
| Burroughs, Edgar Rice | Land That Time Forgot | 0-7607-6886-2 | $7.95 |
| Burroughs, Edgar Rice | Martian Tales Trilogy | 0-7607-5585-X | $9.95 |
| Butler, Samuel | Way of All Flesh | 0-7607-6585-5 | $9.95 |
| Cather, Willa | Alexander's Bridge | 0-7607-6887-0 | $6.95 |
| Chesterton, G. K. | Man Who Was Thursday | 0-7607-6310-0 | $5.95 |
| Childers, Erskine | Riddle of the Sands | 0-7607-6523-5 | $6.95 |
| Cleland, John | Fanny Hill | 0-7607-6591-X | $6.95 |
| Conan Doyle, Sir Arthur | Lost World | 0-7607-5583-3 | $5.95 |
| Defoe, Daniel | Journal of the Plague Year | 0-7607-5237-0 | $5.95 |
| Dos Passos, John | Three Soldiers | 0-7607-5754-2 | $7.95 |
| Franklin, Benjamin | Poor Richard's Almanack | 0-7607-6201-5 | $6.95 |
| Goethe | Sorrows of Young Werther | 0-7607-6833-1 | $5.95 |
| Grey, Zane | Riders of the Purple Sage | 0-7607-5755-0 | $6.95 |
| Haggard, H. Rider | She | 0-7607-5240-0 | $7.95 |
| Hudson, W. H. | Green Mansions | 0-7607-5595-7 | $7.95 |
| Huxley, Aldous | Crome Yellow | 0-7607-6050-0 | $5.95 |

| Jerome, Jerome K. | Three Men in a Boat | 0-7607-5759-3 | $7.95 |
| Lardner, Ring W. | You Know Me Al | 0-7607-5833-6 | $7.95 |
| Lawrence, D. H. | Sea and Sardinia | 0-7607-6583-9 | $7.95 |
| Mansfield, Katherine | Garden Party and Other Stories | 0-7607-6579-0 | $7.95 |
| Maugham, W. Somerset | Three Early Novels | 0-7607-6862-5 | $9.95 |
| Rabelais, François | Gargantua and Pantagruel | 0-7607-6314-3 | $14.95 |
| Radcliffe, Ann | Mysteries of Udolpho | 0-7607-6315-1 | $12.95 |
| Radcliffe, Ann | Romance of the Forest | 0-7607-5753-4 | $7.95 |
| Sabatini, Rafael | Captain Blood | 0-7607-5596-5 | $7.95 |
| Sienkiewicz, Henryk | Quo Vadis | 0-7607-6309-7 | $12.95 |
| Somerville, Edith, and Martin Ross | Some Experiences of an Irish R. M. | 0-7607-6580-4 | $6.95 |
| Sterne, Laurence | Life and Opinions of Tristram Shandy, Gentleman | 0-7607-6305-4 | $9.95 |
| Swift, Jonathan | Modest Proposal and Other Prose | 0-7607-6051-9 | $7.95 |
| Tolstoy, Leo | Gospels in Brief | 0-7607-5762-3 | $7.95 |
| Tolstoy, Leo | What Is Art? | 0-7607-6581-2 | $6.95 |
| Verne, Jules | From the Earth to the Moon | 0-7607-6522-7 | $6.95 |
| Von, Leopold Sacher-Masoch | Venus in Furs | 0-7607-6308-9 | $6.95 |
| Wallace, Lew | Ben-Hur | 0-7607-6306-2 | $9.95 |
| Walpole, Horace | Castle of Otranto | 0-7607-6307-0 | $5.95 |
| Wells, H. G. | Island of Dr. Moreau | 0-7607-5584-1 | $4.95 |
| Zitkala-Ša | American Indian Stories | 0-7607-6550-2 | $5.95 |

## NONFICTION

| Age of Revolution | Winston Churchill | 0-7607-6859-5 | $9.95 |
| American Democrat | James Fenimore Cooper | 0-7607-6198-1 | $6.95 |
| Autobiography of Benjamin Franklin | Benjamin Franklin | 0-7607-6199-X | $6.95 |
| Babylonian Life and History | E. A. Wallis Budge | 0-7607-6549-9 | $7.95 |

| | | | |
|---|---|---|---|
| Birth of Britain | Winston Churchill | 0-7607-6857-9 | $9.95 |
| Book of the Courtier | Baldesar Castiglione | 0-7607-6832-3 | $7.95 |
| Chemical History of a Candle | Michael Faraday | 0-7607-6522-7 | $6.95 |
| Common Law | Oliver Wendell Holmes, Jr. | 0-7607-5498-5 | $9.95 |
| Creative Evolution | Henri Bergson | 0-7607-6548-0 | $7.95 |
| Critique of Judgment | Immanuel Kant | 0-7607-6202-3 | $7.95 |
| Critique of Practical Reason | Immanuel Kant | 0-7607-6094-2 | $7.95 |
| Critique of Pure Reason | Immanuel Kant | 0-7607-5594-9 | $12.95 |
| Dark Night of the Soul | St. John of the Cross | 0-7607-6587-1 | $5.95 |
| Democracy and Education | John Dewey | 0-7607-6586-3 | $9.95 |
| Democracy in America | Alexis de Tocqueville | 0-7607-5230-3 | $14.95 |
| Discourse on Method | Rene Descartes | 0-7607-5602-3 | $4.95 |
| Edison: His Life and Inventions | Frank Lewis Dyer and Thomas C. Martin | 0-7607-6582-0 | $14.95 |
| Egyptian Book of the Dead | E. A. Wallis Budge | 0-7607-6838-2 | $9.95 |
| Eminent Victorians | Lytton Strachey | 0-7607-4993-0 | $7.95 |
| Enquiry concerning Human Understanding | David Hume | 0-7607-5592-2 | $7.95 |
| Essay Concerning Human Understanding | John Locke | 0-7607-6049-7 | $9.95 |
| Essence of Christianity | Ludwig Feuerbach | 0-7607-5764-X | $7.95 |
| Ethics and On the Improvement of the Understanding | Benedict de Spinoza | 0-7607-6837-4 | $8.95 |
| Extraordinary Popular Delusions and the Madness of Crowds | Charles Mackay | 0-7607-5582-5 | $9.95 |
| Fall of Troy | Quintus of Smyrna | 0-7607-6836-6 | $6.95 |
| Fifteen Decisive Battles of the Western World | Edward Shepherd Creasy | 0-7607-5495-0 | $12.95 |
| Florentine History | Niccolò Machiavelli | 0-7607-5601-5 | $9.95 |
| From Manassas to Appomattox | James Longstreet | 0-7607-5920-0 | $14.95 |
| Great Democracies | Winston Churchill | 0-7607-6860-9 | $9.95 |
| Guide for the Perplexed | Moses Maimonides | 0-7607-5757-7 | $12.95 |

| | | | |
|---|---|---|---|
| Happy Hunting-Grounds | Kermit Roosevelt | 0-7607-5581-7 | $5.95 |
| History of the Conquest of Mexico | William H. Prescott | 0-7607-5922-7 | $17.95 |
| History of the Conquest of Peru | William H. Prescott | 0-7607-6137-X | $14.95 |
| History of the Donner Party | Charles F. McGlashan | 0-7607-5242-7 | $6.95 |
| History of the English Church and People | Bede | 0-7607-6551-0 | $9.95 |
| History of Wales | J. E. Lloyd | 0-7607-5241-9 | $19.95 |
| How the Other Half Lives | Jacob A. Riis | 0-7607-5589-2 | $9.95 |
| How to Sing | Lilli Lehmann | 0-7607-5231-1 | $5.95 |
| Hunting the Grisly and Other Sketches | Theodore Roosevelt | 0-7607-5233-8 | $5.95 |
| Imitation of Christ | Thomas à Kempis | 0-7607-5591-4 | $7.95 |
| Influence of Sea Power upon History, 1660–1783 | Alfred Thayer Mahan | 0-7607-5499-3 | $14.95 |
| In His Steps | Charles M. Sheldon | 0-7607-5577-9 | $5.95 |
| Interior Castle | St. Teresa of Avila | 0-7607-7024-7 | $9.95 |
| Introduction to Mathematics | Alfred North Whitehead | 0-7607-6588-X | $7.95 |
| Investigation of the Laws of Thought | George Boole | 0-7607-6584-7 | $9.95 |
| Kingdom of God Is Within You | Leo Tolstoy | 0-7607-6552-9 | $9.95 |
| Lady's Life in the Rocky Mountains | Isabella Bird | 0-7607-6313-5 | $6.95 |
| Leonardo da Vinci and a Memory of His Childhood | Sigmund Freud | 0-7607-4992-2 | $6.95 |
| Letters and Sayings of Epicurus | Epicurus | 0-7607-6328-3 | $5.95 |
| Leviathan | Thomas Hobbes | 0-7607-5593-0 | $9.95 |
| Lives of the Caesars | Suetonius | 0-7607-5758-5 | $9.95 |
| Manners, Customs, and History of the Highlanders of Scotland | Sir Walter Scott | 0-7607-5869-7 | $7.95 |
| Meditations | Marcus Aurelius | 0-7607-5229-X | $5.95 |
| Montcalm and Wolfe | Francis Parkman | 0-7607-6835-8 | $12.95 |
| Montessori Method | Maria Montessori | 0-7607-4995-7 | $7.95 |
| New World | Winston Churchill | 0-7607-6858-7 | $9.95 |

| | | | |
|---|---|---|---|
| Nicomachean Ethics | Aristotle | 0-7607-5236-2 | $7.95 |
| Notes on Nursing | Florence Nightingale | 0-7607-4994-9 | $4.95 |
| On Education | Immanuel Kant | 0-7607-5588-4 | $6.95 |
| On Liberty | John Stuart Mill | 0-7607-5500-0 | $4.95 |
| On the Nature of Things | Lucretius | 0-7607-6834-X | $8.95 |
| On War | Carl von Clausewitz | 0-7607-5597-3 | $14.95 |
| Oregon Trail | Francis Parkman | 0-7607-5232-X | $7.95 |
| Outline of History: Volume 1 | H. G. Wells | 0-7607-5866-2 | $12.95 |
| Outline of History: Volume 2 | H. G. Wells | 0-7607-5867-0 | $12.95 |
| Passing of the Armies | Joshua Lawrence Chamberlain | 0-7607-6052-7 | $7.95 |
| Personal Memoirs | Ulysses S. Grant | 0-7607-4990-6 | $14.95 |
| Philosophy of History | G. W. F. Hegel | 0-7607-5763-1 | $9.95 |
| Political Economy for Beginners | Millicent Garrett Fawcett | 0-7607-5497-7 | $6.95 |
| Pragmatism | William James | 0-7607-4996-5 | $5.95 |
| Praise of Folly | Desiderius Erasmus | 0-7607-5760-7 | $6.95 |
| Principia Ethica | G. E. Moore | 0-7607-6546-4 | $5.95 |
| Principles of Political Economy and Taxation | David Ricardo | 0-7607-6536-7 | $7.95 |
| Principle of Relativity | Alfred North Whitehead | 0-7607-6521-9 | $7.95 |
| Problems of Philosophy | Bertrand Russell | 0-7607-5604-X | $5.95 |
| Recollections and Letters | Robert E. Lee | 0-7607-5919-7 | $9.95 |
| Relativity | Albert Einstein | 0-7607-5921-9 | $6.95 |
| Rights of Man | Thomas Paine | 0-7607-5501-9 | $5.95 |
| Rough Riders | Theodore Roosevelt | 0-7607-5576-0 | $7.95 |
| Russia and Its Crisis | Paul Miliukov | 0-7607-6863-3 | $12.95 |
| Second Treatise of Government | John Locke | 0-7607-6095-0 | $5.95 |
| Theory of Moral Sentiments | Adam Smith | 0-7607-5868-9 | $12.95 |
| Totem and Taboo | Sigmund Freud | 0-7607-6520-0 | $7.95 |
| Tractatus Logico-Philosophicus | Ludwig Wittgenstein | 0-7607-5235-4 | $5.95 |
| Trial and Death of Socrates | Plato | 0-7607-6200-7 | $4.95 |
| Up From Slavery | Booker T. Washington | 0-7607-5234-6 | $6.95 |
| Violin Playing As I Teach It | Leopold Auer | 0-7607-4991-4 | $5.95 |

| | | | |
|---|---|---|---|
| Vindication of the Rights of Woman | Mary Wollstonecraft | 0-7607-5494-2 | $6.95 |
| Voyage of the Beagle | Charles Darwin | 0-7607-5496-9 | $9.95 |
| Wealth of Nations | Adam Smith | 0-7607-5761-5 | $9.95 |
| Wilderness Hunter | Theodore Roosevelt | 0-7607-5603-1 | $7.95 |
| Worst Journey in the World | Apsley Cherry-Garrard | 0-7607-5759-3 | $14.95 |

THE BARNES & NOBLE
LIBRARY OF ESSENTIAL READING

This newly developed series has been established to provide affordable access to books of literary, academic, and historic value—works of both well-known writers and those who deserve to be rediscovered. Selected and introduced by scholars and specialists with an intimate knowledge of the works, these volumes present complete, original texts in a modern, readable typeface—welcoming a new generation of readers to influential and important books of the past. With more than 100 titles already in print and more than 100 forthcoming, the *Library of Essential Reading* offers an unrivaled variety of thought, scholarship, and entertainment. Best of all, these handsome and durable paperbacks are priced to be exceptionally affordable. For a full list of titles, visit www.bn.com/loer.